D0154137

ROARING METROPOLIS

AMERICAN BUSINESS, POLITICS, AND SOCIETY

Books in the series American Business, Politics, and Society explore the relationships over time between governmental institutions and the creation and performance of markets, firms, and industries large and small. The central theme of this series is that politics, law, and public policy—understood broadly to embrace not only lawmaking but also the structuring presence of governmental institutions—have been fundamental to the evolution of American business from the colonial era to the present. The series aims to explore, in particular, developments that have enduring consequences.

A complete list of books in the series is available from the publisher.

ROARING METROPOLIS

Businessmen's Campaign for a Civic Welfare State

Daniel Amsterdam

PENN

UNIVERSITY OF PENNSYLVANIA PRESS

PHILADELPHIA

Published by
University of Pennsylvania Press
Philadelphia, Pennsylvania 19104-4112
www.upenn.edu/pennpress

Printed in the United States of America on acid-free paper
1 3 5 7 9 10 8 6 4 2

Library of Congress Cataloging-in-Publication Data

Names: Amsterdam, Daniel, author.
Title: Roaring metropolis : businessmen's campaign for a civic welfare state / Daniel Amsterdam.
Other titles: American business, politics, and society.
Description: Philadelphia : University of Pennsylvania Press, [2016] | Series: American business, politics, and society | Includes bibliographical references and index.
Identifiers: LCCN 2015038836 | ISBN 978-0-8122-4810-4 (alk. paper)
Subjects: LCSH: United States—Social policy—20th century—Case studies. | Businessmen—Political activity—United States—History—20th century—Case studies. | Social change—United States—History—20th century—Case studies. | Detroit (Mich.)—Politics and government—20th century. | Detroit (Mich.)—Social conditions—20th century. | Philadelphia (Pa.)—Politics and government—20th century. | Philadelphia (Pa.)—Social conditions—20th century. | Atlanta (Ga.)—Politics and government—20th century. | Atlanta (Ga.)—Social conditions—20th century.
Classification: LCC HN57 A63 2016 | DDC 307.76—dc23
LC record available at http://lccn.loc.gov/2015038836

For Farrah and Elliot
and only because of
Kate

CONTENTS

Introduction

Americans concerned about poverty and inequality frequently point to the early twentieth century as a time when new forms of social legislation managed to curb corporate power. But the relationship between business interests and the development of public social policy in that era was far too complex to be captured so neatly. Businessmen of various stripes actually supported the implementation and expansion of a wide range of public social programs throughout the period. In fact, between the end of World War I and the onset of the Great Depression, commercial and industrial elites helped drive social spending in American cities to unprecedented heights.

With a few important exceptions, business interests in the early twentieth century tended to resist the rise of what we now call the social welfare state—an economic safety net woven from programs like unemployment compensation and public pensions for the elderly whose initial consolidation is perhaps most often associated with the 1930s and the New Deal. Yet to varying degrees in the early twentieth century and with particular fervor in the 1920s, business leaders in urban America championed a very different brand of social policy. Rather than state or national programs, they tended to favor local ones. Opposed to most forms of social insurance, they embraced public schooling, the promotion of public health, and the construction of decentralized cities featuring parks, playgrounds, libraries, museums, and single-family homes. Often through a windfall of public spending, these businessmen hoped to remake American cities and in many cases the citizens who inhabited them. Disdainful of most attempts to reduce poverty and economic insecurity through government action, they turned to government-sponsored social policy for altogether different reasons: to foster social and political stability as well as economic growth. Largely resistant to a social welfare state, they sought to build what might be called a civic welfare state, a network of programs that in the minds of elite businessmen promised to further both the goals of urban reform and urban boosterism, to prepare citizens for work and democracy while helping to lure new firms to their hometowns.

Commercial and industrial elites were far from the only political activists in the early twentieth century who supported such programs. But by the end of World War I, urban business leaders had become exceptionally adept at promoting the public social policies that they favored. Prodded in part by these businessmen's political activism, urban budgets skyrocketed in the 1920s. In some cities spending grew by 50 percent adjusted for inflation; elsewhere budgets doubled or even tripled. Across urban America expenditures rose at rates that far outpaced population growth and in many cases spending before the war. The 1920s were hardly a moment of government retrenchment or a time when government growth was limited to Prohibition, early federal forays into economic planning, and the development of a smattering of other programs. On the contrary, business interests helped make the 1920s a moment of aggressive government expansion in urban America.[1]

This book tells the story of how urban business leaders attempted to implement their vision for American social policy in three cities—Detroit, Philadelphia, and Atlanta—that experienced the tumult of the early twentieth century in importantly different ways. It pays close attention to a wide range of political actors, including local unions, middle-class women's organizations, immigrant groups, African American activists, and the Ku Klux Klan. But its main protagonists are successful men of industry and commerce, including a subset of wealthy lawyers and other high-end professionals, who accumulated enough political and economic clout to capture local political office or to steer major local business organizations such as their city's chamber of commerce at a time when white men dominated local government and urban America's largest commercial bodies. It shows how these white business leaders moved from a position of limited political influence when it came to shaping urban social policy in the years preceding World War I to a perch of relative dominance thereafter. It describes how their social policy agenda expanded in the wake of the war and how the configuration of urban political institutions and the unequal distribution of power and economic resources tended to push other political activists to the sidelines in the decade following the armistice.

And yet even as businessmen's political fortunes reached new heights, there was nowhere in urban America where the so-called ruling class could simply rule. Whether in cities that were strongholds of crooked political machines like Philadelphia, in places with relatively free and fair elections like

Detroit, or in communities where disfranchisement had sharply limited the electorate like Atlanta, urban business leaders consistently faced resistance. Everywhere they had to forge alliances. Repeatedly they were forced to compromise. This, then, is a book about wealth, social politics, power, and American democracy in the early twentieth century in its various, often unequal, at times corrupt, and in some instances deeply circumscribed forms.

Like other political actors in the early 1900s, businessmen had an incredible number of alternatives to choose from when considering which social policies to pursue. In the decades following the Civil War, the rapid expansion of factory-based manufacturing had thrown not only American but also European cities into an almost chronic state of crisis. Overcrowding was commonplace. So were poverty and squalor. Beginning in the late nineteenth century and continuing into the twentieth, socially concerned activists on both sides of the Atlantic crafted a stunning array of policy proposals in hopes of ameliorating the social repercussions of industrial capitalism. They focused on everything from the distribution of wages, workplace safety, benefits for the unemployed, and pensions for the elderly to the allocation of housing and the fundamental layout of cities themselves. In addition to the new ideas that sprang from this transatlantic exchange, American businessmen could draw on the United States' already generations-old tradition of using government as a tool for addressing urban social problems, whether through public schooling, the construction of sprawling urban parks like Central Park in New York City and Fairmount Park in Philadelphia, or through legal prohibitions on the consumption of alcohol and other types of behavior that various reformers had attempted to regulate since the earliest days of the republic.[2]

Faced with such a diverse array of options, both old and new, businessmen in the early twentieth century tended to gravitate toward certain kinds of public social programs and to reject proposals for others. They proved particularly resistant to policies that threatened to interfere with employers' ability to determine workers' wages, hours, working conditions, and fringe benefits, at least in the case of the relatively small but growing group of employers who offered them at the time.[3] It was precisely these kinds of government programs that would eventually constitute the nexus of policies that scholars generally refer to as the social welfare state: unemployment compensation, old-age pensions, and other forms of government-sponsored social insurance; laws regulating workers' schedules and pay; and, finally, public assistance to the poor, including payments to single and widowed mothers—early precursors of programs like Aid to Families with Dependent Children and today's Temporary Assistance to Needy Families, the policy commonly referred to as "welfare." To borrow from a widely used definition, social welfare state programs generally serve one of two goals. They either stipulate how employers have to treat, compensate, or otherwise provide for their employees, or they lessen the degree to which certain categories of the economically vulnerable, such as the elderly or unemployed, have to depend on the labor market in order to survive.[4]

Business interests did not unanimously oppose the implementation of all facets of a social welfare state defined along these lines. For instance, in the years leading up to World War I, employers in many cases supported the creation of the nation's first workmen's compensation laws, which many of them saw as a vast improvement over settling disputes related to workplace injuries in the courts. In addition, as the final chapter of this book details, by the early 1920s prominent businessmen in cities across the country had come to embrace the task of aiding the jobless during especially severe economic downturns through a combination of public and private initiatives. Toward the end of the 1920s, a handful of corporate executives began to flirt with the notion of offering public pensions to the elderly, and in the 1930s a few high-profile businessmen would even participate in designing New Deal legislation that created facets of the social welfare state that we know today. But the significance of such exceptions should not be overdrawn. Most businessmen in the early twentieth century were far more likely to oppose than to support calls for public social policies that limited employers' control over their own firms or that lessened the degree to which working-class Americans had to rely on the labor market in order to get by.[5]

Nonetheless, at various points in the early twentieth century and especially in the 1920s, elite businessmen in cities across the country called for heavy government spending on a host of public social programs. In justifying their support for these policies—whether to the public, to politicians, or to one another—these businessmen tended to offer two interrelated arguments on these programs' behalf. The concept of the civic welfare state is meant to connote both of these arguments at once.

First, urban business leaders frequently touted the ability of certain public social policies to mold local residents into good citizens, a concept that in businessmen's minds entailed being a good worker but also more: being law-abiding, being prepared for "responsible" democratic participation, and even being physically healthy. When calling for greater spending on public education, business elites commonly praised schools' potential for preparing the young for both work and democracy. In urging the promotion of residential decentralization through the construction of streets, sewers, water mains, and other basic infrastructure, they frequently contended that dispersing settlement would help cure the crime, vice, and health problems that many of them associated with residential congestion and poor housing conditions. Residential decentralization also promised to encourage homeownership, which many urban business leaders believed had the power to curb working-class radicalism as members of the nation's burgeoning urban proletariat invested in private property, the fundamental building block of the capitalist system. A significant cohort of elite businessmen ascribed to the notion that playgrounds were essential for molding good citizens. Not only would playgrounds keep children safe by providing them with alternatives to playing in the street, but when the nation's first playgrounds were established in the early twentieth century, they were often staffed by public employees who were charged with organizing games and other supervised activities that businessmen and others who supported the playground movement believed would teach children teamwork, dedication, and other values that they considered central to good citizenship.

Local business leaders also lauded parks, libraries, and museums for providing urban Americans with wholesome and even edifying recreational outlets in cities that were replete with potentially debasing temptations. In many cases, they embedded their calls for such initiatives within a broader push for constructing what city planners at the time called the "City Beautiful," an urban form rooted in the construction of grand boulevards, manicured parks, and elaborate public buildings that supporters believed would uplift the urban masses through the power of architecture and urban design.

Next, in addition to this focus on citizenship, local business elites frequently contended that implementing or expanding a certain array of public social programs was necessary for building a city of national or even international standing. They sometimes spoke of achieving this ideal as a good in itself, but much more often they did so as part of an effort to attract new firms to their hometowns. These businessmen realized that their counterparts across the country considered robust social spending in certain areas to be highly desirable. If they wanted to expand their local economies, business leaders felt that they had to remake their cities to reflect what business interests elsewhere had increasingly come to view as integral features of a good city inhabited by good citizens. Thus, the phrase "civic welfare" is meant to connote both business leaders' belief in the power of a certain array of social programs to foster particular visions of citizenship as well as their conviction that pursuing those very same policies would improve the economic well-being of cities themselves.

To be sure, some of the businessmen who appear in the pages that follow supported social spending just to make a quick buck. Constructing a park, a school, or a museum might drive up the value of property near real estate that a businessman owned. Building the infrastructure to promote residential decentralization might also bring water and sewer services closer to a factory that a particular company—searching for cheaper overhead or a way to expand—had built on the outskirts of town. But reducing the social politics of urban business leaders simply to the immediate economic self-interest of individual businessmen would be misleading. It is one thing for an entrepreneur to advocate constructing a school up the road from land that he owns to boost property values. It is quite another for a diverse assortment of businessmen—including at times fierce economic competitors—to more or less collectively champion a multimillion-dollar renovation of an urban school district or another similarly wide-ranging social initiative, which is precisely what business leaders in cities like Detroit, Philadelphia, and Atlanta did repeatedly in the early twentieth century. Simple economic self-interest certainly explains businessmen's motivations to a degree. But understanding the full scope of urban business leaders' political activism demands taking their broader political, economic, and ideological concerns seriously as well—a collection of interrelated interests that the concept of the civic welfare state is intended to underscore.

For some businessmen, the struggle to build a civic welfare state and improve the nation's citizenry was inseparable from another quest: implementing and enforcing regulations on various kinds of personal behavior, like drinking alcohol. But the famous debates that swirled around such proposals in the early twentieth century tended to divide wealthy businessmen more than many other social policy issues. Moguls like John D. Rockefeller Sr. and Henry Ford strongly backed Prohibition, for example, but it was also wealthy businessmen like Pierre DuPont, Henry Joy of Packard, and Alfred P. Sloan of General Motors who led the charge for repeal. Other attempts to regulate personal behavior could breed similar divisions. In urban America, this was in part because the battles that surrounded such efforts could put the two goals at the heart of business leaders' attempt to build a civic welfare state into direct conflict. Campaigns aimed at shaping the comportment of local citizens by enforcing existing laws or passing new ones frequently entailed widely publicized exposés depicting cities as dens of crime, vice, and political corruption—revelations that threatened to undermine business interests' simultaneous push to attract new enterprises to their city. For instance, when a group of especially religious business elites spearheaded an attempt to end prostitution in Atlanta on the eve of World War I, it was the local chamber of commerce that took the lead in limiting the crackdown. With police raids and investigations producing embarrassing headlines day after day, the leaders of the Atlanta Chamber of Commerce feared that bad press would damage the city's reputation and become a drag on the local economy.[6]

Some businessmen persisted in their fight against drinking, gambling, prostitution, and other vices as the early twentieth century progressed. But whether because of the divisions that those efforts tended to breed or due to most businessmen's personal beliefs, urban business elites' social policy agenda tended to focus elsewhere by the 1920s, especially on schooling, recreation, public health, urban decentralization, and city planning more generally. These were the issues at the center of Jazz Age businessmen's campaign for a civic welfare state.

By the end of World War I, urban business leaders' support for many of the public programs that they would advocate in the 1920s was nothing new. But during the war and its aftermath, the chronic urban crisis that they and other political activists had already been fretting over in the opening decades of the century seemed to take a sudden turn for the worse. Cities grew even more crowded, as migrants poured into urban America searching for work in one of the many industries that boomed during the war. In 1919—the first year following the peace—a wave of race riots, strikes, bombings, and bomb threats swept across urban America. In that year, business leaders in cities like Detroit, Philadelphia, and Atlanta called for social spending as arguably never before. But even after the nation had returned to a state of relative calm, elite businessmen in those three cities remained committed to keeping spending levels high. As the 1920s wore on, their reasons for doing so became increasingly tied to the local circumstances that they faced. In Atlanta, the social politics of the city's white business elite grew ever more linked to local boosterism. In Philadelphia, leading business interests redoubled their push for public spending because their immediate postwar effort had met with disappointment and because the city was slated to host a major international fair that elite businessmen hoped would help reverse the city's already recognizable economic decline. In Detroit, the success of the auto industry continued to breed rapid urban growth and with it a host of social challenges that local business leaders believed only government could solve.

At the same time, business interests in all three cities proved far more successful at implementing their policy agenda in the 1920s than they had been in the years leading up to the war. In some cities, like Detroit, this was because business leaders had managed to restructure local government in ways that overwhelmingly favored the wealthy. Elsewhere, businessmen's heightened desire for government growth prodded them to forge new alliances and to reorient their political priorities. In Philadelphia, frustration with political gridlock encouraged local business leaders to overcome their own internal divisions and motivated prominent businessmen who had formerly opposed Philadelphia's corrupt political machine to increasingly make peace with its tactics. In Atlanta, the city's white business leaders—who tended to view African Americans as political subjects, not citizens—generally sought to exclude African Americans from the benefits of the civic welfare state that they hoped to build. And yet on multiple occasions, members of Atlanta's white business elite were forced to make concessions to a small group of African Americans, who despite being disfranchised in most regards still retained the right to vote in special elections, including the bond referenda that white business leaders needed to win in order to finance the government expansion that they so desired.

In the end, these two overarching developments—elite businessmen's heightened commitment to social spending and their enhanced political efficacy—had major consequences for urban policy. Public spending surged in all three cities as local officials funneled money toward social initiatives that urban business leaders favored. Detroit's budget was 340 percent larger in 1929 adjusted for inflation than it had been just before the United States entered the war. All of this growth took place after the armistice.[7] Atlanta's budget grew by 134 percent in the same period and Philadelphia's by 75 percent. In all three cities spending expanded far faster than the local population. Detroit spent 58 percent more per person at the end of the 1920s than it had just before the United States declared war, again adjusted for inflation. Philadelphia spent 51 percent more per person and Atlanta 60 percent.[8]

These figures are all the more impressive because they exclude the costs that governments paid to finance their debts. If those sums were included, the growth of government spending would appear even higher. Cities across the country borrowed with abandon in the 1920s. Detroit's municipal debt grew by over 700 percent. Philadelphia's and Atlanta's each rose by over 200 percent. In all three cities, businessmen called loudly and frequently for debt spending. Indeed, buying now and paying later was elite businessmen's favorite method for financing the major projects that they advocated.[9]

Even so, commercial and industrial leaders in Detroit, Philadelphia, and Atlanta rarely objected to the other main fiscal trend that allowed government spending to grow so rapidly in the 1920s, at least not in a sustained and collective way. The decade's famous prosperity encouraged the extensive development of real estate. The assessed value of property in Detroit grew by over 80 percent between 1919 and 1929 even when inflation is taken into account. Philadelphia's rose by roughly 75 percent and Atlanta's by over 50 percent. Tax rates remained relatively stable in all three cities. Still, as the value of taxable real estate grew, so did the amount of revenue flowing into municipal coffers. By increasing the money available for government services and by enabling cities to finance new debt, these funds allowed local officials to answer businessmen's plea that they spend as never before.

In other cities, public spending followed a similar trajectory. Los Angeles's budget grew by nearly 300 percent between 1916 and 1929 adjusted for inflation with virtually all of this growth following the war. New York's budget nearly doubled. Chicago's rose by 85 percent and Birmingham's by 250 percent. Whether in these cities or elsewhere, increased social spending drove a significant portion of this growth. Overall in the nation's largest cities—those with populations over three hundred thousand—spending per person on schooling rose 73 percent between 1916 and 1929 adjusted for inflation; on recreational programs spending grew 72 percent; on libraries, 47 percent; on hospitals, 44 percent; on sewer systems, 30 percent; and on other facets of public health, 45 percent.

In fact, the pace of government growth was far higher in the 1920s than it had been earlier in the century in many American cities. Spending per person actually decreased by 5 percent between 1904 and 1916 in cities with populations over three hundred thousand adjusted for inflation. By contrast, in a similar twelve-year increment, between 1916 and 1928, spending per person rose 55 percent, again with all of this growth following World War I. Historians tend to treat the first two decades of the twentieth century as more significant than the 1920s in terms of government development. The prewar years were clearly a moment of great policy innovation in urban America, but it was the 1920s that saw the most local government growth.[10]

Table 1.
Rate of Growth in Urban Government Spending Per Capita Before and After World War I

	1904–1916	*1916–1928*	*Population in 1920*
Cities with populations over 300,000	–5%	55%	20,630,251
Cities with populations of 100,000–300,000	–1%	46%	8,532,924
New York	–38%	44%	5,620,048
Chicago	42%	73%	2,701,705
Philadelphia	–2%	56%	1,823,779
Detroit	73%	98%	993,678
Cleveland	47%	27%	796,841
St. Louis	–18%	51%	772,897
Boston	–30%	49%	748,060
Baltimore	41%	17%	733,826
Pittsburgh	30%	42%	588,343
Los Angeles	75%	77%	576,673
Buffalo	58%	70%	506,775
San Francisco	55%	12%	506,676
Milwaukee	65%	68%	457,147
Washington, DC	–21%	45%	437,571
Newark, NJ	32%	70%	414,524
Cincinnati	22%	26%	401,247
New Orleans	33%	69%	387,219
Minneapolis	30%	18%	380,582
Kansas City, MO	–13%	32%	324,410
Seattle	–16%	84%	315,312
Indianapolis	71%	22%	314,194
Louisville	23%	52%	234,891
Atlanta	–18%	55%	200,616
Birmingham	–36%	175%	178,806

Note: Of the twenty-one cities with populations over 300,000 in 1920, sixteen experienced a higher rate of growth in government spending per capita adjusted for inflation between 1916 and 1928 than between 1904 and 1916. The specific cities listed above are those that had populations over 300,000 in 1920 as well the three largest southern cities after New Orleans (the only southern city with a population greater than 300,000 in 1920). Cities are listed in order of population size.

Source: Financial Statistics of Cities Having a Population of over 30,000

It will take more than this one study to unearth the politics that drove these trends in the wide variety of cities that experienced them. In taking the first steps toward that end, this book aims to strike a balance. Instead of digging deeply into the experience of just one city, as so many urban histories do, or touching superficially on a large number, it strives to offer an account that is detailed enough to reflect the unique political environments of individual cities while also shedding light on how various trends played out across urban America's diverse political terrain.

Indeed, by the early twentieth century, American cities were so complex that a historian has to make difficult choices about which facets of that complexity to examine most closely. Following the lead of some of the most influential recent scholarship on American politics, this book especially scrutinizes how local laws and political institutions—from city charters and local political parties to the rules governing municipal spending—shaped urban politics. At the same time, however, the pages that follow seek to remedy shortcomings in that very same body of scholarship. The researchers who first highlighted the importance of such a "state-centered" approach to studying American politics did so in part by critiquing earlier writing on the history of American social policy—specifically on the social welfare state as defined above—that had vastly overstated the role of business interests in propelling that history.[11] Despite their contributions on that front, authors working in this vein have tended to underplay the degree to which businessmen encouraged the development of other facets of American social policy in the early twentieth century, such as public schooling, public recreation, city planning, and the other urban programs that are the main focus here. Thus, whenever possible, this book attempts to underscore how local laws and political institutions—combined with the contingencies of history, shifts in businessmen's political priorities and strategies, and variations in the respective interests and tactics of other political groups—allowed business interests to propel the development of American social policy to an unrivaled degree in certain places and at certain times.[12]

Hence the choice of Detroit, Philadelphia, and Atlanta: by the 1920s, these cities typified some of the main political regimes that were prevalent in urban America at the time—the machine-dominated city (Philadelphia); the politically reformed, largely machine-free city (Detroit); and finally the city of widespread disfranchisement (Atlanta). Taken together, Detroit, Philadelphia, and Atlanta also offer the opportunity to examine a broad assortment of political actors, from professional politicians to grassroots groups. Finally, these three cities featured sharply different economies and economic histories. By the 1920s, Philadelphia was a long-established manufacturing hub that was home to an eclectic collection of factories of widely varying sizes in predominantly older industries. Detroit, by contrast, exemplified the new mass-production economy that had emerged in the early decades of the twentieth century and, unlike 1920s Philadelphia, was a boomtown that featured a single dominant industry. Finally, Atlanta was still primarily a commercial depot—a town with only a fledgling manufacturing sector but with great regional strength in banking, insurance, and the distribution of agricultural commodities—and a city whose economic development still largely lay in the future. Trying to identify a set of places that can fully capture the complexity of urban America in the early twentieth century is a fool's errand. Still, Detroit, Philadelphia, and Atlanta reflect a great deal of that complexity and do so more efficiently than most.

A note on terminology before proceeding: readers attuned to how historians have written about American politics in the early twentieth century might notice the absence thus far of the terms "progressive" and "progressivism," concepts that appear frequently in accounts of the era. I avoid using those terms for a number of reasons, most of all because they have been notoriously difficult for historians to define. This is not to say they are bereft of utility. But historians' lengthy search for the essence of progressivism and for the true identity of the progressives has suggested that both concepts are best suited for painting with broad brushstrokes, not for the pointillism that a nuanced political history demands. They help evoke a complex era in U.S. history when the nation "swam in a sudden abundance" of policy choices, but their usefulness quickly fades when one attempts to differentiate between what the various political actors who waded in those waters—often with wildly different interests, intentions, and visions of reform—respectively chose and why.[13] Nor is it particularly useful to characterize the businessmen who appear in the pages that follow as "corporate liberals"—another term that historians have employed from time to time—because the broad contours of their social politics did not foreshadow (let alone help to constitute) the social politics that would make New Deal liberalism distinct, as the concept "corporate liberalism" tends to imply when used in the context of social policy.[14]

Rather, as the Great Depression was approaching and the New Deal lay just around the bend, business leaders in cities like Detroit, Philadelphia, and Atlanta had chosen a reformist path that they hoped would lead in a very different direction—a social politics that they believed would bolster their political and economic standing rather than set limits on corporate power as New Deal liberalism in part would do. That said, businessmen's political activism prior to the 1930s did help encourage the coming of the New Deal. But as this book's final pages detail, this was largely by accident, not by design.

The early twentieth century was an exceptionally rich political moment, a reformist age that encompassed the 1920s as much as the decades that surrounded them. Historians used to depict the 1920s as an "intermission" that brought the reformism of the early twentieth century to a temporary pause. The pages that follow confirm that this was not the case. Instead, the 1920s in part saw an exceptionally business-friendly strain of reformism flourish in American cities. Appreciating this fact is important not merely in terms of righting the historical record, however. A similar approach to urban issues would live on long after the business leaders who appear in this book would depart the historical stage. Indeed, one of this book's contentions is that drawing attention to the social politics that capitalists embraced in the early twentieth century can help underscore shortcomings in urban social policy today.[15]

But before grappling with the present, it is necessary to get a better handle on the past. We begin in the opening years of the last century, a moment when elite businessmen in cities as diverse as Detroit, Philadelphia, and Atlanta were already attempting to shape urban social policy but more often than not were failing to do so.

CHAPTER 1

At Cross Purposes

Businessmen's Political Activism Before the Armistice

Urban business leaders advocated social spending in a number of areas in the early years of the twentieth century. They lobbied for the expansion and improvement of local school systems. They joined and often led campaigns to construct municipal playgrounds and to improve local health conditions. At their most ambitious, they called for an extensively remodeled city, the "City Beautiful," an urban form designed to include elaborate and interconnected systems of parks and parkways as well as grandiose civic centers featuring ornate city halls, museums, and public libraries. In many cases, business elites hoped to erect these structures on some of urban America's most valuable real estate, stretches of land already occupied by factories, stores, and homes.

Yet whether their plans were bold or modest, pricey or inexpensive, businessmen frequently stumbled in their attempt to implement them in the years preceding World War I. In Detroit, local business leaders' political influence was remarkably limited at the time, a trend that encouraged their involvement in another effort: the so-called municipal reform movement, or the attempt to revamp the basic structure of city government through reforms like expanding the reach of the civil service or abolishing ward-based elections in favor of citywide contests. Municipal reformers generally hoped that such measures would weaken local political machines or dilute the strength of the working-class vote.[1]

Business leaders in Atlanta and Philadelphia were also involved in the municipal reform movement. In fact, in both cities businessmen's support for municipal reform was a root cause of their troubles when it came to shaping local social policy before the war. In Atlanta, business leaders struggled to pull off a nearly impossible about-face—a pivot from denouncing local officials as incompetent and even corrupt when advocating municipal reform to pleading that voters give those same officials more money to spend when championing social spending. In Philadelphia, a handful of especially wealthy businessmen were the principal beneficiaries and even sponsors of the entrenched political machine that other leading businessmen in the city who were bent on municipal reform hoped to dislodge. On multiple occasions, public projects that Philadelphia's commercial and industrial elite almost unanimously favored stalled because of local business leaders' infighting over boss rule.

The tensions that riddled campaigns for municipal reform in cities like Philadelphia and Atlanta compounded the commonplace obstacles that might hinder any call for expensive public projects: the process of gaining eminent domain; legal controversies surrounding government jurisdiction; the architectural and structural problems inherent in planning large-scale public works, not to mention the main challenge that business leaders in Detroit faced—enlisting the support of local officials and the public in the first place. Commercial and industrial elites in different cities confronted varying combinations of these and other dynamics. But the effects were often similar. When it came to shaping local social policy in the years leading up to World War I, urban business leaders notched a record that was far more mixed than the one they would achieve after the armistice.

Struggling to Steer the New Motor City

In the opening years of the twentieth century, the rise of the automobile industry remade Detroit. In 1904, the city was home to an unremarkable smattering of manufacturing enterprises that employed just over sixty thousand workers. By the time the United States entered World War I, the auto industry alone employed twice that many, roughly 40 percent of the total number of factory workers in the city. The rest of Detroit's industrial workforce toiled in one of the city's many other manufacturing firms—building furnaces, producing chemicals, rolling cigars, or processing meat. Detroit was not a one-industry town, but auto manufacturing alone made the city an industrial powerhouse in a stunningly brief interval. In 1900—on the eve of the auto industry's first major growth spurt—Detroit ranked sixteenth among American cities in terms of industrial output. By 1914, it ranked fourth.[2]

The rise of auto manufacturing produced a new group of tycoons. These men eventually displaced the merchants and manufacturers who had made their fortunes in pre-automotive Detroit as the vanguard of the city's business elite. And yet this process was more amicable than one might expect. Detroiters who traced their wealth back to the city's old nineteenth-century economy—rooted in the production of railcars and stoves, in lumber, and in mining—were among the first investors in the city's fledgling car shops. Many of them profited from the car boom and quickly gleaned the importance of building strong social, political, and economic ties to the city's newest moguls. Soon, recently flush automobile executives and the city's old business leaders were comfortably hobnobbing together at Detroit's toniest social clubs and serving alongside one another on various corporate boards. By 1916, the names of a number of the city's new automobile magnates appeared alongside those of Detroit's most established families in Dau's *Blue Book*, essentially a who's who of the local upper crust. Despite the almost revolutionary transformation of Detroit's economy, the city's new and established barons were coalescing into a relatively coherent business class.[3]

There was one important exception to this trend: Henry Ford. Members of Detroit's pre-automotive elite had invested in Ford's early companies, but Ford's first venture flopped, and investors pushed him out of his second when he refused to embrace their vision for the firm. Even after Ford had become an unparalleled success, he remained at odds with many of his corporate colleagues. His competitors were furious when he announced the five-dollar day in 1914, fearing wage inflation throughout the city. They ridiculed his opposition to U.S. involvement in World War I. When Ford endorsed the reelection campaign of Democratic president Woodrow Wilson in 1916, members of Detroit's solidly Republican business elite jeered. Perhaps taking the hint—or maybe out of spite—Henry Ford's involvement in local politics grew increasingly sporadic.[4]

Other car executives, by contrast, grew all the more involved in local affairs. In the run-up to World War I, leaders of the automobile industry took charge of the local business community's most prominent civic organizations. Between 1911 and America's entry into the war, the presidents of the Detroit Board of Commerce were all in car manufacturing. Representatives of the auto industry also dominated the organization's directorate. Meanwhile, auto executives like Hugh Chalmers of Chalmers Motor Company, F. F. Beall of Packard, and A. L. McMeans of Dodge took the helm of the Detroit Employers' Association, the corporate elite's organizational base for waging war on local unions.[5]

It was also one of the city's most successful carmakers, Henry Leland, who established the civic organization that spearheaded the municipal reform movement in Detroit, including the attempt to reconfigure the city's basic political structure by revising Detroit's city charter. Born in 1843 in Vermont, Leland came of age as the industrial revolution was spreading through New England. In his early professional years, he gained a hands-on education as a toolmaker and machinist working in factories throughout the Northeast. In 1890, Leland established a new enterprise in Detroit, where he quickly earned a reputation as an exceptional engineer. When Henry Ford's second company began to struggle in 1902, investors called on Leland to save the firm. Soon, the newly renamed Cadillac Automobile Company gained international fame for producing the first cars with fully interchangeable parts.[6]

In addition to being a master engineer, Leland was a devout Presbyterian, an ardent prohibitionist, and a staunch opponent of organized labor. He was a significant contributor to the Michigan Anti-Saloon League and helped to establish the city's antiunion Employers' Association. An unapologetic elitist, Leland believed that the "better class" of Americans—meaning primarily wealthy, Anglo-Saxon, Protestant men—was most fit to govern.[7]

Unfortunately for Leland, Detroit was becoming less Anglo-Saxon, less Protestant, and more working class with each passing day. Jobs created by the auto boom drew hundreds of thousands of migrants to the city. Most of them were desperately poor. Many of them were Catholic and Jewish peasants from southern and eastern Europe. Between 1900 and 1920, Detroit's population grew from 285,000 to just under one million, and the number of immigrants in the city roughly tripled. By 1920, nearly 300,000 Detroiters had been born in another country.[8]

Initially, these immigrants settled in enclaves throughout older sections of the city. At the time, Detroit elected most of its public officials from neighborhood wards. As the city's largely immigrant proletariat grew, so did its influence on local affairs. A man like Leland, who believed in rule by the "better class," had few sympathies for a political system that gave workers, let alone immigrants, so much sway in local elections. What offended Leland most, however, was the influence that the so-called Voteswappers League had on local politics. The Voteswappers were a band of small-scale political bosses who controlled a number of the neighborhood-based boards that oversaw elections in Detroit and thus were able to manipulate vote counts in favor of their political allies. Worse still for the teetotaling Leland, many of the Voteswappers doubled as saloonkeepers and their primary financial sponsor was the Royal Ark, Detroit's main association of liquor dealers.[9]

Figure 1. Henry Leland, president of the Detroit Citizens League and the Cadillac Motor Company, photographed circa 1920. *National Automotive History Collection, Detroit Public Library.*

In 1912, Leland founded a new political organization that eventually became known as the Detroit Citizens League. Elite businessmen dominated the group's board and quickly adopted charter reform as a leading goal. The Detroit Board of Commerce soon joined the charter fight, while wealthy executives like John and Horace Dodge, Edsel Ford, and S. S. Kresge (whose name would eventually put the *K* in Kmart) all donated large sums to fund the Citizens League's effort.[10]

Detroit's commercial and industrial elite supported charter reform for a variety of reasons. Some shared Leland's distaste for the Voteswappers and their connection to the saloon. Others were weary of the scandals that intermittently rocked the city. Clouds of suspicion hovered over the city's sanitation and street-repair services and over the police department's relationship with local saloonkeepers. At one point, three-quarters of Detroit's city council had been arrested on charges that they had accepted bribes from a regional railroad company. The courts eventually acquitted the lawmakers, but the controversy lasted for over a year.[11]

Business leaders also hoped to streamline a political system that was undeniably cumbersome. Under the existing charter, Detroit was governed by a mayor and a city council that had thirty-six members elected by ward. Government appropriations demanded approval from the city's enormous board of estimates, composed of forty-one officials. Every city department was run by a committee consisting of three members each. It was a system plagued by inefficiencies. Like municipal reformers across the country, businessmen in Detroit wanted city officials to run the government like a private corporation, with efficiency as a primary goal.[12]

But most of all, business elites joined the fight for charter reform because they wanted more political power. Indeed, despite their wealth, leaders of Detroit's business community had a difficult time influencing local politics in the early years of the century. Their failure to shape the local social policy-making process especially attests to this pattern.

Among the commercial and industrial elite's most ambitious social policy proposals in the years preceding World War I was the construction of a new multistructure cultural center just a few miles from Detroit's downtown. Its design was rooted in a movement in architectural and urban planning that had sprung from multiple sources and was just beginning to make its way across the country. Beginning in the middle of the nineteenth century, village improvement associations had begun tinkering with coordinated planning and beautification in small towns in various parts of the nation. In urban America, Frederick Law Olmsted and others had made a splash in the years surrounding the Civil War by designing bucolic common spaces, like New York's Central Park, that they believed could counteract everything from rising class tensions to the hustle-bustle of city life. In Europe, another urban vision was taking shape, one exemplified most clearly by Georges-Eugène Haussmann's reconstruction of large swaths of Paris to fit Napoléon III's dreams for France's Second Empire. In the early 1890s, the American city planner Daniel Burnham drew heavily on Haussmann's ideas in constructing his famous White City at Chicago's Columbian Exposition, a fair marking the four hundredth anniversary of Columbus's arrival in the Americas. Burnham's work inspired a growing collection of planners who hoped to use beautification and urban design to address a variety of forces—from rising inequality to haphazard urban development—that they believed were tearing American cities apart. These planners found additional inspiration in the work of Charles Mulford Robinson, especially from his 1901 *Improvement of Towns and Cities*, a manifesto that argued for the transformative potential of architecture, urban planning, municipal art, and parks. The fledgling City Beautiful movement got an additional boost just after the turn of the century when federal officials decided to redesign portions of Washington, D.C., by elaborating on Pierre L'Enfant's original plan for the city. The main product of that effort was an expanded and reconceived National Mall lined with neoclassical structures and embellished with a large reflecting pool and the monuments that would eventually become the Lincoln and Jefferson Memorials. A few blocks away, the Pennsylvania Railroad agreed to construct a new building of its own, Union Station, in a similar spirit.[13]

Soon cities across the country were crafting their own City Beautiful plans, with various groups vying to tailor the movement to suit their respective interests. Elite women's associations frequently dove into the fray, and so did local commercial groups. City Beautiful projects tended to increase local property values, yet they also promised more from businessmen's perspective. As the lawyer, banker, and wealthy real estate developer Henry Morgenthau contended, proper city planning could ameliorate "disease, moral depravity, discontent, and socialism." Moreover, City Beautiful plans frequently included proposals to construct new parks, museums, and libraries—initiatives that promised to nurture a variety of traits in the local citizenry that business elites found desirable. In cities as diverse as Chicago, Seattle, Los Angeles, and Philadelphia, the City Beautiful movement was propelled in large part by businessmen's civic ambitions.[14]

In Detroit, business leaders' City Beautiful aspirations hinged on the completion of two buildings—a new home for the Detroit Public Library and another for the city's art museum—that were designed to sit across the street from one another and anchor the proposed cultural center. William C. Weber, a Detroit businessman who had made his fortune in timber and real estate, helped lead the campaign for the new buildings. As Weber argued, the cultural center promised to offer everyday Detroiters "high pleasures" as well as "higher ideals," to teach "Detroit residents who could not afford to travel to

Europe or New York" that there was "something better" than working-class "nickelodeons," vaudeville theater, and other forms of mass entertainment.[15]

Yet implementing Weber's vision proved difficult. As was often true in the early twentieth century, Andrew Carnegie donated the seed money for Detroit's new library building, but in the Motor City's case only after years of delay. George W. Radford, a Detroit attorney who served "large moneyed interests," initiated discussions with Carnegie's representatives in 1901. Carnegie quickly agreed to give Detroit $750,000—half for a new central library and the rest for a handful of branch libraries—with the stipulation that Detroit's government purchase the necessary land and allocate $75,000 a year for maintenance. But the deal soon faced resistance from local papers, organized labor, and eventually members of the city council. Opponents decried Carnegie's brutal treatment of workers in his steel mills, particularly during the infamous Homestead Strike of 1892, and argued that accepting funds from the steel titan amounted to taking "blood money."[16]

With political opposition growing, supporters of the library project shifted tacks. They began lobbying for an appropriation from the city itself, all the while hoping to take advantage of Carnegie's offer at a later date. In 1902, Detroiters were asked to approve a $500,000 bond issue to fund construction. The bond issue passed, but the library project immediately hit another roadblock. Members of the city's board of estimates—who met to review the city's budget just once a year and had a reputation for knee-jerk parsimony—agreed to appropriate only $150,000 of the approved funds. The library commission refused to accept the lower amount out of principle and thus received nothing. In 1904, leaders of the Detroit Board of Commerce floated another proposal for the library only to have the city council reject it. Years later, despite ongoing pressure from local business leaders, city officials had yet to accept Carnegie's donation or to provide significant funding on their own. Finally, in 1910, with organized labor and other detractors no longer actively opposing the project, the city agreed to appropriate enough money for Detroit to accept the Carnegie funds. The secretary of the Detroit Board of Commerce, Charles B. Sawyer, traveled to Pittsburgh (Carnegie's hometown) and helped finalize the deal.[17]

Even with Carnegie's money in hand, however, progress on the library remained glacially slow. Some of the delays were inevitable. It took time, for instance, to select an architectural plan. Still, public officials did not start construction until 1915—five full years after the city had finally accepted Carnegie's gift. Then, just months after the city had broken ground, building ceased when local officials failed to appropriate enough money to keep work going. For well over a year, the unfinished building stood as "a gaunt, naked skeleton of steel against the sky" and as a testament to business elites' political inefficacy. Thereafter, World War I brought further delays.[18]

Business leaders' attempt to build a new home for the city's art museum was just as fraught. At the time, the museum was a private entity, but the wealthy businessmen who dominated its board wanted taxpayers to foot the bill for the new building. The Detroit Museum of Art was founded in the 1880s under the leadership of wealthy newspaper publisher James Scripps, a Scripps employee named William H. Brearley, and Thomas W. Palmer, a lumber magnate who also served as U.S. senator. By the early 1890s, the museum's board had convinced city officials to appropriate several thousand dollars to the museum each year. Even so, the city charter capped the amount of funding that public officials could give: $20,000 annually for operating costs. City officials could appropriate additional funds to the museum "from time to time" for special construction projects, but the city council was prohibited from spending more than $50,000 in bond revenue on the museum. Led by cultural center booster William Weber and Dexter M. Ferry Jr. (a wealthy corporate executive and heir to his father's seed distribution company), the museum's trustees wanted to build a monumental structure that would cost far more.[19]

But their attempt to win public funding for the project would backfire. The city's corporation counsel objected to the plan, contending that the city did not have the right under state law to offer additional funds to the museum. In a 1915 test case designed to settle the matter, the Michigan Supreme Court agreed. Moreover, much to the surprise of the museum's trustees, the court outlawed all municipal appropriations to the museum and other private institutions like it. According to the court, even the funding practices outlined under the existing city charter were unconstitutional. For local officials to finance construction of a new building, the museum would have to become a municipally owned entity.[20]

Business leaders also hoped to increase the number of parks and playgrounds in the city, but their efforts fell short on this front as well. In 1913, leaders of the Detroit Board of Commerce hired Rowland Haynes, field secretary of the Playground and Recreation Association of America (PRAA), to survey the city and make recommendations for improving its recreational facilities. PRAA officials were leading proponents of the theory that playgrounds—when supervised by municipal employees who could oversee and coordinate children's play—were singularly promising tools for addressing a host of urban problems. It might seem like an oddly utopian notion in retrospect, but a number of the most influential urban reformers in the early twentieth century agreed. Housing reformer Lawrence Veiller, social activist Jane Addams, and U.S. president Theodore Roosevelt were all strong supporters of the movement, while the muckraker Jacob Riis spoke of playgrounds as one of the most important "counterinfluences to the saloon, street gang, and similar evils."[21]

Figure 2. This photograph appeared in the November 1913 issue of the Detroit Board of Commerce's magazine, the *Detroiter*, amid the board of commerce's prewar campaign for supervised playgrounds. *Courtesy of Baker Old Class Collection, Baker Library, Harvard Business School.*

As for the Detroit Board of Commerce, its members seemed especially sold on the sections of Rowland Haynes's report that argued that play, when supervised by trained adults, could prevent juvenile delinquency and promote good citizenship, particularly among idle boys. As a representative of the Detroit Board of Commerce argued in the organization's monthly magazine, children were like "an unfinished product," and wholesome recreation was a crucial input in their development. "The caliber of our future citizens depends largely upon the boys of today," the author warned. Without playgrounds, the "animal spirits" of local boys were turning toward other "natural outlets," such as "neighborhood gangs, petty thieving," and similar "depredations."[22]

Haynes's report also emphasized the need for a centralized body charged with coordinating recreational initiatives in the city. The board of commerce convinced local officials to establish one in 1914. A leader of the board of commerce's recreation campaign even headed the new commission. But the bulk of businessmen's vision for the city's recreation system remained unfulfilled. In the spring of 1915, the board of estimates declined to appropriate funding for social centers in the city, an initiative that the board of commerce had backed. Moreover, it granted only $15,000 in bonds for purchasing land for new playgrounds even though the board of commerce had wanted much more.[23]

Thus, whether they were lobbying for playgrounds or attempting to build a new library and museum, business leaders in Detroit were reminded that they lacked the political influence that they desired. Charter reform promised to give it to them. Above all, Henry Leland and his corporate brethren sought to implement a charter that would abolish Detroit's ward-based city council and replace it with a much smaller, nine-member body that the electorate would choose as a whole. As Leland and his allies well knew, citywide elections strongly favored wealthy or well-funded candidates who could afford to wage extensive advertising campaigns. The city's largest union, the Detroit Federation of Labor, immediately recognized the proposal as a power grab and opposed it, arguing that workers would lose their voice in city hall without their ward representatives. But other Detroiters viewed the matter differently. Tired of inefficiencies and the potential for corruption in Detroit's existing political system, multiple Polish newspapers endorsed Leland and the Citizens League's proposed charter, as did newspapers in the city's Jewish and Italian communities. A local African American newspaper came out in favor of the business-backed charter as well, contending that citywide elections would allow African Americans to vote as a bloc instead of having their votes split among different wards. Placing the charter question on the ballot required gathering thirteen thousand signatures on a petition. The Citizens League and its allies managed to collect eighteen thousand in short order in part because major employers like Ford, Packard, and Cadillac allowed representatives of the Citizens League to solicit signatures from employees in their plants. A significant number of these workers no doubt signed because their bosses made clear that they were expected to do so. Still, evidence suggests that Detroiters from all walks of life supported the Citizens League's proposals. When the electorate voted on the new charter in June 1918, every single precinct in the city approved it. Political conditions in the city were so poor that many Detroiters were hungry for change. By funneling their wealth toward charter reform, elite businessmen succeeded in determining what that change would look like.[24]

In addition to reconfiguring the city council, the new charter replaced the three-member commissions that had previously administered local affairs with streamlined departments whose heads were appointed by the mayor. It transformed the city's art museum into a municipal entity, thus opening the way for a new building financed by taxpayer dollars. Finally, the charter put the mayor and city council in charge of all city expenditures, free from the oversight of the old board of estimates.[25]

One modification that the city charter did not make was reforming the city's school system—a cause that Detroit's business leaders also embraced in the years leading up to the war. The main thrust of businessmen's involvement in Detroit's educational politics before World War I had less to do with implementing specific policies or expanding local facilities, as it would in the 1920s. Rather, business leaders' primary concern was ridding the school system of ward politics. Their effort paralleled their campaign to redesign the city government more generally, although in the case of school reform businessmen largely followed the lead of female activists in the city, especially members of the Detroit Federation of Women's Clubs, who in turn mobilized behind a wealthy Detroiter named Laura Osborn.

A committed prohibitionist, Osborn shared Henry Leland's distaste for the Voteswappers and denounced their influence on the city's schools. Married to a successful businessman and listed in the city's social register, she joined many of her wealthy peers in fearing the growing political power of Detroit's increasingly immigrant working class. In 1913, Osborn and two male collaborators—an executive at Detroit Edison and a professor at the University of Michigan—convinced state legislators to pass a law restructuring how the city's school district was governed. The Detroit Citizens League and the Detroit Board of Commerce strongly supported the measure, which abolished the existing ward-based school board and replaced it with a much smaller body composed of six members chosen in citywide elections. Opponents of the new law mounted a series of legal challenges that stopped its implementation for several years. Finally, in November 1916, legislators asked Detroit's electorate to weigh in. In the lead-up to the referendum, the Detroit Federation of Women's Clubs waged an extensive campaign with the strong support of the Detroit Board of Commerce and the Detroit Citizens League. The measure carried in 284 of the city's 285 precincts. As in the battle to revise the city charter, wealthy elites led the campaign to reform Detroit's school system, but their success depended on widespread disenchantment with the status quo.[26]

In driving the Voteswappers out of school politics, however, Detroiters opened the door for another clique to run the city's schools, much as they did when they rubber-stamped the Citizens League's charter proposals. Elite businessmen in Detroit failed to realize most of their social policy goals in the years before the armistice. But by successfully transforming how city officials were elected, they established the groundwork for their future political dominance. It was an outcome that business leaders in Philadelphia would have envied.

Stuck in the Gears of the World's Workshop

"Corrupt and contended": that was how muckraking journalist Lincoln Steffens characterized politics in Philadelphia in 1903. Few statements about the city are more famous. And yet Steffens was only partially right. A crooked political machine aligned with the Republican Party dominated Philadelphia's political scene in the opening decades of the century. But the city was also home to a committed municipal reform movement composed of "independent" Republicans who repeatedly tried to loosen the machine's hold on power. First, in 1905, independents helped galvanize public protest to thwart an especially brazen attempt by machine politicians to line their pockets with public funds. Then, in 1911, independent reformers exploited divisions within the machine's ranks and elected their own handpicked candidate for mayor. Finally, in 1919, independents took advantage of yet another conflict within the Republican machine and won a revised city charter that made a number of alterations to Philadelphia's political structure.[27]

Corruption may have been at the center of Philadelphia's political environment, but contentment simply was not. Independents—including the many elite businessmen in their midst—were obviously among the most disillusioned with local affairs. But the city's business community in general had other reasons to gripe. Attempting to shape public policy within such a divided and scandal-ridden political environment was a regular source of frustration. On multiple occasions, progress on some of local business elites' most cherished policy goals stalled after they became focal points in the ongoing struggle between the city's bosses and independent reformers.

Understanding this pattern requires making peace with a tension. Throughout the first two decades of the twentieth century, leading businessmen in Philadelphia agreed on a number of fronts, such as the need to rebuild parts of Philadelphia following City Beautiful ideals. Nonetheless, the city's business elite was deeply divided when it came to other issues, most of all the question of who should run the government and how. On one side of this conflict stood some of the wealthiest men in Philadelphia (and, in fact, the nation), most notably Peter A. B. Widener. In the late nineteenth century, Widener, along with fellow Philadelphians William L. Elkins, William H. Kemble, and Thomas Dolan, had built corporate monopolies that controlled gas, electric, and street railway systems in a number of cities across the country, including in their hometown. In Philadelphia, Widener and his colleagues' economic success had depended on their close ties to machine politicians in the Republican Party—state and local bosses who had helped Widener and his allies win the franchises and other legislation necessary to construct their utility empires.[28]

By the turn of the century, Philadelphia's Republican machine was more centralized and disciplined than ever before. A local politician named Israel "Iz" Durham had recently restructured the city's Republican organization to cut down on intraparty strife. Backed by state party boss Matthew Quay, Durham had successfully maneuvered to gain control of the party's central body, the Republican City Committee. Durham had changed party rules so that he and his closest allies picked the committee's membership. He then put committee members first in line for lucrative patronage posts to ensure their loyalty. Durham also succeeded in giving the Republican City Committee the power to credential the delegates who nominated candidates for local office.[29] According to one observer, once a candidate won Durham's backing, he could skip the party's nominating convention. Instead, he could go off and "rusticate in Florida or luxuriate at the Hot Springs," confident that his nomination was assured.[30]

Whether or not Durham's power ever reached such proportions, the more influence Durham gained, the more party regulars lined up behind him. The number of factions within Philadelphia's Republican organization dwindled. Durham and state boss Matthew Quay never enjoyed absolute authority over Philadelphia's political machine. Nor did their successors, "Sunny Jim" McNichol (who replaced Durham after his retirement in 1906) and U.S. Senator Boies Penrose (who assumed leadership of the state Republican Party after Quay's death in 1904). McNichol and Penrose especially struggled to control George, William, and Edwin Vare, three brothers who held a tight grip on politics in Philadelphia's southern neighborhoods. In the late nineteenth century, the Vares started a family business hauling refuse and ashes in an impoverished South Philadelphia neighborhood known as "the Neck." Over time they built a multimillion-dollar contracting business that performed sanitation and construction work for the city as well as for local companies. The Vares used their profits and their connections to city government to establish a formidable political organization allied with the Republican Party that increasingly controlled South Philadelphia. Durham, Penrose, and McNichol usually collaborated with the Vares. Sporadically, however, the two factions tried to outmaneuver one another. Still, such conflicts played out within a local Republican Party that was more centralized than ever before thanks to Durham's innovations.[31]

Widener and the city's other utility owners had supported this process of party consolidation. Cutting down on rivalries within the Republican Party promised Widener and his colleagues a more predictable legislative process. Utility companies depended on public franchises, and a powerful, well-oiled political machine promised to deliver them. It hardly bothered Widener and the city's other utility moguls that their allies in the Republican machine commonly resorted to voter intimidation and electoral fraud. Men like Widener had spent millions building the city's electric, gas, and transit systems. They preferred to have their investments insulated from the whims of democracy.[32]

While Widener and the city's utility interests backed the political machine, other segments of Philadelphia's business community led the opposition. No single industry dominated Philadelphia's economy as automobile manufacturing did Detroit's. Rather, Philadelphia's factories produced an exceptional assortment of goods, everything from textiles, leather products, and cigars to ships, streetcars, and train engines—an eclectic bounty that led local boosters to brag that their hometown was "the workshop of the world."[33]

The ranks of the city's antimachine "independent" reformers reflected this economic diversity. In 1905, independents established a new political organization, the Committee of Seventy. Its members included owners and top managers of firms that produced machine tools, locomotives, gas fixtures, soaps, and dyes, as well as bankers and merchants who dealt in coal, wool, and other dry goods. Prominent doctors and other professionals also joined the group. Lawyers, most of them well-off, signed up in especially large numbers. In 1911, a similar collection of businessmen and elite professionals united behind the successful mayoral candidacy of independent reformer and manufacturer Rudolph Blankenburg. When independents organized to revise the city charter in 1919, some of the most successful businessmen in the city backed the cause. They included Alba Johnson, president of the city's mammoth Baldwin Locomotive Works; William Disston, vice president of another of Philadelphia's largest factories; Coleman Sellers Jr., a major manufacturer of machine tools; Samuel Fels, a wealthy soap manufacturer; and Ernest Trigg, a factory executive and a director of the U.S. Chamber of Commerce. Trigg was also president of the Philadelphia Chamber of Commerce—a stronghold of antimachine Republicans that helped spearhead the fight for charter reform along with the Committee of Seventy.[34]

Sharply divided over the question of machine rule, Philadelphia's commercial and industrial leaders nonetheless managed to unify behind a number of policy goals. Easily the most ambitious was a sweeping, City Beautiful–inspired plan to expand the city's park system and to construct a network of parkways to increase access to green space throughout the city. Integral to this project was the completion of a downtown boulevard, inspired by the Champs-Élysées in Paris, that would connect the center of the city to Philadelphia's exceptionally large Fairmount Park. Supporters of the downtown parkway hoped to line the roadway with a series of grand monuments and civic structures, including new homes for the Philadelphia Museum of Art and the city's Free Library. A number of local organizations joined forces in support of these plans. Elite businessmen led many of them, including executives of the Pennsylvania Railroad; the owner of one of the city's principal department stores; and a partner in Baldwin Locomotives as well as Peter Widener, his lawyer, John Johnson, and Widener's preferred banker and arguably the most influential financier in Philadelphia, E. T. Stotesbury. In 1904, these businessmen and the civic groups that they helped to run—such as the Fairmount Park Art Association, the City Parks Association of Philadelphia, and the Parkway Association—joined with a number of other local organizations to found a new umbrella group: Organizations Allied for the Acquisition of a Comprehensive Park System (OAACPS). The Philadelphia Chamber of Commerce and other commercial organizations joined OAACPS, as did the city's leading organization of elite women, the Philadelphia Civic Club.[35]

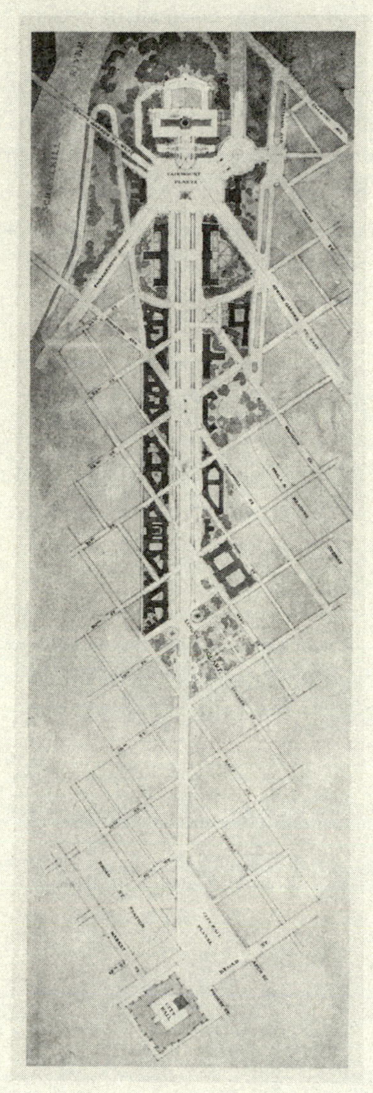

THE PARKWAY
as shown on revised plan recommended by
Mayor Reyburn in his annual message for 1908
and substantially placed on the City Plan in 1909

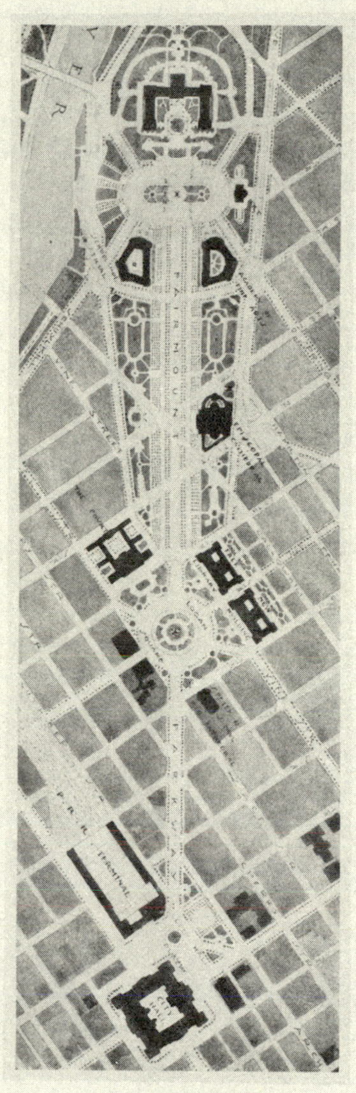

THE PARKWAY
as shown on plan made by Jacques Gréber
for the Commissioners of Fairmount Park in 1917
and now in course of construction

Figure 3. Plans for Philadelphia's downtown parkway, first in 1908 (on the left) and then, as the plans evolved, in 1917 (on the right). *Paul Philippe Cret Collection, The Athenaeum of Philadelphia.*

A handful of municipal departments and public commissions also appeared on OAACPS's roster, most notably the Fairmount Park Commission, a body that Peter Widener and his inner circle controlled. The judges of Philadelphia's court of common pleas—many of whom were closely tied to the Republican machine—appointed the members of the park commission and habitually named Philadelphians tied to the city's utility interests. From this perch, Widener and his close allies directed the planning of the proposed downtown parkway and the civic buildings that they hoped would line it. Widener was especially committed to constructing new buildings for the city's Free Library and art museum. He was a trustee of the library and wanted the new museum to house his extensive art collection along with those of his closest business associates, John Johnson and William Elkins. Completing the new buildings and the downtown parkway would entail the demolition of acres upon acres of existing structures, including working-class homes and a number of factories. Businessmen whose property was slated for removal tended to oppose the plan, but most of the city's business community embraced it.[36]

Figure 4. The intended site of the downtown parkway. The parkway was designed to cut diagonally from where the photograph is taken, through a stretch of structures that would have to be demolished, pass just to the left of the domed building, and end near the edge of the Schuylkill River, just before the river widens and the photograph begins to go out of focus. *Courtesy of PhillyHistory.org, a project of the Philadelphia Department of Records.*

In addition to the downtown parkway, members of OAACPS backed a much more extensive set of proposals authored by a leading advocate of City Beautiful planning, Andrew Wright Crawford. In 1903, Crawford—in collaboration with the well-known architect Frank Miles Day—published a multivolume treatise that called for the construction of the downtown parkway and a set of new parks that would run alongside Tacony and Pennypack Creeks in Northeast Philadelphia and Cobbs Creek in the city's southwest. Crawford's report also endorsed a plan that city officials had already proposed for a new parkway running through the city's largely undeveloped north. The Northeastern Boulevard, as it was commonly called, promised to encourage residential settlement throughout the area and to provide access to the parks that Crawford wanted the city to build there. Crawford also advocated building new parks and parkways in South Philadelphia and on the western bank of the Schuylkill River, one of the city's two principal waterways.[37]

It was an ambitious vision. And as the extensive membership of OAACPS suggests, it was a relatively popular one, at least in corporate and professional circles. Nonetheless, the path toward realizing OAACPS's plans would be far from smooth.[38]

In 1905, Iz Durham was preparing to retire. To secure his and his allies' financial future, Durham concocted an intricate plan to bring millions of dollars into the city's coffers—money that local lawmakers would then funnel back to Durham and his machine associates through city contracts. To get the funds, Durham turned to one of the city's leading utility firms, the United Gas Improvement Company (UGI). Durham proposed to cancel UGI's existing short-term lease on the city's gasworks, which UGI paid for annually, and replace it with a long-term, seventy-five-year lease that the gas company would pay off in a lump sum of $25 million. By some estimates, this was $100 to $125 million less than UGI would have paid under its existing contract. Independent reformers' immediately drew attention to the scam.[39]

To counter the charges of his detractors, Durham contended that the city desperately needed the $25 million from UGI. But the city's existing budget contradicted his claim, so Durham and his allies resolved to make his assertion true. Soon after the gas controversy began, Durham and his allies on the city council introduced legislation providing for the downtown parkway, the Northeastern Boulevard, the park and parkway along Cobbs Creek, and a number of Crawford's and OOACPS's proposals for South Philadelphia.

But Durham's attempt to inflate the city budget simply fed the opposition. In May 1905, in front of a gallery filled with protestors, city councilmen allied with Durham passed bills providing for the park and parkway projects and soon thereafter approved the new gas lease. Local manufacturers opposed to machine rule reportedly gave their workers time off to protest the so-called gas steal. As public anger continued to mount, Durham and the city council abandoned all of the measures.[40]

Crawford's and OAACPS's City Beautiful plans gained a degree of momentum two years later, but only temporarily. During the administration of Mayor John E. Reyburn—a machine politician who took office in 1907—the city constructed the western tip of the downtown parkway and began purchasing land for the proposed parks along Pennypack Creek and Cobbs Creek. The Reyburn administration also completed large portions of the Northeastern Boulevard—a project that proved to be a boon to Reyburn's political allies. A number of machine politicians bought property in the path of the proposed roadway as well as in surrounding areas. They then sold the land needed to build the street back to the city for a sizable profit and watched the values of their remaining property rise as the boulevard was constructed. Political power broker "Sunny Jim" McNichol owned the contracting firm that built the road in exchange for $1.4 million in public funds. In antimachine circles, the project became known as the "McNichol Boodlevard."[41]

After Reyburn left office, however, friction between the city's bosses and reformers once again stymied progress on these and other projects. In 1911, independents successfully exploited a power struggle between the two main factions of the Republican machine and elected as mayor longtime independent reformer and manufacturer Rudolph Blankenburg. Even so, machine politicians continued to dominate the city council. The result was gridlock. Blankenburg attempted to squeeze graft out of the city's political system, while city councilmen allied with the machine clung to the status quo and tried to keep Blankenburg's legislative achievements to a minimum. Bickering over how the city awarded public contracts held up construction on the downtown parkway for the entirety of Blankenburg's four-year term. Similar dynamics hampered progress on the art museum project. Hewing to strict budgetary principles, Blankenburg refused to appropriate funds for the building early in his tenure. When he finally bowed to public pressure and did so, the city council suddenly turned against the proposal in an attempt to humiliate the mayor. Major appropriations for the museum failed to make it into the city's budget until Blankenburg's third year in office. Architectural challenges then brought further delays. Quarrels between Blankenburg and the city council also slowed work on the proposed library, so much so that in 1915—the third year of

Blankenburg's term—the popular preacher Billy Sunday was able to hold a revival on the empty lot where the library was slated to stand.[42]

The machine returned to power in full force under Blankenburg's successor, Mayor Thomas B. Smith. In characteristic machine fashion, Smith funneled money from the city's treasury to his political allies through contracts on public projects, including the downtown parkway. Just a month before the end of World War I, the parkway finally opened to traffic. The commitment of the city's most powerful politicians and its wealthiest citizens had easily swept aside resistance among business owners and working-class Philadelphians displaced by the project. The vehicles that christened the new roadway traveled on pavement that "Sunny Jim" McNichol's construction company had helped to lay just before McNichol died. But they also drove down a street wholly unadorned by the civic structures that local business leaders had hoped to build. Despite progress, the Tacony, Pennypack, and Cobbs Creek park and parkway projects remained unfinished as the nation transitioned from war to peace.[43]

Independent reformers' fight against boss rule reaped a similarly disappointing harvest—a fact that had major consequences for business leaders' political activism in the years that followed. In 1917, another rift developed between the two main wings of Philadelphia's Republican machine—one controlled by the Vare brothers and the other by Boies Penrose (who ruled on his own after his partner "Sunny Jim" McNichol passed away). The fissure stemmed from a municipal primary in the city's Fifth Ward, an area in the heart of what was once colonial Philadelphia. Tensions mounted in the lead-up to the election, as policemen allied with the Vares repeatedly harassed supporters of Penrose's candidate, James A. Carey. As voters cast their ballots, Vare underlings in the city's police department arrested over two dozen Carey backers and closed a number of polls. When Carey and two colleagues went to check on reports of foul play, a group of Vare-hired thugs accosted them. The Vare henchmen eventually opened fire and killed a police officer who had tried to intervene.[44]

The outcry that followed the killing suggested that local sentiment had turned sharply against the Vares. In an attempt to capitalize on public outrage, independent reformers established a new political party—the Town Meeting Party—and ran candidates in the November general election against the Vares' Republican slate. In a rare move, Penrose urged his supporters to vote for the Town Meeting Party's antimachine candidates. But even murder and Penrose's endorsement could not bring independent reformers a decisive victory. The Vares survived the 1917 election, yet so did the fledgling partnership between Penrose and the city's independent reformers. Within a year, Penrose and independents—including leaders of the Philadelphia Chamber of Commerce—had begun to plot a major reformation of the city charter and with it the Vares' demise.[45]

In designing the new charter, independents especially sought to change the composition of Philadelphia's city council, which at the time was a bicameral body with 146 members elected from the city's forty-eight wards. Unlike their counterparts in Detroit, municipal reformers in Philadelphia did not attempt to replace the existing city council with one elected entirely at large. Their newfound ally Penrose would have rejected such a proposal since his power was in part ward based. Still, reformers hoped that the new council would feature at least some at-large representation to dilute ward politicians' strength. They also wanted to reform Philadelphia's civil service system. Under existing law the mayor had the power to appoint the city's three-member civil service commission. Mayors allied with the Republican machine regularly turned the commission into a patronage mill. Independents wanted the city council to appoint a single civil service commissioner by a two-thirds vote. They also proposed bringing the sizable county government (whose jurisdiction was coterminus with the city itself) under civil service law in order to cut a major source of machine patronage.[46]

Yet the legislative process and the whims of Boies Penrose whittled down each one of these proposals. Pennsylvania governor William C. Sproul came out early against anything but token at-large representation in the city council, most likely to mollify machine politicians in the state legislature who opposed abolishing ward power. When a revised charter became law in June 1919, it made no provision for at-large members in the new council. Instead, it provided for a single-chamber body with twenty-one members drawn from the city's eight senatorial districts. The new system apportioned a council member to each district plus another for every twenty thousand voters within a given district's boundaries.[47]

Legislative wrangling also weakened the civil service reforms that independents had initially proposed. Instead of one civil service commissioner appointed by two-thirds of the city council, as reformers had advocated, the final law left the city's existing three-member commission intact. The new charter gave the city council rather than the mayor the power to appoint the commissioners, as reformers had wanted, but by majority rather than supermajority vote. Meanwhile, rural legislators, some of them aligned with Penrose, balked at bringing Philadelphia County under civil service regulations. Many of them were products of county patronage systems and feared that changing the laws that governed Philadelphia would open the floodgates for statewide reform. Once enacted, the new charter brought an additional fifteen thousand city jobs into the civil service system, but county jobs remained unregulated. This loophole left thousands of positions open to patronage appointment, including in the county courts as well as in the offices of the county commissioners, county coroner, the register of wills, and the recorder of deeds. As independents had wanted, the new charter outlawed politicking among the city's police and firemen (a reaction to the murder in the Fifth-Ward primary). But the political activities of other public employees remained largely unregulated, including campaign contributions. Thus, political bosses could continue one of their most lucrative practices under the new charter: filling their war chests with mandatory donations from Philadelphians whom they had placed in patronage posts.[48]

Independents were more successful in implementing some of the administrative and procedural reforms that they sought. The new charter abolished a number of antiquated public commissions and replaced them with new municipal departments featuring clearer lines of authority. Independents also succeeded in revising the city's budget-making process. Still, it is difficult to imagine that independents viewed the new charter as anything but a flawed, compromise document. At best its reorganization of the city council, various departments, and budgetary procedures promised modest gains in the efficiency of the city's legislative process and in its bureaucracy. Many of the charter's other provisions, however, such as the election of councilmen from senatorial districts and the city council's power to appoint the civil service commission, meant that preventing machine domination under the new system would demand winning hard-fought elections to capture and maintain an independent majority in city council—a daunting task considering that the new charter left intact major sources of machine funding and patronage.[49]

Much like in Detroit, the fight to reform Philadelphia's political system included a campaign to change how the city's school district was governed. Antimachine businessmen—working closely with elite female activists and a handful of school administrators—supported this cause as well. Again their efforts were only partially successful. In 1905, independents won state legislation replacing the city's ward-based school system with a small board composed of appointed, rather than elected, members. Yet the new law still left the composition of the new body largely up to machine leaders by giving the judges of the city's court of common pleas the power to appoint the board. These were the same justices who continually named Peter Widener and his corporate allies to Philadelphia's

Fairmount Park Commission. In 1911, independents again tried to reform the city's school system by replacing the appointed board of education with an even smaller body elected at large in the hopes of increasing elite influence. They also sought to give the school board the authority to tax and spend on its own instead of having Philadelphia's city council control the school budget. In the end, independents won legislation reducing the size of the board and freeing it from council oversight. But machine bosses made sure that the judges of the court of common pleas would still determine who ran the city's schools.[50]

Much as they did in the case of the Fairmount Park Commission, the city's judges tended to stack the reconfigured school board with businessmen, wealthy lawyers, and other successful professionals, as well as with Philadelphians whose names appeared in the city's social register, thus satisfying independent reformers' hopes for an elite school board to a degree. Members of the redesigned board also furthered another of reformers' goals. In Philadelphia, the campaign to transform school governance before World War I was part of a broader push to build an educational system that reformers hoped would address the challenges of urbanization, immigration, and training workers in an industrial economy. Between 1911 and 1915, Philadelphia's school budget jumped from just over $7 million to more than $12 million—a major increase. In the 1920s, however, elites on the city's school board would spend far more.[51]

As World War I came to a close, Philadelphia's business leaders remained sharply divided over the question of boss rule. The city's new charter had left major sources of machine power untouched. In fits and starts, public officials had managed to make progress on parts of the City Beautiful plans that elite businessmen had embraced, but many more remained unrealized. Antimachine businessmen and their allies had managed to reform school governance in the city to some degree and to increase educational funding, but local political bosses still retained sway over the city's educational affairs. Whether for business leaders tightly aligned with Philadelphia's political machine or for those strongly opposed to it, there had been few clear-cut victories in the first two decades of the century. In Atlanta, local business leaders' political efforts led to similarly varied results.

Boosters Abroad, Muckrakers at Home

Atlanta's economy never rivaled Philadelphia's and Detroit's in the early twentieth century, but the economic fortunes of the Gate City were clearly on the rise.

By the early 1900s, twelve separate railroad lines converged in Atlanta. They delivered cotton and other agricultural products from the southern countryside to the city's many mercantile enterprises, such as the S. M. Inman Company, one of the world's largest cotton trading firms. In turn, Atlanta's merchants packaged these crops for distribution throughout the nation and overseas. Meanwhile, the value of products manufactured in Atlanta rose more than sevenfold between 1900 and 1919 as the city became home to a growing assortment of cotton and lumber mills and factories producing a range of other goods, from fertilizers and agricultural machinery to the city's signature product, Coca-Cola. As Atlanta assumed its central place in the southern economy, it also became the regional outpost for a number of national corporations and home to many of the South's leading banks and insurance companies.[52]

Atlanta's economic development pleased the well-off bankers, manufacturers, merchants, and high-end lawyers who made up the city's white commercial and industrial elite—a group that was deeply committed to attracting new businesses to the city. But economic growth also brought social upheaval. Indeed, in the opening years of the century, Atlanta's white business leaders especially struggled to reconcile the pristine, boosterish image of the city that they projected in newspapers and journals across the country with the reality that their hometown was riddled with social strife, health hazards, ramshackle schools, and other infrastructure that was buckling in the face of a major population boom. Atlanta's white business elite was particularly fond of bragging about how Atlanta was free of the racial antipathies that plagued other southern cities. In 1906, however, tensions between the city's quickly growing white and African American populations boiled over into a deadly riot that belied those claims. As Atlanta's economy flourished, thousands of rural southerners flocked to the city, many of them hoping to escape the brutal grind of tenant farming and sharecropping at a time when cotton prices were abysmally low. The city's population grew from just under 90,000 to nearly 155,000 between 1900 and 1910. By 1920, another 45,000 people would settle in Atlanta.[53]

Most of these migrants simply traded rural for urban poverty even as many aspects of their lives fundamentally changed. On the farm, parents could work the fields while keeping an eye on their children. In the city, where working-class newcomers toiled in factories, railroad depots, warehouses, or other locations away from their homes, parental supervision became much more haphazard. Anonymity was often impossible in the countryside. In the city, it was unavoidable. Temptations like the chance to get drunk in one of the city's many saloons abounded in turn-of-the-century Atlanta. And so did members of the opposite race. In 1910, Atlanta was one-third African American and two-thirds white. Despite a rising tide of segregation laws, African American and white newcomers to the city tended to live, work, and spend their leisure time in greater proximity to one another than they had in countryside. The combination of a breakdown in traditional forms of supervision, anxiety over urban anonymity, worries over the rampant consumption of liquor and other intoxicants, and the inevitable intermingling of the races continually stoked the racist fears of white Atlantans. In the fall of 1906, white paranoia turned to rage after leading newspapers in the city published a series of sensationalist accounts describing African American men sexually assaulting white women. On September 22, a furious white mob went on a killing spree, chasing down random African American men in the streets and on the city's streetcars. The violence lasted for three days and left at least two dozen African Americans dead.[54]

Before the riot, the city's white business leaders had done little to quell the growing storm of white anger. After the killings, however, leaders of the Atlanta Chamber of Commerce—the most influential commercial body in the city by far—scrambled to restore peace and to limit damage to Atlanta's reputation. They included Sam D. Jones, chamber of commerce president and head of the Atlanta Stove Works; Charles T. Hopkins, one of Atlanta's preeminent corporate lawyers; and James English—banker, manufacturer, and one of the wealthiest men in the city. In the aftermath of the riot, white business leaders like Jones, Hopkins, and English especially called for stricter separation of the races and for the swift adjudication of crimes related to the upheaval. In both cases, the burden fell almost exclusively on the city's African Americans. To curb the purported threat of drunken black predators, the city closed two-thirds of the saloons that catered to African Americans and declared the rest of the bars in the city for white use only. To prove that the city's criminal justice system could enforce the law without the assistance of vigilante mobs, judges convicted black men accused of riot-related transgressions almost automatically and gave them the maximum sentence that the law allowed. By contrast, the small number of white rioters who were indicted enjoyed a presumption of innocence once in court, so much so that few of them were actually convicted and those who were received far lighter sentences than their African American counterparts.[55]

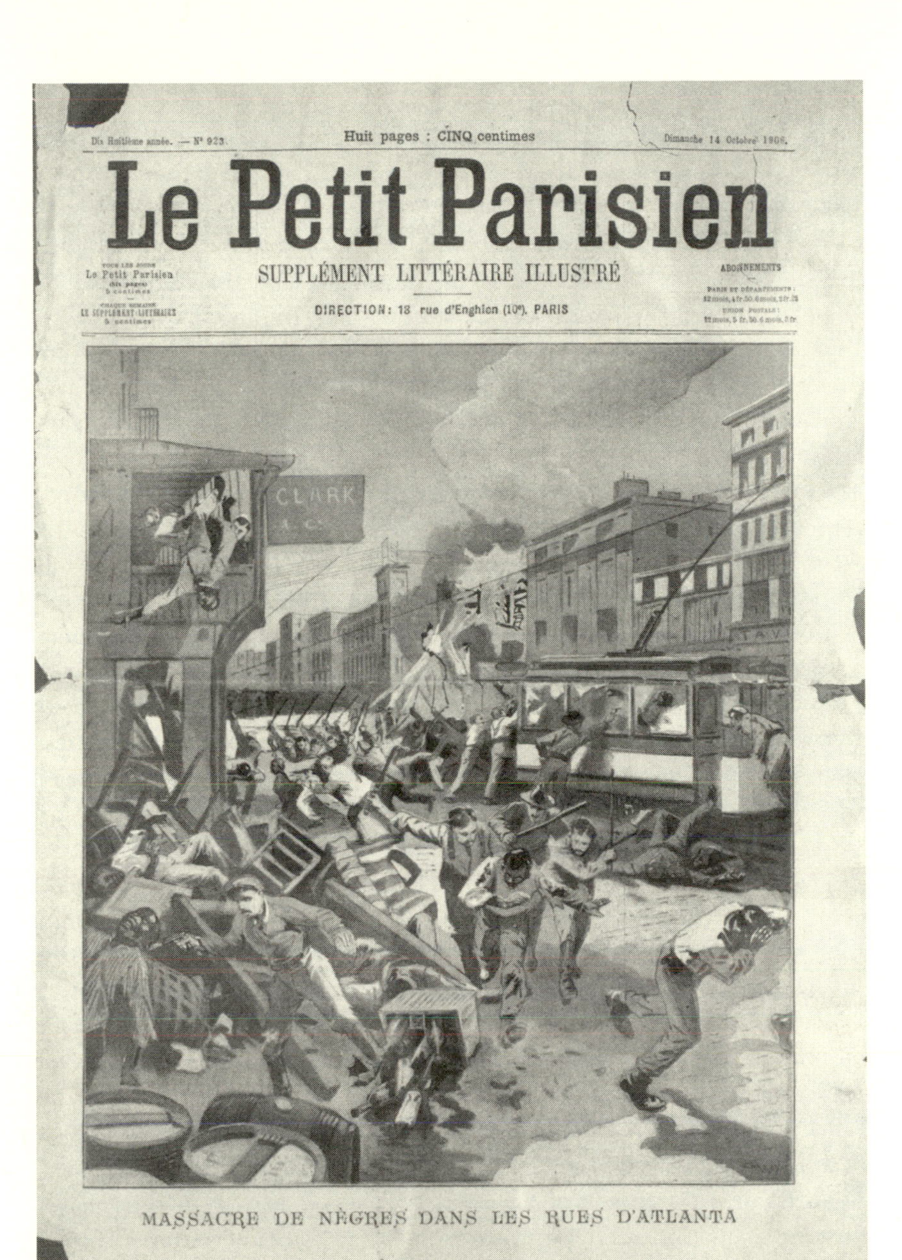

Dix Huitième année. — N° 923.

Huit pages : CINQ centimes

Dimanche 14 Octobre 1906.

Le Petit Parisien

SUPPLÉMENT LITTÉRAIRE ILLUSTRÉ

DIRECTION : 18 rue d'Enghien (10e), PARIS

Le Petit Parisien

LE SUPPLÉMENT LITTÉRAIRE

ABONNEMENTS

MASSACRE DE NÈGRES DANS LES RUES D'ATLANTA

Figure 5. A depiction of the Atlanta race riot in a French publication with the caption "Massacre of Blacks in the Streets of Atlanta." National and international coverage of the 1906 riot prodded Atlanta's image-conscious white business elite to mobilize in the hopes of salvaging the city's reputation. *Courtesy of the Kenan Research Center at the Atlanta History Center.*

The 1906 riot was just one of many developments that made white business elites' boosterish rhetoric ring hollow. Atlanta had one of the worst mortality rates in the country. Forty percent of the city's streets lacked access to sewers and a third lacked water mains. Fifty thousand Atlantans relied solely on outhouses. Other city services were also in shambles. The development of Atlanta's park system lagged far behind other cities. According one investigation, nearly half of the city's thirty schools were completely unsafe while seven others had sections that needed to be condemned.[56]

Controversy also swirled around city officials. One of the city's mayors, James G. Woodward, was caught on multiple occasions visiting prostitutes and had a habit of appearing drunk in public, including at official city meetings and at a conference of the League of American Municipalities. Woodward was a printer by trade, a union man, and a favorite of the city's white working class. He served two terms between 1899 and 1906. In 1908, Woodward managed to win the Democratic primary for mayor for a third time. Soon thereafter, his name appeared in a court case concerning two prostitutes who had gotten into a fight. Woodward was the client of one of the women the night of the incident and was again spotted drunk on the city's streets. In his own feeble defense, Woodward blamed the corn whiskey that a doctor had supposedly prescribed him to stave off pneumonia.[57]

In the months surrounding Woodward's escapade, local business leaders' discomfort with the city's growing array of political and social problems became increasingly clear. Atlanta was a one-party town. Normally, winning the Democratic primary as Woodward had done was the same as winning public office itself. But members of Atlanta's commercial and industrial elite feared the national embarrassment that would follow if voters elected a chronic drunk and an apparently incorrigible john to Atlanta's highest office for yet another term. Using the city's chamber of commerce as their organizational base, a number of the city's most influential businessmen mobilized to draft one of their own to run for mayor. Just weeks before the general election, the sitting president of the Atlanta Chamber of Commerce and the founder of the Coca-Cola Company, Asa Griggs Candler, convened a mass meeting that in turn appointed a committee of twenty-five men to choose a candidate. Former chamber of commerce president J. K. Orr chaired the committee, which also included Candler, corporate lawyer Charles Hopkins, bank president Ernest Woodruff (who would later buy Coca-Cola), and two future presidents of the Atlanta Chamber of Commerce: Victor Kriegshaber, a successful manufacturer of construction materials, and F. J. Paxon of

Davison-Paxon-Stokes, one of Atlanta's leading department stores. Members of the nominating committee quickly decided to back wealthy banker and past chamber of commerce president Robert F. Maddox.[58] In stump speeches before the election, Maddox contended that the "business prosperity, good name and decency of the city was at stake" and urged voters to make the right choice between "decency and indecency; between law and order and lawlessness; between a well and liberally governed city and one in which unbridled license runs riot." With all of the city's newspapers against him, Woodward's campaign barely limped along. Voters chose Maddox by a wide margin.[59]

In the months preceding Maddox's election, a similar cohort of businessmen had begun to mobilize to improve city services. In early 1908, the manufacturer Harry L. Schlesinger published an open letter in the *Atlanta Constitution* calling for a large bond issue to fund a set of initiatives that promised to improve Atlanta's "prestige and prosperity" as well as its citizens "mental and moral . . . development." Schlesinger especially called for new parks, schools, and sewers as well as sidewalks and a new city hall.[60] Soon thereafter, the *Atlanta Constitution* reported being "deluged" with "vigorous and unqualified approvals" of Schlesinger's proposal from the city's "most prominent business men," an outpouring of support that prompted the Atlanta Chamber of Commerce to appoint a committee to evaluate the city's needs.[61] Members of the chamber's committee were reportedly "astounded . . . by the disgraceful sanitary and hygienic conditions under which 50,000 Atlantans were living."[62] They were similarly distraught over the state of the city's school system. Chamber leaders at first accepted the committee's recommendation for a $1,500,000 bond issue—$500,000 for sewers, $500,000 for the city's water system, and $500,000 to build sixteen new schools with playgrounds. After Robert Maddox's triumph in that fall's race for mayor, however, the city's business elite called for double that total. In 1909, the leadership of the chamber of commerce and the Maddox administration launched a campaign to persuade voters to approve $3 million in bonds—the largest bond issue in the city's history up to that time—to be repaid over thirty years from government revenue.[63]

In Atlanta, winning the right to float bonds was an exceptionally difficult task. Victory required the approval of two-thirds of the registered voters of the city. In most cities, including Detroit and Philadelphia, winning bond elections demanded a mere majority vote no matter voter turnout. To emerge victorious in Atlanta, by contrast, proponents of debt spending not only had to win a supermajority of the votes cast but also had to get at least a supermajority of the city's registered electorate to the polls. Over time this requirement proved particularly nettlesome for Atlanta's white business elite, whose strategy for luring new firms to the city focused on improving city services while keeping taxes low—a dual imperative that made debt spending businessmen's leading option for pursuing public sector growth.[64]

As the 1910 referendum approached, the chamber of commerce took the lead in organizing an elaborate campaign to get out the vote. Its leaders sent over eight thousand letters to residents of neighborhoods that would benefit directly from the bond issue and contacted employers throughout the city to encourage them to get their employees to the polls. The city's main union, the Atlanta Federation of Trades, and many of the city's women's clubs also organized on behalf of the bonds. All of these efforts helped make funding available for Atlanta's only major burst of government spending between the turn of the twentieth century and the end of World War I. With the bond money in hand, the city built twelve new schools, constructed its first sewage treatment plants, and greatly expanded the reach of the city's water system. Over nine thousand Atlantans were able to abandon germ-infested outhouses for modern plumbing. Predictably, the city's African American neighborhoods garnered only about 6 percent of the $600,000 in bonds allocated to local schools. But they fared much better when it came to improvements to the city's sewer and water systems. White Atlantans knew that they could not solve the city's public health crisis without dramatically improving African Americans' access to those services. "The disease germ knows no color or race line," the editors of the *Atlanta Constitution* contended. Thanks to the 1910 bond issue, sizable portions of both working- and middle-class African American neighborhoods gained access to running water and sewers for the first time.[65]

The 1910 bond election was a significant victory for Atlanta's business community, but the city's business leaders wanted much more. As leading merchant F. J. Paxon declared during his tenure as chamber of commerce president, "We need more parks, more playgrounds and breathing spots for the people; we need a museum and an art gallery comparable to the Carnegie library," which the city had constructed in 1902. "We want our city so healthy, so attractive, so wholesome and full of charm in every respect that people will come here because it is the best place to live and to educate their children."[66] During the two years of the exceptionally business-friendly Maddox administration, the city took a number of steps in this direction beyond what the 1910 bond issue had provided for. Citing parks and playgrounds as "great preventatives of disease and crime," Maddox oversaw the construction of Atlanta's first municipally run playgrounds and a number of improvements to the local park system that resulted from the city's collaboration with two of the nation's premier landscape architects, John Olmsted and Frederick Law Olmsted Jr.[67]

Nonetheless, within a year of Maddox's departure from office, elite businessmen were clamoring for another large bond issue—including Paxon; William Blalock, the president of Fulton National Bank; Coca-Cola's Asa Candler; and former mayor Maddox himself. A similar collection of merchants, bankers, and manufacturers continued to press for debt spending for years to come. After he became mayor in 1917, for instance, Asa Candler indicated that he was in favor of a $5 million bond issue and even a modest tax increase to help finance the new debt. Yet despite the wishes of men like Candler, Atlanta's budget grew only incrementally until the 1920s.[68]

A number of dynamics undercut business leaders' efforts, but their involvement in the local municipal reform movement was among the most notable. Long disenchanted with the basic design of Atlanta's government, elite businessmen initiated an aggressive drive to revamp Atlanta's political system in 1911. Pursued largely under the auspices of the chamber of commerce, their campaign paralleled those of municipal reformers in Philadelphia and Detroit, except that a large segment of Atlanta's business community embraced the so-called commission plan. First developed in Galveston, Texas, the commission plan entailed the citywide election of a small group of public officials, each of whom headed a city department. After failing in 1911, members of Atlanta's mercantile and manufacturing elite tried to revise the charter again in 1913 but to no avail. In both cases, businessmen who favored commission government had to jettison their original vision due to resistance from organized labor (which feared a loss of working-class political influence) and from local officeholders, including a handful of businessmen who sat in the city council and did not want to risk losing their seats. In both campaigns business leaders eventually endorsed compromise measures that would have implemented some of their goals while also satisfying the demands of their leading opponents. But even these watered-down measures lost at the polls.[69]

The fight for a new city charter compromised businessmen's push for debt spending on multiple occasions. In early 1913, after months of agitation for a multimillion-dollar bond issue, it seemed that local officials were about to call an election in the hopes of gaining voters' approval. But the city's mayor and local business leaders ended up changing strategies. Rather than asking voters to approve a large bond issue, they decided to prioritize charter reform. The exceptionally high threshold for winning bond elections in Atlanta, along with memories of the failed charter campaign of 1911, forced businessmen and their allies in public office to focus on one measure at a time. But in the end, they got neither.[70]

Meanwhile, in arguing for charter reform, local business leaders continually undermined their attempt to get voters to put more money into public officials' hands. In one speech during the 1911 charter campaign, for instance, chamber of commerce leader and wealthy attorney Charles Hopkins denounced the "set of petty grafters and peanut politicians" who were currently running the city and pointed to numerous examples of political favoritism and corruption.[71] After voters rejected charter reform in 1911, members of the Atlanta Chamber of Commerce continued to take the lead in underscoring flaws in the city's political system. In 1912, the chamber's leadership commissioned a study of the city administration. The resulting report exposed a number of problems that provided fodder for the charter fight. But it also offered a host of reasons for local voters not to entrust city officials with more public funds. In trying to convince the electorate to embrace one part of their political agenda—charter reform—businessmen fueled voter resistance to another—debt spending.[72]

Another local reform movement spawned similar dynamics. In 1911, a handful of successful businessmen, including former mayor Maddox, joined with local pastors to form a branch of the Men and Religion Forward Movement (MRFM), a Protestant organization that sought to encourage men's involvement in the church and in moral reform. In Atlanta, the group's first goal was to abolish the city's red-light district. MRFM members also accused a number of public officials of being involved in the city's vice trade. MRFM leaders found a strong ally in the city's police chief, James L. Beavers, who initiated an extensive campaign to shut down the city's brothels. In time, Beavers and his supporters in the MRFM set their sights on other illicit establishments in the city, such as those that violated Georgia's prohibition law, passed in 1908. As the purview of Beavers's moral crusade expanded, however, so did local opposition. A growing segment of the city's business community complained that headlines in local papers regarding Beavers's raids were making Atlanta seem as if it were plagued by crime, an impression made worse by the MRFM's tactic of taking out full-page advertisements to expose illegal activity in the city. Eventually the Atlanta Chamber of Commerce resolved to pressure local newspapers to stop publishing material submitted by the MRFM. The city's mayor tried to rein in Beavers, but the police chief resisted. In July 1915, Beavers was demoted for insubordination after a trial before the mayor and the city's police board. Outraged, members of the MRFM spearheaded a recall campaign to remove the mayor and police administrators from office.[73]

Throughout that fall, the recall effort dominated public debate. Among many measures that suffered was yet another proposal for a major bond issue, this one for roughly $3.3 million, including a million dollars each for schools and sewers, $750,000 to improve the city's water system, and $375,000 for the city's public hospital. The electorate was slated to vote on the bonds on September 30, 1915, but city officials canceled the election as the recall campaign intensified. Voters rejected the recall, but only after the MRFM's moral crusade had pushed debt spending onto the political back burner yet again.[74]

In the meantime, years of accusations of collusion between Atlanta officials and purveyors of vice in the city had further undermined Atlantans' faith in local government. The secretary of the Atlanta Chamber of Commerce, W. G. Cooper, vented about these dynamics in an open letter to the *Atlanta Constitution* in September 1915. Bitter over the ongoing failure to increase public spending in the city, Cooper argued that "several years of severe criticism of the city government . . . has so shaken the confidence of the people in the public officials administering the city's affairs that voters are unwilling to put in the hands of these officials for disbursement the millions of money required to supply Atlanta's needs." Cooper continued, "This severe criticism began about the time when commission government became a burning issue" and surfaced yet again when the "Men and Religion bulletins began" circulating. "City officials, in one way or another, have been under fire for four or five years, almost without cessation."[75]

Cooper blamed the city's newspapers for this barrage of criticism. But the chamber of commerce had engaged in many of the same tactics in its fight for charter reform and so had the businessmen in the MRFM. As in Philadelphia and Detroit, business elites in Atlanta embraced a varied political agenda in the years leading up to the war but one that included internal tensions that compromised business leaders' political efforts on numerous occasions.

New Directions

By the 1920s, elite businessmen's political priorities would notably shift in all three cities. In Detroit, corporate leaders' success in rewriting the city charter would make the question of municipal reform more or less moot in the years that followed. In Philadelphia, the city's independent reform movement would largely dissolve early in the decade. Atlanta's business community would participate in another failed attempt to revise the city's charter in 1922. But when a new movement for charter reform picked up steam a few years later, most of the city's business leaders declined to join. Instead, they resolved to focus their efforts on yet another push to lure new firms to the city in part by improving local social programs through another major bond issue.[76]

As the Atlanta case suggests, the municipal reform movement lived on in the 1920s and so did businessmen's involvement in it, a fact that historians have long known. But historians have rarely examined how businessmen's enthusiasm for municipal reform either before the war or after fit into business interests' larger public agenda, which also included support for public schooling and the construction of parks, playgrounds, museums, and libraries, as well as improving public health by building better sewer and water systems. Judging from the three cities examined here, for many businessmen the desire to achieve a growing number of social policy goals would increasingly trump questions of political process after World War I.

This shift doubtless first sprang from dynamics related to the war itself. Developments on the home front exacerbated many of the social trends that business elites already found distressing. As factories expanded production to supply troops in Europe, a heightened demand for labor drew even more workers to American cities. Surging populations strained municipal services. To make matters worse, the federal government mandated a moratorium on all but the most essential public projects during the war to save material and labor for the fight overseas. Meanwhile, complaints came in from military officials that a large proportion of the men who had reported for duty were physically and intellectually unprepared to serve, a pattern that seemed to confirm many middle- and upper-class Americans' worst fears about the growing inadequacies of the nation's citizenry, especially when it came to the foreign born, who tended to perform poorly on the culturally biased intelligence tests that were used at the time.[77]

Then came 1919, the first year after the armistice. The well-documented tumult that marked that year in part constituted an acute urban crisis from elite businessmen's perspective. In 1919 alone, American workers took part in 2,600 strikes, many of which took place in cities. In general, workers struck for two reasons. First, the cost of living had skyrocketed during World War I and continued to do so for a time after the armistice. Workers needed higher wages to get by, and they were willing to walk off the job to get them. In addition, employers sought to reverse the gains that organized labor had won during the war thanks to a series of federal regulations that had aimed to promote industrial peace in order to maximize production. Membership in the American Federation of Labor, the nation's largest and most influential union, had grown by over two million members during the war. Most employers hoped to restore the open shop after the armistice and to roll back the concessions that workers had won amid the wartime push for industrial harmony.[78]

The first truly major strike took place in Seattle that January. Initially, about thirty-five thousand workers at the city's shipyards struck after negotiations broke down over their wages. Soon thereafter, sixty thousand other Seattle workers walked off their jobs in solidarity. The Seattle General Strike nearly shut down the whole city. It lasted only a week, but more conflicts followed elsewhere. Emboldened by their wartime gains, local unions in more than forty-five cities pledged to form a new political party, the American Labor Party, to push for legislation to permanently alter the balance of power between capital and labor. That spring, violence riddled May Day demonstrations in a number of urban areas, including Boston, New York, and Cleveland. By July, the nation was bracing itself for a national strike. Police forces in Philadelphia and New York implemented twenty-four-hour patrols on the Fourth of July, when the strike was supposedly going to begin. Officials in Chicago called in military reinforcements. A coordinated nationwide walkout never occurred, but strikes continued to break out in city after city. Nearly three-quarters of Boston's police force walked off the job that September and stayed there even as a brief crime wave ensued. Weeks later, 350,000 of the nation's steelworkers went on strike after the chairman of U.S. Steel refused to meet with union officials.[79]

All of these conflicts compounded fears that the radicalism that had brought communist revolution to Russia in 1917 had spread to the United States. With the nation's proletariat already picketing in the streets, a spate of bombings and bomb threats sparked an anticommunist panic. In March, a newspaper in Chicago claimed to have discovered evidence of a looming attack. No bombs went off in the Windy City that spring, but explosions took place elsewhere. In late April, the mayor of Seattle found a bomb in his mail. A senator from Georgia received one that blew off the hands of his maid. On June 2, bombings took place in Philadelphia, Pittsburgh, and six other cities, including Washington, D.C., where a bomb exploded in front of the home of the U.S. attorney general.[80]

It had long been an American pastime to blame radicalism and labor agitation on the foreign born, and immigrants once again took the brunt of the blame. Public officials attempted to round up immigrants suspected of having radical political sympathies. In December 1919, federal officials deported 249 foreign-born political activists to the Soviet Union on a ship nicknamed the "Soviet Ark." Raids targeting immigrants culminated in early 1920, when federal officials arrested over five thousand suspected radicals in a surprise sweep. But much more common than deporting or arresting the foreign born were pledges to redouble efforts to "Americanize" them and promote their assimilation into the nation's political and cultural mainstream.[81]

A series of deadly race riots in over two dozen American towns and cities furthered panic over urban disorder. In Chicago, twenty-three African Americans and fifteen whites died in rioting that followed the fatal stoning of an African American boy who had accidentally drifted into an all-white swimming area in Lake Michigan. Washington, D.C., experienced its own version of the Atlanta riot of 1906 after the *Washington Post* ran a series of trumped-up articles describing African American men attacking white women. The uproar that followed killed six and injured over two hundred more.[82]

Amid all of this instability and continuing into the years that followed, urban business leaders responded in large part by doubling down on their conviction that government—particularly deployed at the local level—was essential for promoting social, economic, and political stability. Viewed from the 1920s, businessmen's vision of a civic welfare state before World War I seems merely incipient, dwarfed by what came thereafter. In some cases, local business leaders were responding to working-class revolts or race riots in their own hometowns. In other cities, business elites turned to government to keep the disorder from spreading to their backyards. Elsewhere, boosterish businessmen viewed the postwar chaos as an opportunity and intensified their efforts to build cities that could lure firms from other towns that were seeking permanent refuge from urban unrest.

Fears of working-class radicalism, worries over the foreign born, and the conviction that city services were insufficient or ill designed to prevent problems like crime and vice all persisted throughout the 1920s. But as time wore on, business leaders' concern for these issues increasingly overlapped with locally specific challenges that urban business elites hoped to overcome, including relentless population growth in Detroit, the early signs of economic decline in Philadelphia, and evidence that the efforts of Atlanta's boosters were falling short. These and other dynamics kept heightened social spending at the forefront of business leaders' public agenda in all three cities throughout the 1920s, even as businessmen's distress over the war and its immediate aftermath grew less sharp. And in all three cities, business leaders would prove considerably more successful in implementing their policy objectives in the 1920s than they had been before the armistice. Even so, political realities would continually remind them that the power to shape public policy was a privilege that could not be assumed but had to be continually won.

CHAPTER 2

Detroit

Businessmen at Large

At the end of World War I, roughly one in three residents of Detroit was a first-generation immigrant. More than a third were children of at least one foreign-born parent. About forty thousand African Americans lived in the city. The vast majority of Detroit's population was working class, and over half was Catholic.[1]

Yet when the city held its first elections under its new charter, the results would have better suited a place that was Detroit's demographic inverse. The contest took place in November 1918, just as the last shots were being fired in Europe. Of the nine candidates who won Detroit's first at-large elections for city council, none were foreign born. Just one had been born to immigrant parents, and only two were Catholic. All of the winners were white, and all were men. The city's leading union, the Detroit Federation of Labor (DFL), ran a slate of candidates in the race for city council, but every one of them lost. Henry Leland's business-dominated Detroit Citizens League, by contrast, supported all nine candidates who won out of the sixty-six who entered the race. Nearly all of the winners were businessmen. Five of the incoming councilmen were corporate executives, two were realtors, and one was a banker. The remaining councilman, Fred Castator, had previously served as deputy assistant labor commissioner for the state of Michigan. Though Castator was supposedly the Citizens League's labor-friendly pick, the DFL had denounced Castator going into the election while the Michigan Manufacturers Association had supported him. The DFL eventually claimed Castator as an ally, but in 1918 he was a businessmen's candidate. The composition of the city council had changed markedly since the eve of charter reform, when the council had included saloonkeepers, a druggist, a plumber, a barber, and several other members of the city's petite bourgeoisie. In 1917, elections for the city's new at-large school board brought similar changes to that body, except that a woman, Laura Osborn—leader of the prewar movement to reform the board—succeeded in winning a seat.[2]

Business leaders managed to implement large swaths of their vision of a civic welfare state in 1920s Detroit because the city's new political structure gave candidates with access to wealth an advantage that proved difficult for other political actors to surmount. Except for a brief interval between 1924 and 1926, candidates backed by the Detroit Citizens League held a supermajority on Detroit's city council throughout the 1920s. Out of the seventeen councilmen who served between 1919 and 1929, ten were identifiable as corporate executives or businessmen in real estate, insurance, and banking.

Viewed from another angle, businessmen's dominance of Detroit's city council appears even more pronounced. In the eleven-year period between 1919 and 1929, the members of the nine-member council collectively served ninety-nine years in office. Businessmen served sixty-five out of those ninety-nine years. The remaining councilmen who served in the 1920s included three professional civil servants, a doctor, a dentist, former deputy assistant labor commissioner Castator, and finally Robert Ewald, a union man who managed to fight his way onto the city council early in the decade. In time, however, Ewald grew palatable enough to business interests to earn repeated Citizens League endorsements, suggesting that even the most worker-friendly councilman in 1920s Detroit walked a line between capital and labor.[3]

Candidates backed by the Detroit Citizens League also held a supermajority on the city's school board at all times during the decade, and all but three of the board members who served during the 1920s were listed in the city's social register. The superintendent of schools during the period was a former director of the Detroit Board of Commerce and was the board of commerce's choice to head the schools. Finally, Detroit's mayors, when they were not business executives themselves, forged close ties to the city's commercial and industrial elite.[4]

Of course, businessmen's political power could be neither constant nor absolute in a mass democracy like Detroit's. A number of dynamics compromised business leaders' influence during the decade, including a crisis in municipal finances, a grassroots insurgency led by the local branch of the Ku Klux Klan, and the sporadic political mobilization of organized labor. Indeed, there was a moment in the middle of the 1920s when it was unclear who would rule Detroit. Only a series of unforeseeable developments—including a working-class mayor who moved to broaden his base after nearly losing an election—enabled local business leaders to regain clout.

Yet despite slips in businessmen's political influence, it is difficult to identify another political force in 1920s Detroit that truly rivaled the city's business elite. The political fortunes of the Ku Klux Klan declined as quickly as they had arisen. Open-shop campaigns tended to sap organized labor's political strength and narrow local unions' political priorities. Insofar as they organized based on ethnicity, local immigrants rarely overcame the steep odds that they faced when trying to shape public policy in the city. Detroit's largest immigrant group, Poles, constituted just 5 percent of the city's population in 1920, a meager proportion in a political system based on citywide voting. The most prominent organization in Detroit's quickly growing African American community, the Detroit Urban League, depended in large part on the support of wealthy white benefactors and tended to shy away from challenging the city's white business leaders in the public sphere. Meanwhile, female activists, galvanized by the city's vast network of women's associations, fought most of their battles in the 1920s on the state and federal levels rather than in the local arena.

Lacking strong political organizations that could channel their demands, most Detroiters' principal opportunity for shaping public policy came intermittently and indirectly at election time. Other than selecting among candidates, the electorate's primary intervention in the policymaking process arose in a number of citywide referenda on major public improvement projects that entailed high levels of debt spending. Albeit often in elections with low turnout, voters approved the vast majority of the ballot initiatives enabling increased government expenditures that were put before them in the 1920s, suggesting that there was a basic consensus among Detroiters that the city needed more and better public services. Yet these referenda were worded in the most general terms and allowed voters to register only all-or-nothing, yea-or-nay votes on policies that were largely of elite design. At best, voters' participation in bond referenda constituted oblique assertions of political power and highly abstract expressions of policy preferences. Most residents of 1920s Detroit barely had a voice in the city's policymaking process due to the scarcity of effective and engaged political pressure groups. Members of Detroit's commercial and industrial elite, on the other hand, had far less trouble making themselves heard as they sought to use local government to create the city and the citizenry that they desired.

Behind the Wheel, 1919–1922

In the first elections under Detroit's new charter, voters not only elected every single candidate on the Citizens League's slate for city council. They also chose one of the most well-known corporate executives in the city to serve as mayor. James Couzens had made his fortune as the general manager of the Ford Motor Company, where he worked until 1915. Over the years, Couzens had gained a reputation for being a maverick who was willing to take worker-friendly stances even if they put him at odds with his corporate brethren. While at Ford, Couzens helped dream up the five-dollar day, a policy that most employers in the city opposed. During a nationwide unemployment epidemic at the start of World War I, Couzens publicly chastised his fellow industrialists for not doing more to aid the jobless. In the 1918 mayoral campaign, Couzens ran on a platform calling for municipal ownership of the city's street railway system. To show solidarity with Detroiters struggling in the face of high fares, Couzens boarded a streetcar and refused to pay. Other local citizens followed suit, sparking a wave of confrontations across the city. A number of local executives who opposed municipal ownership of Detroit's street railways accused Couzens of opportunistic rabble-rousing. Henry Leland and the Detroit Citizens League chose to back another candidate for mayor.[5]

Still, despite such instances of friction, Couzens and the rest of Detroit's commercial and industrial elite agreed in a number of realms. Couzens relied heavily on his corporate colleagues for input and advice throughout his term. At times Couzens denounced members of the business-dominated city council when they did not follow his lead, but he and local legislators moved in tandem on most major issues, a pattern that led to accusations in the local press that the city council was merely a rubber stamp for Couzens's agenda. In fact, Couzens and the city council's tendency to agree was indicative of a relatively robust consensus among elite Detroiters about what the city needed most.[6]

Detroit's population had skyrocketed during the war as the city's booming economy had drawn ever more people to the city. Between 1910 and 1920, the number of Detroiters grew from 465,766 to 993,768. By 1930, the city would boast 1,568,662 residents. Detroit's geography was expanding at a similarly rapid pace. Between 1910 and 1920, annexations of nearby territories increased the size of the city from 41 square miles to 78, a number that would continue to grow until the city encompassed 138 square miles in 1930. Most of this new land was undeveloped. The throngs of newcomers who arrived in Detroit during the war and its immediate aftermath continued to crowd into the city's densely populated core, an increasingly congested island in a sea of open land. Because of a shortage of classrooms, more than fifteen thousand grade-schoolers were able to attend only half-day sessions in 1919. By one account, over half the city's school-aged children were not in school at all. Reports of crime and juvenile delinquency had increased during the war, a trend that elite Detroiters associated with the population boom and the concomitant shortage of housing, schools, recreational outlets, and other city services. As the Red Scare and militant strikes swept across the country in the wake of the armistice, the anxieties of Detroit's business leaders peaked. Connecting postwar radicalism with the foreign born, businessmen's long-standing worries about immigrant assimilation intensified.[7]

Once in office, Couzens and his elite colleagues on the city council and school board moved quickly to address these issues. In his first year as mayor, Couzens convened what he called a "reconstruction meeting" that brought together "250 bankers, manufacturers," and public officials to find ways to resurrect what an advertisement for the forum called Detroit: "a civic giant flat on its back."[8] The city's commissioner of public works called for $20 to $25 million in new debt spending to improve the city's sewer system and millions more to build and improve roads, alleys, and sidewalks. Alex Dow, an executive at Detroit Edison and the city's water commissioner, demanded millions more for new water mains. Frank W. Blair, the president of the Union Trust Company, proclaimed that the city had to spend nearly a quarter billion dollars to meet its needs. James Vernor, a local manufacturer and president of the city council, declared, "The Council is ready to go the limit as far as construction work is concerned." The president of the Detroit Board of Commerce—Allan A. Templeton, a successful auto parts supplier—pledged his organization's support.[9] Soon thereafter, an editorial in the board of commerce's weekly publication called for a cascade of spending: "Instead of a slow and deliberate program of public improvements, it is necessary to do a great number of things all at once." "Immense bond issues must be sold."[10]

And indeed they were. In August 1920, voters approved the Department of Public Works and the Water Commissioner's request for a windfall of bonds, $37 million in all. By the time Couzens left office at the end of 1922, the city had built 100 miles of sewer mains and another 200 miles of lateral sewers at a cost of over $30 million. It laid 170 miles of road and spent more than $18 million to improve the city's water system.[11] While most of this new construction did not follow a formal city plan—Detroit would not officially adopt one until 1925—promoting residential decentralization formed a guiding principle. As Couzens attested, it is "the consensus of opinion that there is more immorality being caused by people huddled together in small rooms, who are robbed of normal home life . . . than from any other cause."[12]

Couzens was right that he expressed a commonly held view. The fight against overcrowding and residential congestion in American cities sparked some of the most definitive political movements of the early twentieth century, such as the struggle to improve tenement housing in places like New York City. Urban reformers fashioned an assortment of proposals to reduce residential density in urban America during the era. The most straightforward was simply promoting development away from central cities. For business leaders in places like Detroit (as well as Philadelphia and Atlanta), this approach was particularly alluring. Fostering decentralization through government action served the varied goals of a diverse assortment of business interests: real estate developers hoping to turn a profit; manufacturers who sought to erect bigger factories in outlying areas; corporate higher-ups who sought a suburbanesque lifestyle for themselves and for the growing number of middle-class, white-collar workers whom local companies employed; employers who wanted healthier and therefore more productive workers; and, finally, businessmen who feared that congested, dilapidated neighborhoods were hotbeds of vice, crime, and political radicalism. A political cartoon that appeared in the Detroit Board of Commerce's monthly magazine in 1919 underscores how local business leaders viewed housing conditions in the city as a threat to political stability (Figure 6). The cartoon shows a hand holding a candlesnuffer shaped like a single-family home—an architectural form that entails residential decentralization. The house is labeled "Home for Workmen." The candle that the house is about to extinguish features a skull and crossbones and the words "Bolshevism" and "Unrest." By using government to build infrastructure like water mains, sewers, and roads in a decentralized pattern, Detroit's business elite in part sought to encourage the development of a city composed of freestanding homes inhabited by workers averse to radical politics.[13]

Figure 6. A cartoon from the June 30, 1919, issue of the Detroit Board of Commerce's magazine, the *Detroiter*. Detroit's business elite believed that constructing new housing, ideally in a decentralized pattern, was essential for quelling working-class radicalism and protest. *Courtesy of Baker Old Class Collection, Baker Library, Harvard Business School.*

Couzens and the new city council also moved to expand the city's recreation system. In the spring of 1919, they won voters' approval of a plan to spend $10 million in bond revenue to construct new playgrounds, playing fields, and to extend the city's park system. Representatives of the Detroit Board of Commerce cheered the measure, which included initiatives that they had lobbied for before the war, including supervised play areas. "Not only good health but good citizenship is served by this playground policy," an editorial in the board of commerce's magazine proclaimed.[14] The business leadership of the Detroit Citizens League echoed this sentiment and added that providing more recreational outlets could address two other issues facing the postwar United States: suspected bolshevism and the consequences of Prohibition. "Red Radicalism is rampant in the land, including Detroit," leaders of the Citizens League warned in its monthly publication, the *Civic Searchlight*. "One of the best weapons for fighting against radicalism and for completing the solution of the saloon problem lies in a generous supply of recreation facilities."[15] Mayor Couzens echoed the Citizens League's conviction that publicly funded recreation was an important substitute for the pub. He also pointed to yet another benefit of constructive play: its potential for assimilating immigrants into "American" culture. As Couzens awkwardly put it, the city's new parks and playgrounds were among Detroit's "best Americanization factors."[16]

Meanwhile, members of the city's elite school board were busy implementing an ambitious agenda of their own. Elected in the spring of 1917 with the backing of the Detroit Citizens League, the new at-large school board faced a difficult road early in its tenure. World War I coincided with the board's first year and a half in office, drawing political attention away from the schools. Then, just months after the armistice, Detroit's superintendent accepted an offer to lead Chicago's school district. The search for his replacement opened a brief division between the new elite board, the Detroit Board of Commerce, and the city's multimillionaire mayor. The board of education initially extended an offer to Randall Condon, the superintendent of Cincinnati's schools. But Mayor Couzens and the board of commerce favored Condon's main competitor for the post, Frank Cody, a longtime Detroit educator and a former director of the Detroit Board of Commerce. Under the new charter, the mayor and the city council retained oversight of the school district's budget, a power that Couzens gladly used to overturn the school board's new hire. Just weeks after the board of education extended an offer to Condon, Couzens vetoed the action based on a series of technicalities, including that the school board had failed to stipulate a specific tenure for the new superintendent and that the salary that board members had promised Condon was in excess of what the city council had approved. Taking the hint, Condon withdrew his candidacy. As Couzens and the board of commerce had wanted all along, Frank Cody became Detroit's new superintendent of schools. But the rift between Couzens, the board of education, and Cody healed quickly. Convinced that Couzens and the board of commerce's instincts about Cody's appointment had been right, the school board continued to renew his contract until 1942.[17]

In fact, within months of assuming his new post, Cody and members of the Detroit Board of Education had found enough common ground to undertake a broad survey of the city's school system and to agree on a far-reaching set of new policies, including an unprecedented amount of construction. As was true of many educators at the time, Cody and members of Detroit's school board viewed schools primarily as mechanisms for training children for democratic citizenship while simultaneously preparing them for the increasingly hierarchical world of work. Cody and board members' new plan discarded the school system's existing practice of building six-year elementary schools and six-year high schools. Instead, they adopted a proposal to build elementary schools to serve the kindergarten through sixth grades, three-year intermediate schools, and three-year metropolitan high schools, or the 6-3-3 model. They resolved to convert all elementary schools to fit the "platoon" design, in which students moved from class to class and activity to activity instead of remaining in the same room for the majority of the day. Among other justifications for platoon schools, Cody and members of the school board explained that the model provided "a half hour daily in the auditorium for every child" when "an effort is made to socialize and Americanize him."[18] Cody and the board believed that civic goals should inform elementary education more generally as well. "During the early years of school life," they contended," it is important that all children acquire a common fund of ideas, ideals and habits of thought and action in order that there may be social and national solidarity."[19]

Cody and the school board hoped that new intermediate schools would ease students' transition from elementary to high school. Most of all, intermediate schools promised to keep older children from dropping out of the system when students were in a "critical period" of their development, according to Cody and the board.[20] School officials in Detroit reasoned that separating young adolescents from elementary students and high schoolers would help educators better tailor curricular offerings to meet student interests, especially by offering vocational courses that might make staying in school seem financially worthwhile. Separate intermediate schools would also provide the physical space necessary for "the organization of classes of like ability."[21] New metropolitan high schools, in turn, would differentiate students even further through an increasingly hierarchical curriculum, including more vocational education.[22] Following an influential set of guidelines that the National Education Association had released in 1918, school officials in Detroit resolved to focus the city's high school curriculum on teaching "health . . . home making, citizenship, the proper use of leisure time, character formation and vocational education."[23] Intellectual goals went unmentioned. School officials experimented with a number of different curricular structures in the city's high schools during the decade to achieve these ends. At first, they designed a shared core curriculum that was supplemented by a variety of electives, many of them vocational, including shop, mechanical drawing, and home economics. Later, the common curriculum fell out of favor. Instead, administrators funneled high school students into one of four tracks: college preparatory, commercial, technical, or general, which school leaders described as "a course on citizenship and in the vocations."[24]

The school district's commitment to curricular differentiation and sorting students into different tracks found further expression in 1921, when Detroit's school system began administering IQ tests to all members of the first grade. Previously Detroit's schools had used the IQ test solely as a diagnostic device for students whom teachers had identified as potentially needing special care. Now, the district resolved to use the test to divide all of the city's schoolchildren into X, Y, and Z groups. IQ testing continued to spread as the decade wore on. By 1926, students in the first, third, sixth, and twelfth grades were all tested and in some cases in the eighth and ninth grades as well. Ninety thousand students were tested in 1926 alone. By the end of the decade, Detroit's school district had grown deeply gradated at all levels of the system with its structure and curriculum tightly focused on preparing children to assume their "proper" place in the labor market and to perform what school officials deemed basic civic duties.[25]

Detroit's business leaders enthusiastically embraced Cody and the elite school board's new program, which furthered business elites' broader attempt to use government programs to mold Detroiters to fit businessmen's vision of the ideal citizen-worker. Couzens and the business-dominated city council allocated unprecedented sums in support of school officials' agenda. Between the 1919–1920 school year and that of 1920–1921—when the school system began to implement its new construction plan—appropriations to the board of education shot up from $9.8 million to over $31 million. Teacher salaries doubled, appropriations for maintenance costs grew, and over $17 million in bonds were allocated to finance new construction, up from $2.4 million the year before.[26] When the school district's building initiative came under attack in some quarters, leaders of the Detroit Board of Commerce quickly rose to the defense. "To say that we must stop building schools is utterly ridiculous." Halting school construction, the businessmen warned, would amount to "civic suicide."[27]

As the largest piece of the city budget, the precise amount allocated to Detroit's schools was contested intermittently in the years that followed. Nonetheless, school spending remained high throughout the 1920s and school construction proceeded at a brisk pace. Between 1920 and 1929, Detroit built forty-four elementary schools, eleven intermediate schools, and five high schools and made improvements to many more. Cody and the board of education also made major headway in moving the city's school system to the 6-3-3 model. By the end of the decade, there were close to three times as many K–6 schools in the system as there had been at the beginning of the 1920s. The number of intermediate schools had more than tripled. The goal of creating high schools that served only grades ten through twelve had proven more elusive. There were only two at the end of the decade. The vast majority of high school students still attended facilities that housed ninth through twelfth grades. Even so, Detroit's school system left the 1920s fundamentally transformed.[28]

Under Couzens, the city also completed the new library building that business leaders had first called for two decades earlier. Opened in 1921 on the city's Woodward Avenue, the imposing marble edifice featured intricate exterior carvings, oversized bronze doors, and enough space to house over three-quarters of a million books. The city's health department also extended its reach. In 1919, department officials provided prenatal care to fewer than five hundred women. In 1922, when Couzens left office, it provided services to over ten thousand, thanks in part to the federal government's 1921 Sheppard-Towner program, which aimed at improving maternal and infant health through federal matching grants. The health department also increased the number of nurses working in the city's schools, initiated nutrition classes for underweight students, and ramped up efforts to vaccinate schoolchildren against diphtheria. Facing a shortage of hospital beds just after the war, the city built extensions to the city's two public hospitals and constructed a new sanitarium. Couzens and the city council also expanded Detroit's public market system in order to improve access to fresh and affordable food at a moment when the cost of living was on the rise throughout the United States.[29]

Thus, immediately upon capturing city hall and the city's school board, Detroit's newly empowered business elite moved aggressively to address a host of social issues. In their minds, the city that they had won control of politically was riddled with social problems. Immigrants needed assimilating. Children lacked adequate preparation for work and citizenship. Business leaders' current and future employees were too often trapped in densely populated neighborhoods filled with crime, vice, and disease—threats to political stability, productivity, and profits. Detroit and its citizenry needed saving; civic welfare was at stake. Business elites viewed the local state as the most attractive tool for the job—even more so now that business interests themselves controlled local government. Expanding public health services; building schools, playgrounds,

Figure 7. The new Detroit Public Library building soon after its completion in 1921. *Courtesy of the Burton Historical Collection, Detroit Public Library.*

and the new central library; constructing roads, sewers, and water mains to alleviate residential congestion were all projects that business leaders believed were good for local citizens. An air of benevolence often infused their rhetoric. But this does not mean that they acted contrary to their own interests. Rather, business leaders sought to use government to build a city that would serve their own political and economic goals while believing that Detroiters in general would also benefit from this quest.

Before leaving office, Mayor Couzens followed through on his campaign promise to municipalize Detroit's street railway system. Couzens sometimes spoke of purchasing the street railways and extending railway service as yet another front in the battle against residential congestion. But his primary motivation was distaste for how the city's private streetcar franchise was run. Formerly a member of the city's street railway commission, Couzens had come to believe that all so-called natural monopolies, like local gas, electric, and rail systems, would best serve the public as municipally owned entities. More than any other issue at the time, the street railway question divided Detroit's business elite. A significant cohort of local businessmen fretted that a government takeover of local streetcar companies might serve as a precedent that would threaten their own private property. This fissure, however, did not prevent the city's business leaders from agreeing in many other regards.[30]

Couzens resigned as mayor at the end of 1922, when the governor of Michigan tapped him to fill a vacated seat in the U.S. Senate. Detroit's business leaders had enjoyed an incredible amount of influence under the Couzens administration. Now, rocky terrain lay ahead.[31]

Losing Control, 1923–1925

In March 1923, Detroit's city controller announced that the Couzens administration's buying spree had brought the city to the edge of its debt limit as stipulated by the nation's principal bond exchange in New York. According to the controller, nearly $40 million in bonds approved under Couzens could not be sold on the New York market, which by state law linked the amount of debt that a city could float to a percentage of the assessed value of local property. At least in the short term, Detroit had to cease work on all but the most necessary government projects. In the spring of 1923, just over a year after Detroiters had reelected James Couzens in a landslide, the public turned sharply against him. That April, in a special election to determine who would serve out the final months of his mayoral term, Couzens's handpicked successor lost by more than a two-to-one margin. Soon after taking office, the new mayor, Frank Doremus, urged "rigid economy" to pull the city through the financial crisis.[32]

The city's fiscal woes persisted, however, and continued to shape local politics in the coming months. Elected merely to finish Couzens's tenure, Mayor Doremus soon had to run for reelection. He faced little opposition, but the races for city council were fiercely contested. In the end, four incumbents lost their seats, all of them to challengers who had denounced the city's spending habits. It was the Detroit Citizens League's worst performance in an election during the decade. Few Detroiters missed the irony that the first three years under the new charter—meant to usher in greater businesslike efficiency and rule by the "best men," as the Citizens League might have put it—had led the city toward a fiscal crisis. In part, the sitting council's attempt to move forward on one last project widely associated with the city's business elite had helped usher in the defeat. Despite the city's budget constraints, just weeks before the primary, city councilmen approved a measure to allocate nearly a half million dollars to help fund the construction of the art museum that elite businessmen had called for before the war. In the aftermath of the elections, local papers pointed to the misstep as a "strong factor in the voting."[33]

Yet even as voters repudiated how Couzens and the incumbent, business-dominated city council had run city affairs, the upshot of that fall's elections was hardly a working-class coup. Going into the contest, five candidates won the backing of the Detroit Federation of Labor, the city's main union. The DFL's core membership in the 1920s consisted of skilled workers like electricians, ironworkers, carpenters, and others in the building trades who toiled outside of the auto industry. (Autoworkers would not successfully unionize until the 1930s.) In the city council elections of 1923, three candidates backed by the DFL won, but Robert Ewald—an ally of organized labor who had won a council seat in a 1920 special election—was one of the incumbents ousted. Viewed through the dichotomous lens of capital and labor, neither emerged as the clear victor in the 1923 elections. Instead, the results expressed widespread frustration with a city council that had risked the city's financial health.[34]

In what must have seemed like a harsh irony for the councilmen who lost their seats, Detroit's budget crisis proved short lived. The mid-1920s were high times for the local real estate market. As the assessed valuation of property in Detroit rose, so automatically did the amount of bonds the city could sell in New York. Even as the city returned to fiscal stability, however, Detroit's political climate remained in flux, especially from the point of view of the city's commercial and industrial leaders. Mayor Doremus, who had fallen ill even before his reelection in 1923, soon resigned for health reasons. An election to replace him was called for the fall of 1924.[35]

In the meantime, business leaders struggled to influence the city's acting mayor, Joseph Martin, as well as the newly elected city council. In early 1924, the board of commerce, shaken by the fiscal crisis and perhaps worried that the incoming council would be less likely to do its bidding, established a new governmental committee in the hopes of shaping the city's budget. The new body brought together nearly two dozen local organizations—predominantly business-oriented groups. Recognizing that the city could not spend as freely as it had in the past, the committee recommended trimming expenditures in some areas while continuing to fund programs especially dear to the city's business elite. The Detroit Citizens League was a member organization of the new committee. As one of its representatives explained, the new body "adhered to the principle that the tax-rate, while it ought to be kept down, if possible, is . . . not the question of primary importance." After all, the representative of the Citizens League reasoned, "a low tax rate might be . . . very poor economy" since "the suppression of crime would require additional money . . . school authorities must be supported," and the city's recreation system also demanded additional funding.[36] When the governmental committee announced its budget recommendations, however, Acting Mayor Martin reportedly told the group to "mind its own business."[37] As members of Detroit's business elite looked toward the upcoming mayor's race, many of them hoped to elect someone more open to their input.

As it turned out, the 1924 election was one of the most tumultuous in Detroit's history. Even after the dust had settled and a new mayor was chosen, it remained unclear what sorts of alliances he would forge and whose interests he would serve. Unlike earlier elections under the new charter, the 1924 contest focused on religion, race, and ethnicity. The quick rise of Detroit's Ku Klux Klan was largely responsible for this shift. After establishing a local branch in Detroit in 1921, the Klan made quick work of exploiting the fears of native-born whites regarding Detroit's quickly growing African American and immigrant populations. By 1923, Detroit's KKK claimed over twenty thousand active members, a number that continued to grow. As the 1924 mayoral contest began to unfold, two Catholic candidates emerged as frontrunners: Joseph Martin, the acting mayor, and John Smith, a longtime activist in local Republican politics who had served most recently as Detroit's postmaster. From the anti-Catholic Klan's perspective, it was a contest between two evils. So the hooded order entered the fight, drafting Charles Bowles as its candidate, a political novice with no name recognition. Few in the media considered Bowles a serious contender until his surprisingly strong showing in that September's primary. With the top two vote-getters proceeding to the general election, Bowles came in third, but he nonetheless garnered 74,000 votes to Martin's 76,000 and Smith's 90,000. Bowles's unexpectedly strong finish catapulted his name into the headlines, so much so that he and the Klan resolved to win the mayoralty through a write-in campaign that November.[38]

The general election left local business leaders without a clear candidate. John Smith was a product of Detroit's working-class and largely immigrant

East Side and was an outspoken labor ally, but as postmaster he had worked closely with the board of commerce and had garnered that organization's effusive praise. Joseph Martin had rejected the input of the board of commerce's governmental committee earlier that spring, but as head of the department of public works under Couzens, he had earned a reputation for efficiency that made him seem like the best choice to some local businessmen. Finally, Charles Bowles remained an unknown entity. Some business leaders, including Citizens League founder Henry Leland, favored Bowles as the Protestant alternative to the Catholic Smith and Martin and perhaps also embraced the bigoted platform of "one hundred percent Americanism" that Bowles's association with the Klan implied.[39]

As the election approached, Smith campaigned hard throughout working-class Detroit, delivering countless speeches in the city's immigrant and African American neighborhoods. Meanwhile, the Ku Klux Klan mobilized its supporters in one of the most extensive grassroots campaigns that Detroiters had ever seen. In late October, Klan proponents and detractors clashed downtown as Bowles supporters bombarded an anti-Klan protest—honking their car horns, waving Bowles placards, exploding stink bombs, and chanting Bowles's name. Detroit policeman resorted to tear gas to disperse the crowd. Just days before the vote, fifty thousand Klansmen reportedly rallied in nearby Dearborn. The election grew all the more heated because the Detroit Federation of Labor mobilized with newfound vigor. Rallying extensively around Smith and former councilman Robert Ewald—who was running in a special election for a vacant council seat once again—the DFL organized to fight the Klan threat and also the candidacy of Joseph Martin. Detroit's Klan was vocally antiunion, and the DFL had grown to despise Martin due to his harsh treatment of city workers when he was the commissioner of public works under Couzens. Leaders of the DFL divided up the city and sent captains to organize in each division. Through neighborhood meetings, rallies in union halls, and by distributing 250,000 copies of its newspaper, the *Detroit Labor News*, the DFL made its positions known as never before.[40]

When the votes were counted, the majority's wishes were clear—and terrifying. The Klansman Bowles had beaten Smith by roughly seven thousand votes with Martin finishing far behind. But some of Bowles's supporters had been careless when writing in their choice for mayor. The city's election commission—intent on preventing a Klan victory—discounted nearly seventeen thousand ballots because of small discrepancies in the spelling of

Bowles's name and declared Smith the victor. The DFL-backed candidate for council, Robert Ewald, also won.[41]

Smith's prize, however, was merely a year in office. After all, the 1924 election was only for the privilege of completing Mayor Doremus's half-expired term. Smith knew that the Klan would attempt to prevent his reelection. And this time he could hardly count on eking out another victory based on a technicality. Once in office, the working-class darling moved to broaden his base. In so doing, he adopted a framework that allowed business interests to regain an unrivaled role in influencing the overarching trajectory of public spending in the city.

In one of his first speeches after taking office, Smith appeared before what was likely a room of familiar faces at the Detroit Board of Commerce thanks to his time as postmaster. He took the opportunity to emphasize that his administration would be a business administration. In a move that the board of commerce later called "one of the finest steps ever taken by a public official in this city," Smith announced that he was appointing a committee of five of the city's most esteemed businessmen to make a survey of the city's financial conditions and to make recommendations for a ten-year plan for city expenditures. Smith named National Bank of Commerce president and Packard investor Richard P. Joy as the committee's chair. He also appointed John Ballantyne, treasurer of Dodge Brothers and former head of Merchants National Bank; Richard H. Webber, the head of the J. L. Hudson Company, the city's largest department store; Charles H. Hodges, president of the Detroit Lubricator Company; and Detroit Trust president Ralph Stone. In the ensuing months, Smith went on to appoint more business-dominated committees to examine municipal affairs: one to study traffic, another to study aviation, and one to improve sanitation in the city. As a founding member of the Detroit Citizens League cooed, under Smith Detroit's government increasingly relied on "committees of business men" to examine local problems and to propose solutions.[42]

The elite businessmen on Smith's finance committee released their ten-year plan in June 1925. The mayor wholeheartedly endorsed the committee's report, which hewed closely to business leaders' past priorities. It included an ambitious proposal for infrastructural expansion, $60 million for school construction, the extension and maintenance of recreational facilities, and funding to complete the new art museum building, as well as improvements to the city's two public hospitals. All told, the committee approved the expenditure of $450 million over ten years for public improvement projects alone (the equivalent of more than $6 billion in 2015). Already recommending a high rate of spending, the committee also advocated that some projects be put on hold, including the construction of a new civic center on the downtown waterfront. Later that summer, when the city council voted to proceed with the civic center project, Smith proved his fidelity to his corporate advisers and vetoed the measure, citing the unassailable judgment of his finance committee as justification.[43]

In the fall of 1925, Smith and Bowles once again lined up for what was sure to be a bitter fight. Joseph Martin, bruised by his 1924 defeat, declined to enter the race. The city council was up for election as well. Racial tensions had surged over the previous months. In April 1925, a mob of whites gathered in front of a home that stood on the city's Northfield Avenue, throwing enough stones to break every window in the house where a group of African Americans had rented a room. That June, when an African American doctor, Alexander Turner, bought a home a few blocks away, another angry white mob gathered. This time the crowd staked its ground outside the newly purchased property even before Turner's moving truck arrived. By nighttime over a thousand white Detroiters had swarmed around the house. Fearing for his life, Turner pledged to sell to a white buyer and fled along with his family, but not before members of the crowd began to throw bricks and other objects and injured Turner. Similar incidents followed during the remainder of the summer. That fall, one turned deadly. On September 8, 1925, the African American doctor Ossian Sweet moved into a house in a predominantly white neighborhood on the east side of the city. Again, a group of seething whites gathered on the African American homeowner's lawn. Amid screams and the crash of objects hurled against the house, shots rang out, killing one white man and wounding another. By the next day, the whole city was fixated on the shooting. Members of Detroit's KKK were convinced that the Klan's political stock would soar.[44]

The city held its primary just weeks after the confrontation at Sweet's house. In one sense, the results suggested a Klan victory. With only two candidates in the mayor's race, Bowles automatically moved onto the general, as did John Smith. The Klan endorsed five candidates for council, and all of them earned the right to appear on November's ballot. But only two of those winners were Klan candidates pure and simple. The Klan had endorsed three-term incumbent Fred Castator; former councilman and well-known political figure Sherman Littlefield; and Robert Ewald, who in turn had repudiated the Klan's support. Castator, Littlefield, and even labor's ally Ewald had also received endorsements from the Detroit Citizens League, while the Detroit Federation of Labor had listed both Ewald and Castator among its favored slate. Local newspapers called the October primary a Klan triumph. In fact, voters' intentions were not altogether clear.[45]

The general election clarified the ambiguity. The Detroit Federation of Labor mobilized extensively on behalf of Smith, but labor's endorsement did not stop the mayor from bandying about his new alliance with Detroit's business community. When Smith's opponents tried to smear him as a lackey of the Wayne County Republican machine, Smith claimed that if he was working with "a gang" it was composed, not of party hacks, but of the types of business elites whom he had placed on his many new committees.[46] With business interests increasingly behind him, Smith defeated Bowles by thirty thousand votes. According to precinct-level analysis by the *Detroit Free Press*, new support in blue-blood neighborhoods had helped push Smith over the top. In the KKK's one undeniable triumph, Klansman Phillip Callahan finished ninth in the city council race, barely winning a seat. The other unabashed Klan candidate, Andrew Brodie, lost. The three remaining men whom the Klan had backed for council but who had also enjoyed strong support from other voting blocs all emerged victorious. But the question of whether these men would do the Klan's bidding once they took office soon turned moot. Following Bowles's defeat, the Detroit branch of the Ku Klux Klan went into a tailspin after its leader got into a pitched battle with the KKK's national headquarters. The fight made for splashy headlines in Detroit's papers, as both sides accused the other of more and more egregious derelictions. According to local pundits, Detroit's Klan soon wilted like a "dead flower."[47]

The Detroit Federation of Labor also saw its brief moment of political influence come to an end in the aftermath of the 1925 election. That said, even the DFL's showing in the 1925 contest had been mixed. The union had backed a winner in John Smith, but only three of the six council candidates that the DFL had favored won seats, and two of them had also garnered the support of the Detroit Citizens League and the Ku Klux Klan. Still, the 1924 and 1925 elections were political high points for the union. For most of the decade, the perennial antiunion activities of local employers put DFL members on the defensive, forcing the union's leadership to channel what little political energy it could muster toward a handful of carefully selected issues. More often than not, this meant that worrying about the trajectory of social spending in the city took a back seat to bread-and-butter issues like pressuring public officials to use union contractors, protecting the rights of municipal employees, and trying to elicit pro-union pledges from political candidates. The DFL frequently used the editorial page of its *Detroit Labor News* to opine on various social policy issues, ranging from the activities of the school board to public officials' attempt to monitor local dance halls. But beyond publishing editorials, the union rarely tried to organize working-class voters on behalf of specific social policy goals. In fact, unlike its chief political rival, the Detroit Citizens League, the DFL failed to take a public stance on the majority of social spending initiatives that appeared on the local ballot in the 1920s even as the union repeatedly tried to galvanize workers around other political issues. When the city's electorate was asked to approve $37 million in bond issues for sewers and water mains in August 1920, the Detroit Citizens League circulated three hundred thousand copies of its main publication, the *Civic Searchlight*, in part to urge voters to approve the measure. By contrast, the editors of the *Detroit Labor News* did not take a position. In the same election, however, they endorsed a ballot initiative allowing the city to regulate private detectives, a favorite tool of antiunion employers seeking to identify labor activists. Later in the decade, the DFL was likewise silent about a referendum on selling $30 million more in bonds to expand the city's water system, even as union leaders voiced support for a measure to ensure that the city's curbs were made from stone cut in Detroit.[48]

Similarly, the DFL did not weigh in on a single school board election between the end of World War I and 1925. Thereafter, the union primarily engaged in school politics less to shape specific educational policies than to influence employment practices on school-related jobs. Elaborating on its endorsement of two candidates in the 1925 school board election, the DFL decried the current board of education's use of unlicensed engineers on city work and nepotism in city hiring but did not mention a single pedagogical issue. In another school election, the DFL explained its endorsement of its favored candidate by citing his union membership and his experience in construction. The only educational positions noted in the endorsement were the candidate's prosaic stances that school buildings should be standardized and that the city should provide enough classrooms for all the city's children. Only in 1929, when the DFL backed four candidates for school board, did endorsements in the *Detroit Labor News* discuss pedagogy at any length. Still, employment issues remained a leading concern. The DFL backed two of the candidates in part because they promised to fire all married female teachers in order to create more job openings in the city's schools. In much the same vein, it was rare for the DFL to underscore the specific policy stances of candidates for mayor or city council. Instead, nearly all of the endorsements that appeared in the *Detroit Labor News* during mayoral and council races emphasized candidates' attitudes toward municipal employees and, in some cases, that candidates had once been union members themselves.[49]

Perhaps the greatest indicator of the DFL's political fragility, however, was that Mayor Smith increasingly ignored the union after winning reelection in 1925. Indeed, the editorial page of the *Detroit Labor News* eventually denounced Smith for failing to give the union its due when it came to political appointments even though there "was plenty of evidence that . . . big business elements received ample recognition."[50] The DFL was right. Smith proved far more concerned with deepening his ties with the local business community than with cultivating the support of organized labor, doubtless in part because the tempestuous elections of 1925 and their immediate aftermath had cut in a clear direction. Not only had elite support helped reelect Mayor Smith, but the Detroit Citizens League had backed eight out of nine winners in the city council race. As the KKK went into rapid decline and the DFL became an increasingly marginal political force, members of the incoming council would have all the more reasons to do the Citizens League's bidding as time progressed. With Smith positioning himself as a businessmen's mayor, and with candidates tied to the Citizens League running the city council, elite businessmen in Detroit would once again enjoy a clear, although not absolute, hold on power.[51]

A New Moment of Authority, 1926–1929

When Mayor Smith began his second term in 1926, the fiscal crisis of the early 1920s was a fading memory and the Detroit Board of Commerce was still characterizing many aspects of government expansion as "absolutely necessary."[52] Under Smith and the new council, government spending quickly reached new heights, much as the businessmen on Smith's finance committee had wanted. School construction boomed. A new set of additions were built at the city's public hospitals, and the department of public health continued to extend its services. Local officials also allocated over a million dollars to improve the city's parks and playgrounds. All told, the number of acres in Detroit's recreation system grew nearly tenfold in the 1920s, from 57 before World War I to 547 on the eve of the Great Depression. In 1929, the recreation department boasted that local residents had visited the city's parks, playgrounds, and social centers over eleven million times during the preceding year—more than three times as often as ten years prior. Meanwhile, business leaders remained convinced of the power of play. "Recreation is not a fad," a board of commerce editorial declared during Smith's term, years after it had initiated its first campaign for more parks and playgrounds. "It is a factor that makes the difference between good and bad citizens."[53]

Smith and the new council doubled appropriations to the city's art commission—enough to finish the art museum that business leaders had long desired. They also resumed heavy spending on basic infrastructure. Under Smith, the city laid over four hundred miles of pavement, eighty-five miles of sewer mains, nearly four hundred miles of lateral sewers, and over a thousand miles of new water pipe providing service to nearly fifty thousand new homes. Unlike earlier in the decade, however, much of this infrastructural expansion was guided by an official city plan that Smith and the city council approved in the spring of 1925.[54]

The origins of Detroit's new "master plan" lay in the early 1920s. As one of his final acts as mayor, James Couzens had appointed a new rapid transit commission to determine an agenda for infrastructural and especially road construction in the city. The chair of the commission, Sidney Waldon, was a millionaire who had served as vice president of both Packard and Cadillac. Three other high-ranking corporate executives and a former city engineer

Figure 8. The new home of the Detroit Institute of Arts opened to the public in 1927 across the street from the Detroit Public Library's new building. The Detroit Institute of Arts: The Architecture *(Detroit, 1930), plate 5.*

made up the remainder of the commission. Waldon envisioned using the master plan to build a "new kind of city . . . where there will be sunlight and air" rather than overcrowding and congestion as well as "rapid transit on rails and rubber." To this end, he and the rapid transit commission drew up a sweeping proposal to construct 120-foot thoroughfares and 204-foot superhighways throughout the metropolitan area. The plan was not simply meant to make Detroit friendlier to automobile traffic, however. Rather, it also called for the construction of a subway system in the center of the city that would connect with a new network of aboveground rail lines five miles from the city's downtown.[55]

Within months of the master plan's release, voters approved a proposal to purchase the land needed to construct the boulevards and highways that Waldon and his colleagues envisioned. Despite strong business backing, however, the subway system was never built. The board of commerce, the Detroit Employers' Association, the Detroit Real Estate Board, and the Citizens League all endorsed the subway proposal. Downtown merchants hoped that subways would alleviate traffic in the city's old commercial district by removing cumbersome street railway lines. Factory owners believed subways would make their employees' commutes easier and more reliable. Henry Ford was especially enthusiastic about the proposal since the subways promised to connect his River Rouge plant in nearby Dearborn with the vast majority of Detroit's street railway lines, easing the commute of Ford employees from all parts of the city. The subway and rail plan additionally promised to facilitate the social project of urban decentralization despite the fact that buying an automobile remained out of reach for many working-class Detroiters. Because of the incredible expense of subway construction, public officials resolved to build the new system in increments. When voters were asked to approve the first stage—the construction of thirteen miles of subway at a cost of $91 million—they rebelled. Galvanized in part by a collection of homeowners' associations, nearly three out of every four voters rejected the measure.[56]

Yet even without the new subways, the implementation of the rest of the master plan ensured the continued fast-paced decentralization of Detroit. This is not to say that Detroit was cured of residential congestion. On the contrary: the massive amount of funding that the city spent on basic infrastructure during the 1920s primarily subsidized the private construction of homes in Detroit's less developed areas for people who could afford them. Most of Detroit's poorest residents remained trapped in the city's oldest neighborhoods, which—despite heightened settlement away from the old urban core—grew increasingly overcrowded amid a relentless population boom.

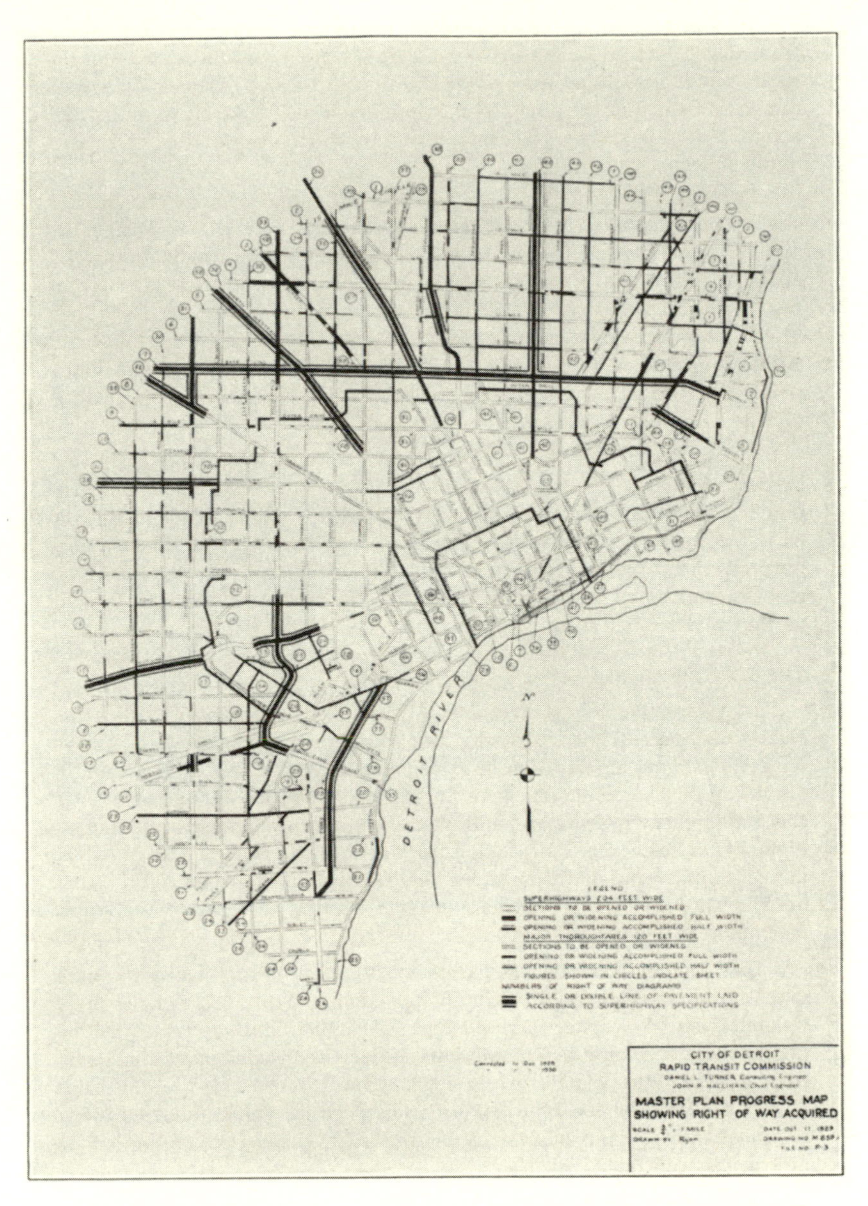

Figure 9. Detroit's 1925 master plan prioritized decentralizing settlement and diffusing traffic. This map depicts the plan as originally adopted (both the darkly and lightly lined roadways) as well as progress that the city made toward implementing major portions of the plan by the end of the 1920s (indicated by the darkly lined roadways). City of Detroit, Vehicular Traffic in Detroit in 1930 *(Detroit: Detroit Rapid Transit Commission, 1930). Courtesy of the Bentley Historical Library, the University of Michigan.*

Perhaps predictably, African Americans and the poorest working-class immigrants suffered most from this pattern. New federal laws drastically curtailed immigration to the United States in the 1920s, but the growth of Detroit's foreign-born population continued nonetheless, as jobs in the city's bustling economy attracted immigrants who had initially settled in other American cities. The number of first-generation immigrants in Detroit rose from roughly 290,000 to nearly 400,000 between 1920 and 1930. Like their predecessors, many of these immigrants squeezed into Detroit's densely populated older neighborhoods. Meanwhile, Detroit's African American population tripled during the decade. White homeowners and real estate agents conspired to keep African Americans isolated in an emerging racial ghetto. As a condition of membership in the all-white Detroit Real Estate Board, realtors pledged not to sell houses in predominantly white communities to African Americans, while white homeowners in new and old neighborhoods across the city signed covenants promising to keep their houses out of African American hands. As a result, the vast majority of African American Detroiters remained stranded in the city's old East Side in a desperately poor neighborhood known as Black Bottom. Despite the hostility endured by Ossian Sweet and others, some, mostly middle-class African Americans managed to move into other areas of the city that had better housing stock. In the mid-1920s, about 7,000 of the city's 120,000 African American residents lived on the city's West Side. In addition, a smattering of working-class African Americans had established residential outposts near or beyond the city limits, including near the city's Eight-Mile Road. For the most part, however, the combination of a real estate market rigged against African Americans and the continued growth of the city's poor population made a mockery of elite businessmen's attempt to rid Detroit of its most congested neighborhoods simply by promoting private construction in a decentralized pattern.[57]

In the face of such abysmal conditions, African Americans especially organized to try to improve their lot. By the end of the decade, African Americans constituted nearly 8 percent of the city's population—a potentially influential electoral bloc. But leading African American organizations in the city rarely focused their political efforts on mobilizing the city's swelling African American population to challenge the city's dominant power structure. There were important exceptions to this pattern, to be sure. The local branch of the National Association for the Advancement of Colored People (NAACP) at times organized to fight housing discrimination and especially—in collaboration with the NAACP's national headquarters—to successfully defend

Ossian Sweet and his family in a trial that garnered national attention. The local branch of Marcus Garvey's popular Universal Negro Improvement Association—an early black nationalist organization—boasted a sizable membership early in the decade and regularly critiqued the city's white elite. But the preeminent African American organization in 1920s Detroit—the Detroit Urban League—embraced a more accommodationist approach. Many of the middle-class African American men and women who joined the Urban League blamed the rising tide of racism and segregation in Detroit on the customs and behavior of the thousands of southern black migrants who streamed into the city during the decade in search of a better life. As the head of the Urban League contended: "Why is segregation increasing? Chiefly on account of the loud, noisy, almost nude women in 'Mother Hubbards' standing around on the public thoroughfares. There are dirty white people of course, but white people are the judges and colored people are being judged." Leaders of the Urban League focused the bulk of their efforts on trying to change the way African American migrants from the South dressed, how they comported themselves in public, and how they spent their leisure time. In addition to trying to reform their behavior, the Urban League was especially committed to helping migrants find jobs. In this effort, the Urban League collaborated with the elite, all-white Detroit Employers' Association, which funded the Urban League's employment bureau throughout the 1920s. White employers saw African American migrants as a promising source of labor and believed that an organization like the Urban League could form an efficient clearinghouse for matching those migrants with jobs. The Urban League also relied heavily on contributions from the city's largest charitable organizations, such as the Associated Charities of Detroit and the Detroit Community Fund. Wealthy white elites dominated the boards of both organizations, including corporate executives like Edsel Ford and Richard Webber, the president of J. L. Hudson.[58]

Of course, leaders of the Urban League did not simply accept every racial indignity that was thrown African Americans' way. They protested the harsh treatment of African Americans by the police and at times tried to mediate racial conflicts between African Americans and whites over housing. But given its guiding ideology—which prioritized education and uplift over confrontation—and the fact that it relied so heavily on white financial support, Detroit's leading African American organization rarely challenged white business leaders in the political sphere.[59]

Meanwhile, female political organizations—whether African American or white—tended to prioritize state and federal issues over local ones throughout much of the decade. When working on the local stage, moreover, organized women's groups in Detroit seemed to favor educational and charitable activities over direct engagement with city hall. To be sure, female activists aggressively lobbied local officials in some instances. For example, the city's largest women's organization, the Detroit Federation of Women's Clubs (DFWC), successfully pressured city hall to establish a women's division of the Detroit police department. Women's clubs also convinced local officials to institute harsher laws against gambling, to strengthen food safety regulations, and to improve the living conditions of female inmates in local prisons. But the DFWC and its member organizations focused most of their energy in the local arena on volunteer work, not on pressure-group politics. Some of women's volunteer activities took place in collaboration with public officials. For instance, DFWC volunteers assisted city workers in their efforts to promote better health in the city's schools throughout the decade. With the encouragement of local officials, the DFWC also helped spearhead "Safety Week," an annual event that aimed to reduce traffic accidents, primarily through a combination of law enforcement and education. The DFWC was similarly integral to a government-backed campaign against smoke pollution and another aimed at curbing the city's rat population. In both cases, women's main contribution consisted of educating the public about methods of prevention.[60]

But the DFWC and its member organizations pursued most of their volunteer activities independently of city government. Detroit's women's clubs sponsored various forms of charity work, from feeding and clothing the poor to providing them with Christmas gifts. The DFWC's public health division organized educational talks in various parts of the city. The DFWC and its member organizations also sponsored debates, classes, lectures, and study groups so that female members could gain information regarding the main political issues of the day. But the DFWC's strong commitment to educating female voters rarely morphed into an attempt to tell women how to vote. The organization did not endorse candidates and failed to take a public stance on many of Detroit's most pressing political issues, whether municipal ownership of the city's streetcars, infrastructural expansion and the master plan, or even major school board policies. In general, the DFWC's member organizations, including the local branch of the League of Women Voters, followed a similar course. With the city's most influential women's organizations favoring educating their members over mobilizing them politically, it is hardly surprising that women did not emerge as an effective voting bloc in the local arena. Although leading female activists at times urged women to throw their electoral weight behind female candidates, only one woman won a seat in local government—Laura Osborn, who gained office in 1917 and continued to serve on the school board for several years thereafter. By contrast, the city elected and then reelected as mayor one of the city's most outspoken opponents of women's suffrage—former congressman Frank Doremus—despite the pleas of many female activists.[61]

And yet these patterns applied only to local politics. The DFWC and many of its member organizations remained keenly focused on state and federal policy both on their own and as part of the efforts of their parent organizations, the Michigan Federation of Women's Clubs and the General Federation of Women's Clubs. Even as they failed to mention a single local issue, members of the DFWC's legislation department reported contacting both state and federal lawmakers to voice their support for an array of bills, most of them concerning the welfare of women and children. On the federal level, these included a child labor bill for the District of Columbia, the Sheppard-Towner bill providing federal funding for maternal and infant health, and a bill to provide federal support for education. The DFWC also wrote state legislators asking that they augment pensions for single and widowed mothers, raise the age of marital consent, increase movie censorship, and adopt a number of deeply disturbing eugenics laws: one preventing the marriage of the "feeble-minded," another promoting their sterilization, and one calling for the construction of farm colonies to house the mentally handicapped.

A onetime legislative chairman of the DFWC, Lucia Grimes—formerly a leading Michigan suffragist—spearheaded many of these state-level efforts. In 1920, Grimes and other prominent female activists formed the Legislative Council of Michigan Women, a consortium of leading female groups in the state that aimed to maximize women's influence in Michigan politics. The priorities of the legislative council paralleled those of the DFWC and emphasized a combination of laws to protect women and children, to fund free vaccinations, to promote eugenic interventions by the state, and to stifle vice, especially gambling and the consumption of alcohol. In the end, Grimes's legislative council achieved only a mixed record. Roughly 30 percent of the legislation that it favored passed in 1921 and 50 percent in 1923 before its influence began to wane even further. Still, women's substantial, direct engagement in Michigan politics stood in sharp contrast to their approach to local affairs.[62]

As women set their sights on forging change in the state capital and in Washington, back in Detroit, Mayor John Smith's political star was in decline. Despite his best efforts, by the end of his first full term in 1927, Smith's connections with powerful segments of the city's business community had frayed, primarily due to disagreements over how to police crime. Claiming that the national prohibition of alcohol was too difficult to enforce and that the attempt to do so drained police resources, Smith banned so-called tip-over raids, where policemen barraged illegal drinking establishments and arrested all offenders. Instead, he thought that illicit bars were inevitable in a city the size of Detroit and ordered police to enforce prohibition laws only in the case of disorderly drunks. But the dry leadership of the Detroit's Citizens League wanted the prohibition law executed in full. The Citizens League and a number of other local organizations, like Detroit's Council of Churches, also decried Smith's failure to curb prostitution in the city. Together, they sponsored a study by the American Social Hygiene Association that claimed that there were over six thousand prostitutes at work in Mayor Smith's Detroit. Led by the Citizens League, a group of wealthy businessmen began gathering funds to draft city council president and founding member of the Citizens League John Lodge for mayor. Lodge's credentials as a business-friendly lawmaker were pristine. Even the large number of corporate Detroiters who were opposed or indifferent to the Detroit Citizens League's crusade against prostitution and illegal drinking had little difficulty abandoning Smith for Lodge. By the fall of 1927, Lodge's backers had gathered over fifty thousand signatures on the petition to nominate him.[63]

In the lead-up to the mayoral primary, the Detroit Federation of Labor proved too disenchanted with John Smith to support him with the same enthusiasm that it had shown two years earlier. The union even attempted to lure another candidate into the race—future U.S. Supreme Court justice Frank Murphy. After Murphy declined, the DFL eventually made peace with Smith's candidacy as the lesser of two evils, but only after a long delay, so much so that the union failed to take a position on the mayoral primary until just days before the election. By contrast, Lodge's business supporters poured money and energy into the fight, which Lodge won in a landslide. Heading into the general election, Smith made a desperate attempt to energize his former working-class base by trying to turn the contest into a referendum on Prohibition, which most working-class Detroiters opposed. The DFL reiterated its support for Smith heading into the November vote, but Lodge's corporate backers reportedly provided enough funding to publicize their candidate's record "into all of the homes of the city."[64]

In successfully electing Lodge, the city's commercial and industrial elite placed a clear ally in the mayor's chair. Moreover, candidates backed by the Detroit Citizens League triumphed once again in the races for city council that had coincided with the mayoral contest. In comparison to previous administrations, Lodge's two-year term did not bring as dramatic a rise in social spending as earlier years. But this comparatively modest growth rate did not signal a turn to fiscal conservatism among the city's business leaders and their allies in public office. During his first months in office, Lodge assumed control of a city that was on the brink of exceeding its debt limit once again, forcing another temporary slowdown in government spending. Eventually New York's state legislature upped the limit on the amount of bonds cities could sell on the New York market, and Lodge quickly came out for new debt-financed projects. In 1928, Lodge and local business leaders convinced the electorate to authorize $30 million more in bonds to improve the city's sewer system. But this victory was quickly followed by a defeat. It was during the Lodge administration that voters rejected the expensive subway proposal that corporate Detroiters had advocated as part of the city's master plan. If the mayor and his corporate allies had gotten their way, Detroit's budget would have kept up its fast-paced growth. Indeed, during his last year in office, Lodge released an ambitious ten-year plan that called for spending $540 million on public improvements, including $50 million for school construction, $6 million for parks and playgrounds, and more than $100 million on basic infrastructure. As the decade came to a close, Detroit's businessmen could feel satisfied that an ally willing to implement large portions of their agenda was running city hall.[65]

In the Motor City of the 1920s, the combination of at-large elections and the weakness of rival interest groups deeply engaged with local politics allowed elite businessmen to disproportionately shape public policy and thus to implement large portions of their vision of a civic welfare state. Whether through extragovernmental groups like the Detroit Board of Commerce or quasi-governmental bodies like Mayor Couzens's "reconstruction meeting" and Mayor John Smith's finance committee, many of the most ambitious government projects undertaken in 1920s Detroit originated in the minds of local business elites. Drawn largely from the same social milieu, members of Detroit's school board and city council as well as the city's mayors proved effective partners in furthering business leaders' social policy agenda. Even as everyday voters were asked to weigh in on some of the city's most ambitious projects through referenda on public debt, without effective pressure groups, most Detroiters enjoyed only a peripheral role in the city's social policymaking process.

And yet this combination of institutional ecology and interest-group politics explains how businessmen achieved so many of their goals only within the unique context of Detroit. Elsewhere in urban America, business leaders exercised outsized influence within very different political environments. And among northern cities at the time, perhaps no other political world contrasted with Detroit's as sharply as Philadelphia's, where one of the nation's most infamous political machines remained a potent force on the municipal stage.

CHAPTER 3

Philadelphia

Money and the Machine

Soon after the end of World War I, the writer Christopher Morley visited the downtown parkway that elite Philadelphians had first proposed decades before. Morley praised the "excellent ruthlessness" with which the city had demolished acres of existing factories and homes to make space for the parkway. But according to Morley the road was still surrounded by "open fields of splintered brick and gravel pits." He had to rely on his imagination to visualize how the boulevard would "appear five or ten years hence, lined with art galleries, museums and libraries, shaded with growing trees, leading from the majestic pinnacle of City Hall to the finest public estate in America," meaning Philadelphia's Fairmount Park.[1]

The unfinished parkway that Morley described was a testament to a broader trend. Despite years of effort, much of the agenda that Philadelphia's commercial and industrial elite had embraced before the war remained unrealized as the nation transitioned to peace. Even so, the ambitions of Philadelphia's business leaders grew rapidly in the months following the armistice, much as they did in Detroit. Not only did leading businessmen in Philadelphia share Morley's hope that the city would complete the civic structures slated for the downtown parkway. They also called for a barrage of new projects. In 1919, for instance, after canvassing members, leaders of the Philadelphia Chamber of Commerce proposed a set of "Urgent Needs for the City," a list that included improvements to Philadelphia's water and sewer systems, "proper school facilities for every child and the Americanization of all resident aliens," as well as more and better rapid transit that would in part encourage residential decentralization.[2] Within months, the chamber added to its wish list the expenditure of $30 million over five years to improve the city's roadways and the construction of a large municipal stadium, the city's first. The chamber also launched a campaign for an elaborate fair to mark the 150th anniversary of the signing of the Declaration of Independence. Philadelphia's business leaders hoped that the celebration would spur the completion of a number of permanent improvements closely linked to their vision of a civic welfare state: the new art museum, library, and other structures along the downtown parkway; the expansion of City Beautiful–style planning to new areas of the city; and as plans for the fair evolved, the reclamation of acres of swampland in Philadelphia's far south, a project that promised to accelerate residential decentralization by making land available for constructing over forty thousand new homes.[3]

Completing these and a variety of other projects grew even more important to local business leaders in the years that followed. Before the war, various trends had suggested that Philadelphia's economy was stagnating. Wartime production brought a temporary turnaround, but indicators soon confirmed that major industries in the city stood on shifting ground. In addition to addressing issues like immigrant assimilation, poor health conditions, and working-class discontent (anxieties shared by their counterparts in Detroit), business leaders' attempts to increase social spending in Philadelphia aimed at reversing the city's economic decline by making the city more attractive to business. In the context of Philadelphia (and even more so Atlanta, as the next chapter describes), the concept of the civic welfare state helps draw attention to two dynamics at once: first, businessmen's quest to foster the development of citizens of a certain type and, second, businessmen's boosterish efforts to improve their city's economic health—a concern that was less pressing for business leaders in Detroit amid the Motor City's fast-paced economic growth.

The question remained, however, whether members of Philadelphia's business elite could prod local officials to implement their expanding agenda. Recall that Philadelphia had just adopted a new city charter—the product of an unlikely alliance between independent reformers (including a number of leading businessmen) and a faction of the local political machine led by Boies Penrose. Independents had won a handful of the changes that they had wanted through charter reform, but they had also failed to abolish major sources of machine funding and patronage. The new charter left Philadelphia's sizable county government untouched by civil service regulations and thus left thousands of county jobs open to patronage appointment. Aside from policemen and firefighters, municipal employees could still take part in local politics, and local political bosses could still force workers whom they had placed in patronage posts to fill the party's coffers with mandatory contributions. Independents had hoped to redesign Philadelphia's city council so that it would include at least some at-large representation—a reform that would have weakened local political bosses whose power was rooted in the ward system. The new charter, however, stipulated that city councilmen were to be chosen from state senatorial districts. Whether or not machine politicians could successfully organize across those districts (which were far bigger than the city's political wards) remained unknown. What was certain was that charter reform had not, by itself, struck a deathblow to boss rule. Rather, independent reformers would have to win control of the new system by electing representatives sympathetic to their goals.

In the first elections after the war, independent reformers continued to cultivate the same alliance with Penrose that had produced the new city charter and its many shortcomings. Choosing the lesser of two evils, independents hoped that joining forces with Penrose might at least put the other main faction of the city's political machine, led by the Vare brothers, out of business. In the fall of 1919, independents—along with Penrose and his followers—managed to win a slim majority in Philadelphia's city council and elect their chosen candidate for mayor: a man named J. Hampton Moore. Yet by the end of Moore's terms, a variety of dynamics—from political gridlock and Moore's political shortcomings to Boies Penrose's death—had left independent reformers so flummoxed that they could hardly agree upon a candidate to run as Moore's successor.

The Vares and their followers took advantage of these developments and soon made clear that they could deliver on many of local business leaders' most cherished policy goals. Frustrated with years of government inaction, elite businessmen who had once been staunch independent reformers increasingly switched allegiances and embraced machine governance. The Philadelphia Chamber of Commerce, formerly a bastion of independent reform, became a close collaborator and vocal supporter of the machine-dominated administrations that governed Philadelphia for the remainder of the decade. Once divided over the question of boss rule, Philadelphia's commercial and industrial elite increasingly consolidated behind the city's political machine. This trend heightened business interests' influence on local affairs, but it further marginalized other political actors in the city, such as white women's associations, immigrant groups, and African American activists, some of whom had benefited from earlier rifts between independent reformers and machine politicians. Meanwhile, as the political goals of local business leaders and machine politicians converged, elite businessmen in Philadelphia saw their vision of a civic welfare state take material form.

Moore Troubles

In the 1919 Republican primary—usually the only contest that mattered in Republican-dominated Philadelphia—independent reformers and Boies Penrose settled on Congressman J. Hampton Moore as their candidate for mayor. Moore represented Philadelphia's Third Congressional District, a stretch of land that lay along the city's northern waterfront, home to a number of Philadelphia's manufacturing plants. Moore had served in Congress since 1906 and had established himself as a pro-tariff and antilabor stalwart, the type of politician that Philadelphia's manufacturers adored. As a congressman, Moore had fought against immigration restriction, the income tax, child labor laws, the creation of the Federal Trade Commission, and the Clayton Act's exemption of organized labor from antitrust prosecution. Much to the entertainment of his corporate supporters, he had rarely taken such stances quietly. In railing against the Clayton Act, Moore "reportedly shook his fist under the nose of Samuel Gompers" (the head of the American Federation of Labor, the nation's largest union) "and told him that organized labor could 'go plumb to hell.'" When opposing the Adamson Act of 1916 limiting the working hours of railroad employees, Moore decried the measure as a "political dodge" aimed at winning "400,000 labor votes." In urging Moore for mayor, independent Republicans, so many of them local manufacturers, thought they were backing a man who would protect their economic interests and who also had the backbone to resist orders from local bosses like Penrose.[4]

Initially Penrose and his allies were reluctant to accept Moore's candidacy for precisely that reason. They feared that Moore would ignore their mandates and even attempt to build a political organization of his own. But Penrose and his machine collaborators knew that the Vare brothers would choose a daunting opponent. Between his name recognition, his support among businessmen, his potential to garner votes among independents, and his political experience, Moore emerged as a compelling candidate.[5]

The Vare brothers tapped local judge John M. Patterson to run as Moore's opponent. It was a shrewd choice. Patterson's longtime connection to Penrose and his followers promised to steal support from his opponent's base.

Patterson had also served as a member of the 137-member committee to revise the city charter. His participation in the charter reform campaign may have chafed the Vares, but it also gave Patterson the bona fides to potentially capture independent votes.[6]

The October 1919 primary resulted in a virtual dead heat, with Moore edging out Patterson by just over a thousand ballots. Elections for city council gave the Penrose-independent alliance a slight majority in the city council. Out of twenty-one members, ten of the incoming councilmen were Vare loyalists, leaving Penrose and the independents a majority of just one. Out of these, however, only a few were true independents; most were professional politicians aligned with Penrose. In short, the first elections under Philadelphia's new charter had produced yet another city council dominated by machine politicians. Independents could only hope that their choice for mayor had the political acuity necessary to navigate the new council without pushing any of Penrose's followers into the Vares' column. Within months, however, "Hampy" Moore made clear that he was not up to the job.[7]

Moore's difficulties began during negotiations over his administration's first official budget. In Pennsylvania, the state government set the salaries of most county employees. But during the war, salaries for county jobs had lagged, so Philadelphia's city government had offered annual bonuses to county workers in order to compensate. As the mayor and the city council hammered out the municipal budget in the fall of 1920, disagreement over these bonuses led to a standoff. County officials, particularly leaders of the county-run municipal court, submitted a budget request that effectively continued the wartime bonuses. Citing a wasteful system of patronage, Mayor Moore used the line-item veto to excise the court's request.[8]

Moore was right that jobs with the municipal court were intricately tied to machine politics. The court's roster was filled with the names of machine loyalists, and its head judge, Charles Brown, was a major player in Philadelphia's Republican machine. But Moore chose the wrong time to pick a fight over patronage. The mayor hoped to have Penrose's backing in the budget battle since many Vare men were on the municipal court's payroll. But Penrose had other priorities that fall—above all forging a united Republican front as state and national elections approached. According to one local newspaper, Penrose was "looking forward to the rich treasure of federal patronage" that the election of a Republican president might bring, much of which would come under Penrose's control at the state and local levels. Additionally, Penrose—who was also a U.S. senator—was running for reelection that November. In an opportunistic twist, Penrose moved to enlist the Vares' backing for his campaign. With their eyes on federal patronage as well, the Vare brothers signed on. In the meantime, Penrose left Moore dangling in the budget fight. Outraged at Moore's attempt to cut a major patronage slush fund, the Penrose men on the city council joined with the Vare faction and overrode Moore's veto of the court's budget request by the required three-fifths majority.[9]

Infuriated by the rapprochement between the Vare and Penrose forces, Moore took a number of futile steps to consolidate loyalty within his administration and to construct an organizational base of his own. In December 1920, he ordered department heads to weed out employees who were sympathetic to the Vare-Penrose alliance. Just after Christmas, the director of the department of public works demanded the resignation of forty employees. The head of the department of public safety transferred over a dozen reputedly anti-Moore detectives to foot patrol. The Moore administration particularly targeted employees from the city's Fifteenth Ward, political home of Charles Brown, head of the municipal court. By New Year's Eve, local newspapers reported that the jobs of nearly two hundred city workers were on the line. A small group of ward politicians who opposed the Vare-Penrose détente established a downtown headquarters to act as a "rallying point" for pro-Moore forces. But despite his best efforts, Moore garnered only nominal support from the city's ward heelers. Moreover, his attempt to consolidate power further antagonized Penrose's adherents and helped to solidify the machine bloc in the city council. Matters grew worse for Moore after Penrose died in 1921 and many of Penrose's followers ran for cover by pledging allegiance to the Vares.[10]

Just as important, Moore's attempt to strengthen his hold over municipal employment cost him support among his independent base. As the 1920 budget fight initially unfolded, leading independent groups had rallied behind Mayor Moore and denounced the city council for overriding his veto of the municipal court's budget request. The Philadelphia Chamber of Commerce and the Civic Club (the city's leading organization of elite, female independents) had both voiced their strong support for the mayor. Soon thereafter, however, Moore moved to change local civil service rules to make it easier for him to hire and fire municipal employees—part of his attempt to weaken the Vare-Penrose alliance and to tighten his grip over the city's bureaucracy. Independent reformers decried the move, furious that Moore would undercut the few, hard-won civil service reforms that they had managed to insert into the city's new charter.[11]

The 1920 budget fight and its aftermath put Moore in a delicate political position. The Penrose camp of the local machine had shifted from ally to adversary. Moore's much less potent independent base had begun to turn against him amid his scramble for power. With three years left to govern, a more adept politician might have recovered. But Moore did not. Whether out of principle or hubris, Moore rarely negotiated with his foes on the city council or with the machine's representatives on powerful city commissions. Policymaking became a matter of serendipity rather than compromise. If Moore and the city council's priorities happened to align, then legislation passed. Moore also failed to win back the support of the city's independents. In fact, he increasingly alienated the most financially powerful among them.

Indeed, Moore's governing style hamstrung a number of projects important to the city's business elite, including the fair to mark the 150th anniversary of the Declaration of Independence. One of the city's most successful merchants, John Wanamaker, had first called for the sesquicentennial celebration in 1916. The war interrupted the planning process, but prominent businessmen, including leaders of the Philadelphia Chamber of Commerce, redoubled their commitment to Wanamaker's proposal soon after the armistice. Philadelphia's leading advocates of City Beautiful planning quickly enlisted prominent architect Paul Cret to design a proposal utilizing the downtown parkway and Fairmount Park as sites for the sesquicentennial. Cret's plan called for the completion of the art museum, Free Library, and other civic structures along the parkway, the beautification of the banks of the Schuylkill River (which neighbored the roadway), and for the expansion of parkland surrounding the downtown boulevard. Mayor Moore refused to accept Cret's proposal until the city entertained other options. Much to the chagrin of local business leaders, the debate over where to hold the fair dragged on for more than a year.[12]

Moore also upset other groups whose support was essential to the fair's success. In January 1921, the mayor named a planning committee and appointed himself as its head. In drawing up the list, however, Moore failed to confer with the city council. Instead, he simply selected names from a roster that the chamber of commerce had helped to draft. This move put Moore in good stead with the chamber, but his failure to include local lawmakers in the selection process snubbed the very officials who would have to provide a good deal of the funding for the event. Just after naming the committee, Moore asked the city council for an initial appropriation of $50,000—a pittance considering the sesquicentennial would eventually cost close to $20 million. The city council balked, sparking a fight that took nearly two months to resolve.[13]

Moore's relationship with the fair's planning committee also soured. After an early fundraising attempt fell flat, instead of helping to build support,

Moore publicly "flayed" members of the committee, which included some of the most successful businessmen in the city—men like Samuel Rea, the president of the Pennsylvania Railroad, and Ellis A. Gimbel of Gimbel Brothers, the department store chain.[14] In the spring of 1922, another member of the sesquicentennial planning committee—the wealthy editor Edward Bok—asked U.S. Secretary of Commerce Herbert Hoover to act as the sesquicentennial's director general. Offended that he had not been asked to fill that position, Moore reportedly unleashed "a hurricane of criticism . . . upon persons making many suggestions and doing little work to further the Sesquicentennial."[15] Moore also resigned as head of the planning committee, although for a time he maintained his post on the event's board of directors.[16]

Without a clear leader and with the planning process stumbling, even some of the fair's early supporters started to turn against the event. In the summer of 1922, Samuel Vauclain, president of Baldwin Locomotive Works, declared his opposition to the fair in a public telegram. Just a year earlier, Vauclain had recommended a director for the celebration. Now he proclaimed that such an exhibition was no longer necessary in a technologically advanced age in which "wireless, telephone and moving picture films" allowed the city to advertise its accomplishments to the world.[17] A few months later, Vauclain assumed leadership of a new "Town Pump Party," which, according to Vauclain, was designed to gather "about the town financial pump and guard against it being sucked dry for the benefit of useless enterprises," meaning the sesquicentennial.[18] When Vauclain officially accepted his new position at a public rally, E. T. Stotesbury, the most eminent financier in the city, sat next to him and enthusiastically applauded. Stotesbury had previously served as the financial director of the sesquicentennial's planning committee. Now he would become one of the event's most visible opponents, albeit only for a time.[19]

Moore was not solely responsible for all of this turbulence. From the beginning, members of the planning committee disagreed over the appropriate size and style for the sesquicentennial. As delays mounted, committee leaders began to bicker over whether there was enough time to pull off the event. In June 1922, Edward Bok proposed delaying the exhibition until 1927 instead of the summer of 1926 as originally planned. Alba Johnson—former president of Baldwin Locomotive Works, past president of the chamber of commerce, and vice president of the sesquicentennial committee—temporarily resigned in protest. Such squabbles put the event's prospects further in doubt and likely suggested to former supporters like Vauclain and Stotesbury that the sesquicentennial might become an expensive fiasco.[20]

But Moore certainly made matters worse. In February 1923, Moore once again expressed his disapproval of the event's planning committee and resigned from the sesquicentennial's board of directors. Later that year, he publicly demanded that planners halt a major fundraising drive that was then in full swing. He also called a public meeting in city hall to reassess the entire endeavor.[21] Leaders of the fair's planning committee declined to attend out of protest. Ernest Trigg—executive of a local lumber company, former president of the chamber of commerce, and a leader of the sesquicentennial planning effort—complained that the mayor's stance toward the festival "had been apathetic, to say the least."[22] Participants in the meeting were asked to vote whether to hold a large-scale exhibition. The final tally was 43 for and 403 against. The headline in the *Philadelphia Public Ledger* the next morning read, "Town Meeting Votes Down Big Sesqui, 10 to 1." With only a month left in office, Moore had organized a high-profile forum for the sesquicentennial's most vocal detractors.[23]

Moore played a similarly unconstructive role in the city's already troubled quest for a new art museum. Before his death in 1915, the wealthy utility mogul Peter Widener (then head of the Fairmount Park Commission, which oversaw the museum's construction) had asked his "family architect," Horace Trumbauer, to draw up plans for the new building. Three wings formed the core of Trumbauer's design—one to house the paintings of each of the city's leading art collectors: Widener, his business partner William Elkins, and Widener's lawyer, John G. Johnson. By 1917, Johnson had lost confidence that the city would construct the new building. Just before his death, he withdrew his offer to house his art collection in the new museum. Soon after taking office, Mayor Moore and Peter Widener's son, Joseph, got into a row over Johnson's collection. In addition to the new art museum, Joseph Widener called on the city to construct a smaller gallery on the downtown parkway that could house Johnson's paintings in a way that might satisfy the spirit of Johnson's will. Moore scoffed in characteristically "blunt language" at the notion of the city paying for two galleries and publicly confronted Widener at a hearing of the city's Art Jury. Furious, Widener revoked his father's pledge to donate the family's vast art collection to Philadelphia's museum. Instead, he eventually gave his father's holdings to the National Gallery in Washington, D.C.[24]

Meanwhile, construction of the new museum barely moved forward during Moore's term. Many of the delays were out of the mayor's control, such as difficulties obtaining building materials. But Moore slowed down the process further by pursuing an extensive inquiry into the financial practices of the Fairmount Park Commission in relation to the museum project. Moore's inquisition exposed tremendous waste in the commission's contracting practices. Some contracts had not been properly advertised or awarded to the lowest bidder. In at least one instance, work had been paid for twice. The park commissioners commonly used "continuing contracting," or feeding a new job to a contractor originally hired for a different task without re-advertising for the lowest bid. These revelations helped explain the museum's ballooning costs. Before the war, the park commissioners had claimed that the project would cost $3 million. In November 1922, they announced that $8.5 million was necessary just to complete the building's exterior. Finishing the interior would cost millions more.[25]

Yet Moore's inquiry proved almost all bark. State laws in Pennsylvania governing public contracting were much less rigorous for work done by the Fairmount Park Commission than by City Hall. Unable to affix legal blame or to provoke changes in state laws, Moore let the inquiry fizzle after the head of the park commission, E. T. Stotesbury, pledged to abide by the same contracting practices that other city departments were legally obligated to follow. As the editors of one of the city's leading newspapers complained, the "vehement fulminations of the Mayor" had resulted only in a meager pledge "to be good."[26]

As Moore pursued his investigation, a number of deadlines related to the museum's completion were fast approaching. In 1919, William Elkins's son died and his will made the gift of his family's artwork contingent on the city's completing the new museum in five years. In 1921, another wealthy donor, John McFadden, made a similar bequest. Additionally, proponents of the sesquicentennial still hoped that the new museum would serve as one of the fair's structural centerpieces. The city's independent reformers were doubtless aghast at the findings of Moore's exposé. But the businessmen among them, especially those who supported the sesquicentennial, were likely just as displeased that the mayor's inquiry had delayed a time-sensitive project merely in exchange for an unenforceable promise.[27]

Other projects dear to the city's business leaders stalled during Moore's tenure. Before his death, Peter Widener—who was also a trustee of the city's Free Library—had arranged for Horace Trumbauer to design that institution's proposed new home as well. Once in office, Moore forced Trumbauer's firm to cut costs and redesign the original plan. Trumbauer significantly reduced the size of the proposed building and the consulting engineer on the project abandoned his earlier idea of using masonry walls to support the new structure in favor of using a less expensive steel frame. Once the revised plans were approved, however, the steel proved hard to obtain. Workers did not lay the cornerstone of the new building until Moore's last year in office. Similarly, the city made little headway in constructing a long-planned subway under Broad Street, the city's main north-south thoroughfare, which was in part designed to facilitate access to the city's undeveloped outskirts. Moore took on the subway project in earnest only late in his term. Thereafter, quarrels with machine politicians in the city council undermined the project.[28]

Still, the Moore years were not completely fruitless from business leaders' perspective. Moore oversaw the opening of a major new rapid transit line—the "Frankford El," which ran from the city's far northeast through downtown and connected with another high-speed line that ran deep into the city's west. Officials also made significant headway on the Cobbs Creek Parkway and Pennypack Park projects that elite businessmen had first championed before the war as part of their City Beautiful plans.[29]

But the most significant steps toward realizing businessmen's vision of a civic welfare state during Moore's tenure came in a domain wholly outside of the mayor's control: the city's school system. Despite the efforts of independent reformers, Philadelphia's board of education was still appointed by the judges of the city's court of common pleas—a body closely affiliated with the city's political machine and the same group that continually named corporate allies of local political bosses to the Fairmount Park Commission. In appointing the school board, the judges generally chose a combination of well-connected socialites, corporate executives, well-off professionals in medicine and law, and a handful of professional educators and machine politicians. The school board's composition was especially elite in 1922, when its members adopted an ambitious school construction plan that guided the district's building efforts through the rest of the decade. Of the fifteen school board members serving in 1922, five were current or former bank executives and five were lawyers, at least three of whom lived in high-end residential areas. A doctor also sat on the board; he lived in the city's upscale Rittenhouse Square neighborhood and was listed in the city's social register, as was the board's sole female member. Only one professional educator and two professional politicians were board members at the time.[30]

The 1922 school construction plan called for building forty new elementary schools, eighteen junior high schools, and one senior high school, as well as additions to twelve other schools over three to four years, with a "minimum cost of approximately $36,000,000." The school board also resolved to raze parts of Philadelphia's outmoded educational plant, including ninety-four "old buildings and 39 sites unused and unusable." Thereafter, board members pledged to spend another $25 million on school construction just to keep up with increasing enrollment. They especially sought to eliminate overcrowding and part-time sessions in the city's school system, a problem that was particularly acute "in the foreign and congested districts" where shorter school days threatened to compromise educators' Americanization efforts.[31]

School board members also hoped to revamp the city's educational landscape following the most cutting-edge pedagogical ideas of the day. Their guide in this effort was Edwin C. Broome, the superintendent whom they had hired in 1921. Broome adhered to many of the same tenets that Superintendent Frank Cody and Detroit's elite school board followed in the Motor City. Broome advocated platoon schools at the elementary level, the construction of additional junior high schools, and building new and elaborately equipped comprehensive senior high schools—measures embedded in the board of education's 1922 construction plan. Much like Frank Cody and Detroit's school board, Broome insisted that this agenda would help educators adjust students to their future economic stations and civic duties.[32] Indeed, Broome emphasized the social and civic purposes of education above all else. He once listed the main goals of schooling as, "1) The development of clean-minded manhood and womanhood. 2) The impartation of such knowledge and the development of such skills as are necessary for intelligent and worthy citizenship," and finally, "3) The development of sound and vigorous bodies, and a training in the practice of healthy living."[33]

Leaders of the Philadelphia Chamber of Commerce had listed improving the city's school system as an "urgent need" just after the armistice and thus had reason to cheer Broome and the school board's new program. But Philadelphia's business leaders wanted more from local government than just schools and the smattering of initiatives that the Moore administration managed to implement. As the end of Moore's term approached, businessmen of various types mobilized to elect officials who could execute this broader agenda. Many of them—including a number of notable business elites like E. T. Stotesbury and others tied to local utility companies—allied themselves with the machine from the start. Others, including the leadership of the chamber of commerce, attempted to draft an independent alternative for mayor. Wary of electing another J. Hampton Moore, however, chamber leaders and other independents failed to galvanize around a viable candidate.[34]

The Allure of Cooperation and Action

At the beginning of the 1923 campaign, questions lingered about how the Vare machine would perform in that fall's election. Edwin Vare—for years the functional head of the Vare organization—had died only months before. Local pundits wondered whether William, the youngest and only remaining Vare brother, could retain the loyalty of ward leaders who had formerly pledged their allegiance to his brother or whether Edwin's passing would trigger a political free-for-all. Moreover, despite Penrose's death, a number of the late senator's former lieutenants still reigned in parts of the city, a reality that threatened further infighting that might compromise the Republican machine's efforts that fall.[35]

With these weaknesses in sight, local independents began to organize. The chamber of commerce formed a special committee to choose a candidate and to help lead an independent campaign. Discussions initially focused on drafting the city's director of public works. After he declined to enter the race, the chamber of commerce and other independent organizations tried to convince another well-known local official to run: Judge John Patterson, the Vare-backed candidate for mayor in 1919. Much like they had when they had first backed Moore, independent reformers hoped that Patterson could peel away enough support among machine followers to win. But William Vare saw the Patterson threat coming. In one of his first tests as the machine's heir apparent, he successfully maneuvered to prevent any of his underlings from defecting to Patterson's camp. Fearing defeat, Patterson stepped aside.[36]

With Patterson out of the race, independents' hopes quickly dimmed. Unable to enlist a competitive candidate, they instead tepidly endorsed Powell Evans, a prominent municipal reformer, manufacturer, and former vice president of the Philadelphia Chamber of Commerce who had declared his candidacy earlier that summer.[37] Yet even among his corporate colleagues Evans was disliked. Many considered him "temperamental" and feared that he would prove a "second 'Hampy Moore' in his contact with council because of his somewhat arbitrary and imperious methods."[38]

Ambivalent about Evans's candidacy, an antimachine campaign barely limped along. William Vare, meanwhile, continued to prove that he had the clout to unify members of the Republican machine. Reports suggested that Vare was willing to spend generously on the campaign, and ward politicians eagerly lined up to gather their share of the booty. A few former Penrose men succeeded in strong-arming Vare into backing a handful of their choices for seats on the city council and for a few other local offices, but by election day nearly all of the city's machine politicians had unified behind an agreed-upon slate, including Vare's choice for mayor: longtime machine loyalist and the city's receiver of taxes, W. Freeland Kendrick.[39]

From the start, the Vare organization played up Kendrick as a businessman's candidate. Vare had decided on Kendrick long before, but it was a group of businessmen who first publicly called on him to run. At a staged stop at Kendrick's office, roughly fifty men presented Kendrick with a petition listing nearly two hundred signatures from local leaders who supported his candidacy and put on a show of drafting Kendrick to run as their Cincinnatus. As the campaign continued, this original group, the "W. Freeland Kendrick Business Men's Committee," grew to include a mixture of less eminent bank executives, real estate men, contractors, and small manufacturers, as well as a number of well-known business elites, including the South Philadelphia real estate mogul Albert M. Greenfield; Jules Mastbaum, realtor and president of the motion picture giant the Stanley Company of America; and even a handful of former independent Republican businessmen who had served on the committee that had helped to revise the city charter.[40]

Attuned to widespread disenchantment with gridlock under Mayor Moore, Kendrick built his campaign around the slogan "Cooperation and Action."[41] He elaborated on the motto in his stump speeches by using business metaphors, touting the mayor and city council as the board of directors of a "three billion dollar corporation" and noting that "without co-operation and harmony in that board, the interests of the corporation and of its stockholders can neither be properly safeguarded or advanced." Working together, Kendrick promised, he and members of the city council would complete an array of policies dear to the city's business community, including the art museum, the Free Library, and other projects planned for the downtown parkway. Kendrick pledged to improve the city's water supply and rapid transit system; execute a comprehensive sewage plan "to protect the health and lives of [the city's] citizens;" build a "great and modern" public hospital; and develop the city's far south since "Philadelphia, like all other cities, is feeling keenly the need for additional houses for its citizens."[42]

As election day neared, the unity of the Republican organization, the weakness of the independent movement, and widespread fatigue with an antimachine mayor pointed toward a Kendrick victory. Sensing catastrophe, Kendrick's opponent, Powell Evans, spent election night at his estate in Devon—a wealthy enclave roughly twenty miles west of Philadelphia. Kendrick carried every single ward in the city, including formerly independent bastions in West and Northwest Philadelphia. The official tally gave Kendrick 280,604 votes and Evans merely 55,487. Just as important, the Vare organization won all but one seat on the city council. Campaign finance records underscored businessmen's growing disenchantment with the independent cause. Kendrick's business committee collected $61,000 for its candidate. Powell Evans had to pay for his campaign largely on his own.[43]

Even the Vare organization was reportedly "dazed by Kendrick's great sweep."[44] With election returns suggesting that Kendrick had won the support of a large number of formerly independent Republican voters, the mayor-elect moved to shore up his support among them. In the months surrounding his inauguration, Kendrick sent additional signals to the Philadelphia Chamber of Commerce that he would cooperate with the organization and work on its behalf. He tapped chamber vice president Dr. Wilmer Krusen to serve as his director of public health and another chamber vice president, E. J. Lafferty, as the city's purchasing agent. Kendrick also pledged himself to one of the chamber of commerce's pet endeavors, the sesquicentennial, calling for a fair that would be "big and dignified."[45]

In the end, however, it was Kendrick's execution of an array of public projects—the sesquicentennial and much more—that won the chamber of commerce over to the machine's side. Overall, adjusted for inflation, government spending in the city grew nearly 60 percent during Kendrick's term, excluding funds to finance the city's debt. The sale of unprecedented sums of municipal bonds fueled most of this new spending. Under Kendrick, Philadelphia's debt soared by more than $200 million, a trend that local business elites, including leaders of the chamber of commerce, largely applauded.[46] A year and a half into Kendrick's term, an article in the chamber of commerce's monthly magazine looked back at the election of 1923 as a watershed in the city's history, a moment "when Philadelphia shook itself loose from the lethargy that . . . had held in abeyance many projected improvements" and a time when "few had the temerity to believe that within a period of eighteen months so much would actually have been accomplished."[47] Harkening back to Kendrick's campaign slogan, the chamber proclaimed that the mayor had succeeded in garnering "the necessary co-operation" and had, in turn, furnished "the necessary action." Chamber leaders were similarly pleased that Kendrick stuck to his campaign pledge to "confer with representatives of the city's business and industrial life" regarding pressing municipal problems.[48] Throughout his term, Kendrick appointed chamber of commerce leaders to various public bodies and investigatory committees, whether to study traffic, revamp the city's building code, or to serve on the city's gas commission.[49] Surveying Kendrick's many accomplishments in 1927, an editorial in the chamber of commerce's *News Bulletin* giddily exclaimed, "Surely Philadelphia shows no sign of lagging in its march of progress!"[50] Just as surely, the Kendrick administration had succeeded in converting the chamber of commerce—formerly a den of antimachine reformers—into one of local political bosses' leading cheerleaders.

Kendrick's success in building a broad alliance between his administration and Philadelphia's business leaders lay in identifying overlap between the agendas of elite business interests and power players in Philadelphia's Republican machine. In many cases, the groundwork for this strategy had been established well before. The city's utility owners had long relied on machine politicians to help them realize their public goals and, when possible, local political bosses had moved to implement the policy objectives of their longstanding corporate sponsors. Funding for projects especially important to the city's utility interests, like the art museum and the Free Library, rolled in unencumbered under Kendrick. Both buildings were largely constructed

Figure 10. The new Free Library of Philadelphia building, which opened on the downtown parkway in 1927. *Courtesy of PhillyHistory.org, a project of the Philadelphia Department of Records.*

during his term. The new home of the Free Library opened its doors in 1927 and the art museum in early 1928.[51]

Yet Kendrick also succeeded in merging the machine's agenda with that of elite business interests in the city more generally. Doing so promised a great deal from machine politicians' perspective. Finding ways for local bosses to do the bidding of formerly antimachine businessmen might hobble the city's independent movement once and for all by co-opting some of its wealthiest supporters. In the case of the sesquicentennial, for instance, Kendrick and his allies in the city council cancelled plans to hold the fair in the city's Fairmount Park and instead used the event as an opportunity to reclaim an enormous expanse of marshland in South Philadelphia. The southern sections of the city had long been the center of the Vare machine's political power. South Philadelphia was also the turf of some of the Vares' wealthiest benefactors in real estate. Even with the change in venue, however, chamber of commerce leaders and the sesquicentennial's other business supporters were thrilled to finally get their fair.

Figure 11. The new building of the Philadelphia Museum of Art, which opened on the downtown parkway in 1928. *Courtesy of PhillyHistory.org, a project of the Philadelphia Department of Records.*

Indeed, Kendrick's inauguration brought a near immediate turnaround in the exhibition's fate. Within months of taking office, Kendrick moved to reorganize the sesquicentennial's planning committee. Leading members of the chamber of commerce, like former chamber president Ernest Trigg, remained in charge. But other businessmen closely tied to machine politicians, like South Philadelphia real estate dealer Albert Greenfield and movie theatre magnate Jules Mastbaum, assumed new prominence in organizing the event. Kendrick also convinced the fair's wealthiest detractors to drop their opposition. After a closed-door meeting with Kendrick in April 1924, both E. T. Stotesbury and Samuel Vauclain declared a newfound enthusiasm for the sesquicentennial provided that it result in permanent improvements of "real lasting benefit to the city" rather than a set of expensive, temporary structures.[52]

When it came to using the sesquicentennial as an opportunity for pursuing durable public improvements, the Kendrick administration came through. The lowland in the far south of the city where Kendrick and the sesquicentennial's planners decided to hold the fair originally lay almost fifteen to sixteen feet below the grade of South Broad Street, the main road leading to the site.[53] In preparation for the event, the city spent $4.5 million to haul "thousands of tons" of dirt to fill in over 3,000 acres of land, a number that would rise to over 4,500 as the city continued the project in the months following the sesquicentennial.[54] The Philadelphia Real Estate Board called the undertaking "perhaps the largest operation directly concerning realty on which the City has ever engaged" and predicted that reclamation of the area would lead to the construction of tens of thousands of homes as well as a burst of commercial and industrial development.[55]

The city also used the sesquicentennial as an opportunity to build an enormous municipal stadium with seating for a hundred thousand spectators and standing room for thousands more—a measure that the chamber of commerce had first called for just after the armistice. Planners designed the horseshoe-shaped structure to stand on a tract of the filled-in lowland where the sesquicentennial was held (and where Philadelphia's stadium complex still stands today). This decision delayed the project, as construction had to wait until contractors hauled in enough dirt. Work on the new arena did not begin until June 1925, only a year before the fair was scheduled to open. Some engineers said the city would never finish the structure on time. But a combination of new construction methods developed during the war and $2 million in public money sped up the process. The following year the stadium hosted perhaps the only event at the sesquicentennial that spawned an enduring memory: Jack Dempsey and Gene Tunney's first title fight.[56]

Figure 12. The site in South Philadelphia where the sesquicentennial was eventually held before the enormous swampy area had been filled in with dirt. *Courtesy of PhillyHistory.org, a project of the Philadelphia Department of Records.*

In fact, as an event unto itself, the sesquicentennial was "a colossal flop," to quote one historian. Despite Kendrick's and the sesquicentennial planning committee's best efforts, the fair never recovered from the long delays of the Moore years. Many exhibits were unfinished when the exposition opened on May 31, 1926. Bad weather and poor publicity kept potential visitors at home throughout the summer. In retrospect, it also seems that Americans had grown weary of the types of exhibitions that formed the sesquicentennial's main attractions—displays of "primitive" cultures and the triumphs of modern manufacturing and agriculture—and instead favored more modern forms of entertainment and spectacle, from home radio to motion pictures. Despite being a failure in the short term, however, by laying the groundwork for a major new recreational outlet for the city—the municipal stadium—and by opening up land for an onslaught of residential development in Philadelphia's southern outskirts, the sesquicentennial greatly furthered the realization of businessmen's vision for the city.[57]

In addition to reclaiming land in South Philadelphia as part of the sesquicentennial, the Kendrick administration encouraged Philadelphia's decentralization in other ways. By the time Kendrick left office, the city had all but completed the northern half of a lengthy subway running under Broad Street, and it had begun work on a southern route. The new subway officially opened

Figure 13. Philadelphia's municipal stadium soon after its completion as part of the 1926 sesquicentennial celebration. The stadium, which was later named after President John F. Kennedy, sat on filled-in marshland, where Philadelphia's stadium complex remains today. *Courtesy of PhillyHistory.org, a project of the Philadelphia Department of Records.*

for business in September 1928, running cars from the center of the city to Philadelphia's less developed far north. The construction of the Broad Street subway came on the heels of the Frankford El's opening earlier in the decade. Along with the city's construction of sewers, water lines, and streets, both of these projects provoked extensive construction in Philadelphia's less populated north, northeast, and western sections.[58]

Real estate developers predictably celebrated these trends. When it came to residential construction, the city's real estate men favored single-family dwellings over multifamily tenements or apartment houses. They wanted to preserve Philadelphia's reputation as a "city of homes." As the leaders of the Philadelphia Real Estate Board argued, "The real solution of the housing problem is to encourage intelligent heads of families to build homes in Philadelphia's vacant outlying tracts, to develop new home sections, where children will have the influences of real home life and the comfort of real homes." Only then would Philadelphia maintain its "reputation for productive industry, content, good-workmanship, steadiness, dependability, good manners and neighborliness."[59] The president of the Philadelphia Real Estate Board put the matter more bluntly: "Home ownership will create a citizenry which will, at all times, support and uphold government."[60]

Kendrick and other members of the Republican machine rarely bothered to justify their promotion of residential dispersion. For them, building the infrastructure to foster residential decentralization was primarily a matter of furthering their material and political interests. The Broad Street subway and the Frankford El were boons to the wealthy utility moguls who had long sponsored the political machine. The Philadelphia Rapid Transit Company gained exclusive franchises to run both lines. Supplying gas and electricity to new neighborhoods offered utility companies more opportunities to turn a profit. In addition, bringing modern infrastructure to undeveloped parts of the city allowed ward politicians from those areas to show their constituents what they gained by voting for them. Together, these dynamics led to a series of projects that helped push settlement away from Philadelphia's urban core. Nearly all of the wards in the center of the city lost population during the 1920s. By contrast, the eleven wards furthest from downtown Philadelphia, including wards in South, West, Northeast, and Northwest Philadelphia, captured all of the city's demographic growth during the decade and gained many Philadelphians who relocated from the city's center. Moreover, Philadelphia largely remained a "city of homes." In 1929, the Philadelphia Real Estate Board counted over four hundred thousand houses in the city and only four thousand or so apartment buildings.[61]

Meanwhile, local officials with ties to the Republican machine continued to deliver in another policy realm important to the city's business elites, especially those who ran the Philadelphia Chamber of Commerce. In the wake of adopting a new school construction plan in 1922, members of Philadelphia's board of education proceeded to spend $62 million on new buildings. By 1929, the district would build fifty-three new elementary schools, sixteen new junior high schools, a trade school, a vocational school, and three new comprehensive high schools, including one, Overbrook High School, that was twice the size of any other school building in the city when it was designed. Representatives of the chamber of commerce gushed that the flurry of school construction was "like pure romance" and continued, "Never have the accomplishments of the Board of Education . . . meant so much to Philadelphia."[62]

Alongside the school board's efforts, the Kendrick administration ushered in one of the most formative moments of government expansion in Philadelphia's history. Yet Kendrick's term was also a time of tremendous political corruption. Politically connected contractors won jobs on major projects like the Broad Street subway and the Free Library building. The Vare Construction Company earned between $15 and $20 million in contracts from 1924 and 1928, most of them related to work for local utility companies as they extended services throughout the city. Voter fraud was rampant. For instance, in the wake of a primary election for county offices in 1925, the board of registration commissioners requested an official investigation of irregularities at the polls. The inquiry eventually brought jail sentences for four election officials; another two were arrested and eight were removed from office. In one of the city's voting divisions, "it was charged that 40 percent of the vote had been cast by a 'phantom phalanx' from jails, hospitals, vacant houses, [and] graveyards."[63] When William Vare ran for the U.S. Senate in 1926, an investigation uncovered almost twenty-five thousand fraudulent names on the city's voter rolls, including "dead people, nonnaturalized foreigners, and children."[64]

The issue of political malfeasance came to the fore in the mayoral election of 1927. Accusations of cost overruns and graft, including on work related to the sesquicentennial, plagued Kendrick's final year in office. But more offensive to many Philadelphians was the candidacy of Harry A. Mackey, Vare's right-hand man and the campaign manager of Vare's corrupt 1926 senate run—a scandal that had made national headlines. Sensing a chance to capitalize on the Vare organization's excesses, J. Hampton Moore entered the race. His campaign was poorly funded, suggesting a lack of business support. Even so, Moore made a surprisingly good showing in the Republican primary, winning twelve out of forty-eight wards and 166,110 votes. Mackey gathered 248,000 votes, although election fraud in Vare controlled areas no doubt upped his tally. Moore remained in the race for the general election, but in November he performed worse than he had in the primary—losing all but two wards. The final count gave Mackey 296,618 and Moore 133,784. As the 1920s came to a close, a machine mayor who had gained national notoriety for running an abjectly corrupt senate campaign governed the nation's third-largest city. Unlike earlier in the century, no meaningful antimachine reform movement emerged in protest among the city's business leaders. Most of Philadelphia's upper crust had come to prefer boss rule to government inaction.[65]

Figure 14. The downtown parkway in 1929. The photograph is taken from the top of Philadelphia's city hall. The new art museum appears in the distance at the end of the parkway. The Free Library is just behind the domed building on the right. This photograph is taken from almost exactly the same vantage point as Figure 4 (see Chapter 1). Comparing the two images underscores the number of buildings that were demolished as part of the project. *Courtesy of PhillyHistory.org, a project of the Philadelphia Department of Records.*

On the Margins

The consolidation of Philadelphia's business elite behind machine politicians and the heightened power of Philadelphia's political bosses had a number of negative consequences for other political forces in the city. For example, in the years just after the armistice, portions of the city's quickly growing African American population had benefitted from the split between the Vares and the alliance between independent reformers and Boies Penrose. Between 1920 and 1930, Philadelphia's African American population grew from just over 130,000 to more than 200,000, or roughly 11 percent of the city's total. By the 1920s, African Americans in Philadelphia had been members and supporters of the Republican machine for decades. Many African Americans had moved to the city from the South, where African Americans' allegiance to the party of Lincoln remained strong. More importantly, most of these migrants were poor, as were many black Philadelphians more generally. Neighborhood political leaders tied to the machine had access to municipal jobs and in some cases offered them to African Americans in exchange for political support. Additionally, the machine's precinct captains and ward bosses sporadically provided free food and coal to local residents and could potentially intervene with the police or local judges if needed. Such instances of machine benevolence were infrequent, and the number of African Americans placed in public jobs was never proportionate to their numbers in the local population. Moreover, those African Americans who did find work with the city were forced to toil at the lowest levels of the municipal hierarchy in sanitation and similar jobs. Nonetheless, given the severity of African American poverty, the mere promise of potential employment, coal, food, cash, or legal help was enough to encourage many African Americans to support machine politicians, who readily exploited African Americans' economic vulnerability in their search for votes.[66]

Native-born, white Anglo-Saxon Protestants primarily controlled Philadelphia's Republican organization in the early twentieth century. But a handful of African American politicians wielded influence at the neighborhood level. A saloonkeeper named Amos Scott was arguably the most successful African American politician in the city when World War I came to an end. Scott was a close associate of the Vares, having met William Vare long before when both men were working as hucksters in South Philadelphia. Over the years, Scott and the Vare brothers cultivated a mutually beneficial relationship.

Scott rounded up support for the Vares among the city's African American community, and in return the Vares placed Scott in public jobs and offered him financial support, enough for Scott to open his own saloon. Scott's bar doubled as a political club and eventually became one the main seats of African American political power in the neighborhoods just south of downtown, where a large portion of the city's African American population lived.[67]

Just after the war, however, Scott's relationship with the Vares temporarily soured. Leading up to the municipal elections of 1919, the Vares promised to back Scott for police magistrate. But the Vares eventually pushed him off the ballot after an especially powerful white ward boss demanded that one of his underlings get the position instead. Angry that the Vares had slighted Scott, a number of African Americans resolved to vote against the Vares' candidate for mayor and instead support J. Hampton Moore. When the Vares' candidate lost the election by just over a thousand ballots, local pundits attributed the outcome to this African American protest vote.[68]

For a brief interval thereafter, Moore and the Vare machine competed to woo African Americans into their respective camps. In the elections of 1920, the Vares successfully backed two African American candidates for seats in the statehouse. It was the first time that the bosses had slated African Americans for the state legislature since 1914. In a 1921 election, the Vares moved to right their earlier misstep and threw their support behind Amos Scott's candidacy for police magistrate. Scott won as well. Meanwhile, Mayor Moore drew attention to how poorly the city's political machine served Philadelphia's African American population. Moore repeatedly decried conditions in the city's principal African American neighborhoods and blamed the dilapidation on the Vares' political monopoly in many of those areas. When African American leaders pointed out that the city owned one of the worst blocks in African American Philadelphia—a hotbed of prostitution and gambling known as "Hell's Half Acre"—Moore vowed to raze the area and turn it into a recreation center.[69] A number of residents still inhabited the shanties that stood on the stretch of municipal property. The city gave them several months to find new homes and enlisted African American reverend R. R. Wright Jr. as "volunteer agent of the mayor in aiding their relocation."[70] Thereafter, the city made the rare move of awarding the contract for clearing the land (which sat at Tenth and Lombard Streets) to an African American contractor. But members of the Vare machine refused to be outdone. In early 1922, Charles B. Hall, the most powerful Vare man in city council, pledged to build a $100,000 recreation building on the site, an exceptionally large appropriation for such an amenity, about a sixth of the recreation bureau's total budget that year.[71]

Over time, however, as the strength of the independent reform movement waned and the machine's hegemony waxed, African Americans received far less attention from white politicians. In 1924, the two seats in the state legislature that African Americans had won in 1920 were up for grabs again. At first, the Vare machine slated two white candidates for the posts. Only sustained protest by black politicians kept the seats in African American hands. After this show of strength, African American employment in municipal jobs rose throughout the decade as the Vare machine continued to reward a handful of African Americans for their support. Overall, however, as the machine's power grew unchecked, white politicians allied with local political bosses found it increasingly easy to ignore African Americans' political demands.[72]

A major facet of African American activism during the decade concerned the Philadelphia school board's practice of establishing separate schools for African American students. Throughout the 1920s, the overwhelming majority of African American schoolchildren in Philadelphia attended schools that served whites as well. If the population of a school became more than 95 percent African American, however, the district would shift all of the white teachers out of the building, replace them with African American teachers, and declare the school for African American students alone. In other cases, the school board segregated newly constructed schools from the start.[73]

The issue of separate schooling was a divisive one for local African Americans. Philadelphia's school board generally prohibited African American teachers from instructing white children. Thus, some African Americans in the city viewed separate schools as a rare professional opportunity for African American teachers. But other black activists resolved to end segregation in Philadelphia's schools. During the 1920s, the local branch of the NAACP launched a multiyear effort to force Philadelphia's board of education to integrate the city's teaching force and school buildings. But with no meaningful opposition to machine rule, local bosses had come to view African American support as less integral to their political success. The machine-appointed school board largely ignored the NAACP's protests. Philadelphia continued to establish segregated schools for African American students until the late 1930s.[74]

Immigrant populations in Philadelphia likewise struggled to influence local affairs. Jewish immigrants from Eastern Europe and Italians came to

Philadelphia in sizable numbers in the early years of the century. Most of them settled in the highly congested, older sections of the city that were strongholds of machine politicians allied with the Vares. As was the case for African Americans, most of the immigrants who came to Philadelphia were poor, and supporting the local political machine provided a potential avenue to municipal jobs, legal protection, or material aid. The majority of Jewish immigrants who came to Philadelphia from Eastern Europe voted for machine candidates throughout the 1920s. In exchange for backing local political bosses, Eastern European Jews gained a number of municipal posts during the decade, but Jewish immigrants remained second-class citizens within Philadelphia's Anglo-Saxon-dominated Republican organization. The preeminent exception was Albert Greenfield, whose family had immigrated to Philadelphia from Ukraine in the late nineteenth century. Greenfield made millions in real estate and eventually became one of William Vare's chief benefactors. When Vare ran for the U.S. Senate in 1926, Greenfield contributed $125,000 to the campaign. The Vare machine returned the favor on multiple occasions. Greenfield's main property holdings were in South Philadelphia. The development of the swamplands for the sesquicentennial was in part a sop to him. When the machine mayor Harry Mackey created Philadelphia's first city planning commission in 1929, he named Greenfield as a member. But Greenfield was an unusual case. Few other immigrants from Eastern Europe benefited so extensively from boss rule.[75]

The political experience of Italian immigrants was similar. By 1920, there were over one hundred thousand Italian immigrants in Philadelphia. Most Italians had settled in the southern section of the city, the political base of the Vare machine. Italians' main employment niche was in construction, often on public projects. The *padrone* system—in which a labor broker matched batches of Italian immigrants with various construction jobs—flourished in Philadelphia in the early twentieth century. Employers with short-term labor needs, like contractors working on public construction projects, relied heavily on the *padrone* system to secure temporary labor. Political boss William Vare's own construction company was a major employer of Italian workers. A number of Italians also gained permanent jobs within the city government. As was the case for the city's African Americans, however, most of these positions were at the lowest echelons of the municipal workforce. Indeed, only a handful of Italians were able to leverage their connections to the Vare machine to a significant degree. During the 1920s, Italians managed to capture a police magistracy and a judgeship on the city's court of common pleas. But the Republican Party never slated an Italian candidate for the U.S. House of Representatives, let alone the U.S. Senate. Only two Italians held seats in the Pennsylvania state legislature in the 1920s, and one of them served just a single, two-year term. The other was the son of Philadelphia's leading Italian powerbroker, Charles C. A. Baldi, who had used his access to large pools of Italian voters and unskilled laborers to forge strong ties with the Vares. Baldi was also the only Italian to serve on the city's school board during the decade.[76]

In part because of these dynamics, Italians in Philadelphia proved open to other political alternatives. In 1928, Philadelphia's beleaguered Democratic Party slated an Italian named Biagio Catania for a seat in the Pennsylvania House of Representatives. Democrats in part hoped that Catania's candidacy would help garner Italian support for Al Smith, the Democratic candidate in that year's presidential election. Italians in Philadelphia voted in large numbers for Smith, and Catania became the first Democrat to represent South Philadelphia's "Little Italy" in the Pennsylvania statehouse. As the Democratic Party's star ascended in the 1930s, more and more Italians would bolt Philadelphia's Republican machine. But this lay in the future. Throughout most of the 1920s, Vare's stranglehold on local politics left Italians with few political options.[77]

Female activists of various backgrounds also struggled to make their mark in the political sphere. Soon after women joined the electorate in 1920, Philadelphia's political bosses made clear that any favors doled out in working-class neighborhoods were contingent on an entire household's political loyalty. Working-class women who hoped to get a public job or whose husbands were employed in local government were effectively forced into backing the machine. Female Republican clubs spread throughout working-class Philadelphia, including in immigrant and African American neighborhoods, as women organized to distribute campaign literature and to get out the vote for machine candidates on election day. Some women who supported local bosses earned benefits in exchange. By the end of the 1920s, roughly two thousand women worked for the city, primarily in clerical positions, as social workers, or at the city's public hospital. Many more women worked for the city's school district, but these positions were less closely tied to machine patronage. A few women managed to win higher-level offices in the city. In 1924, the judges of the court of common pleas appointed a second female member to the city's school board. That year, voters elected the city's first female magistrate. Women served as assistant directors of the city's department of public welfare, and one woman, Sadie Turner Mossell Alexander, who was African American, served as an assistant city solicitor.[78]

Meanwhile, female activists involved in the independent cause—most of whom were middle- and upper-class, white Anglo-Saxon Protestants—found it difficult to gain recognition from their male collaborators. Women were deeply involved in J. Hampton Moore's run as the independent candidate for mayor in 1919.[79] Once in office, Moore failed to repay the favor. A year into his term, a mass meeting of independent women demanded that the mayor begin appointing women to his administration. Sarah Lowrie—one of the meeting's organizers and the head of the Philadelphia League of Women Voters—warned that Moore was at risk of losing his support among independent women and demanded "to know what the Mayor will do for us." Furthermore, she complained that the mayor had not "taken women into the inner councils of city affairs by appointing us to boards or commissions."[80] But despite the efforts of Lowrie and other female independents, Moore made only a few token appointments of women during his term.[81]

After Moore left office, women continued to struggle to gain recognition within the independent movement. In the election of 1923, a number of female independents declared their candidacy for various offices, but the male-dominated committee organizing the independent campaign initially refused to include any of them on its slate. At the meeting where the candidates were selected, Elizabeth Groben, who was running for city council, denounced the committee from the floor. "The nominating committee told me yesterday that the time is not ripe for a woman to sit in council," Groben declared. "When will the time be ripe?" "Now! Now!" her female supporters reportedly chanted.[82] The committee ended up dropping the male candidate whom it had originally endorsed in favor of Groben. The supporters of another female candidate, Edith Fales, demanded that the committee back her as well. Afraid that women would abandon the independent cause, the committee agreed. But both Groben and Fales ended up on a ticket that the Republican machine defeated from top to bottom. Plenty of female activists remained committed to the independent cause thereafter. For instance, women helped lead the antimachine campaign against Harry Mackey, the Vare candidate for mayor in 1927. Mackey's eventual victory, however, further marginalized the city's independent movement, including its female supporters, this time for the remainder of the decade. In sum, the machine's ability to elicit the support of working-class women largely through promises of patronage rather than pledges to enact certain policies, combined with political bosses' success in driving the independent movement to the periphery of local politics, tended to push female activists toward the edges of Philadelphia's policymaking process.[83]

Meanwhile, in labor circles Philadelphia was known as "scab city" and "the graveyard of unionism"—monikers that hint at organized labor's lack of clout.[84] Soon after the turn of the twentieth century, employers in the city's largest industrial sector, the metal trades, formed the Metal Manufacturers' Association (MMA) to crush existing unions among the city's metalworkers and to prevent the formation of others in the future. The city's largest metalworking firms, including Midvale Steel and Baldwin Locomotive Works, declined to join the MMA but only because they did not have to. Companies like Midvale and Baldwin had already found ways to undercut union organizers in their shops. By the time the United States entered World War I, members of the MMA had dislodged labor organizations from their firms as well. According to one leading historian, employers in Philadelphia's metalworking industries "completely controlled" the labor market by the 1920s.[85] Unions enjoyed a degree of strength in some sectors of Philadelphia's economy during the decade, including parts of the textile industry and in the printing trades, but not enough to act as an effective political lobby. Local bosses regularly ignored Philadelphia's unions without suffering at the polls.[86]

By contrast, the relationship between elite businessmen and machine politicians grew so close in the 1920s that their alliance produced results strikingly similar to those achieved by business interests in Detroit—a city where local business leaders' access to power was far more direct. Indeed, despite vast differences in the political climates of Detroit and Philadelphia, the combination of businessmen's political activism and business leaders' vision of a civic welfare state helped to produce monumental new art museums and libraries in both cities, as well as ambitiously reconstructed school systems, new recreational outlets, and an increasingly decentralized urban landscape.

Of course, regardless of these parallels, Philadelphia and Detroit remained on sharply different economic trajectories—a reminder that local government spending by itself cannot determine a city's economic fate. Deindustrialization eventually crippled both places, but Detroit's long-term descent would not begin until after World War II. Philadelphia's economic troubles were already apparent in the early twentieth century—certainly in the 1920s. Local business leaders' policy triumphs during the decade did little to insulate Philadelphia from various regional, national, and international economic trends. Profits in Philadelphia's once robust textile industries shrank. Employment in metalwork decreased by 25 percent. The city's shipbuilding industry was hit hard in the 1920s, as vessels built during the war more than met demand in the wake of the armistice. The spread of diesel and electric capabilities in the railroad industry destabilized onetime behemoths like Baldwin Locomotive Works and other local manufacturers focused on steam technology. Beyond failing to adjust to such macro-level trends, Baldwin Locomotive encouraged Philadelphia's incipient deindustrialization in another, more straightforward way: by decamping for a nearby suburb late in the decade.[87]

Such instances of capital mobility whetted the boosterish appetites of businessmen in other cities. In 1920s Atlanta, business leaders redoubled their generations-old effort to attract new firms to their hometown. Much as they did in Philadelphia and Detroit, elite businessmen in Atlanta viewed government as an essential tool for developing a business-friendly city. Yet in their quest to fund new government programs, Atlanta's business elite faced a distinct set of political obstacles.

CHAPTER 4

Atlanta

City Building in Black and White

In the spring of 1919, the Atlanta Chamber of Commerce invited over a hundred businessmen to a meeting to discuss the question, "What's the Matter with Atlanta?" According to the chamber's president and soon-to-be head of Coca-Cola, Samuel Candler Dobbs, attendees replied with a refrain strikingly similar to the one that business leaders in northern cities like Detroit and Philadelphia were voicing at the time. As Dobbs reported in the chamber of commerce's monthly magazine, "The general consensus of opinion was that . . . Atlanta needs better schools, better streets, more parks, and an adequate fire department, police department and waterworks." "In fact," he continued, "Atlanta is a very needy city."[1]

Despite this common starting point, business leaders in Atlanta traveled a very different political path than their counterparts in Detroit and Philadelphia. The successful merchants, bankers, and manufacturers who still formed the core of Atlanta's white business elite remained deeply committed to keeping taxes low as a way of luring new firms to the city—a top priority for elite businessmen in 1920s Atlanta and one that was inseparable from their commitment to building a civic welfare state. As had been the case before the war, concern over the tax rate led Atlanta's white business leaders to put an almost exclusive emphasis on debt spending to fund major public projects. In 1918, local officials managed to convince state legislators to lower the threshold governing bond elections in the city. Gaining the right to float bonds still demanded the assent of two-thirds of the voters participating in a bond referendum. But now those voters had to constitute only half of the registered electorate, not two-thirds, as state law had formerly stipulated. Even so, winning a bond election in Atlanta remained an exceptionally difficult task, particularly in comparison to cities like Philadelphia and Detroit, where a simple majority, no matter voter turnout, could carry a bond referendum. To pass bonds in Atlanta, the city's white business leaders had to stage elaborate campaigns and forge broad coalitions to get a majority of the registered electorate to the polls and earn a supermajority of their votes.[2]

White business elites' search for allies in these struggles encouraged political alliances that, while not wholly absent in either Detroit or Philadelphia, proved much more formative in 1920s Atlanta. The strict laws governing bond referenda especially encouraged local businessmen to work alongside newly enfranchised women in Atlanta. Moreover, on multiple occasions white business leaders aggressively solicited the support of African Americans in the city, a small group of whom still retained the right to vote in special elections like bond referenda despite white attempts to disfranchise black voters in Georgia more generally. Repeatedly during the decade, African Americans used their limited access to the ballot to shape the trajectory of public spending in the city. In both 1921 and 1926, they leveraged their electoral power to bargain for new school facilities for African American children. In other bond elections they forcefully opposed measures that they thought either harmed or did nothing to help Atlanta's African American population. Ironically, African American voters exerted the most sustained political influence not in the northern cities discussed in depth here but in Atlanta, the commercial center of a region infamous for African American disfranchisement. Meanwhile, in most instances white business leaders had little trouble enlisting the backing of the city's main union, the Atlanta Federation of Trades, because of that organization's overall support for social spending.

Yet even though the politics of bond referenda crossed class, gender, and in some cases racial lines, most often wealthy, white businessmen initiated such campaigns and, when they won, successfully maneuvered to exert an unrivaled influence over how bond money was spent as well as over other significant aspects of local social policy. Other interest groups in Atlanta often advocated the extension of local services, but it was not until white business leaders called for windfall spending that lawmakers placed the two most expensive bond initiatives of the decade on the ballot. Moreover, in both of these campaigns, white business leaders successfully lobbied local officials to create a special bond commission dominated by elite businessmen to oversee the projects involved. Similarly, early in the decade, the Atlanta Chamber of Commerce convinced the mayor and city council to create a city planning commission that successful white businessmen controlled, including in 1922, when the planning commission adopted an extensive zoning ordinance aimed at enforcing residential segregation, promoting homeownership, and encouraging housing construction in a decentralized pattern, one similar in both its form and its civic goals to what took shape in Detroit and Philadelphia.

As these instances suggest, for the most part Atlanta's white business leaders had little trouble enlisting the support of local officeholders in furthering their agenda. That said, the chamber of commerce and its wealthy allies failed to convince public officials to build a new art museum for the city and instead had to settle for converting a privately donated home into a gallery. Additionally, powerful businessmen bickered almost perennially with the city's school board over its inability to live within its allocated budget. These conflicts likely slowed the pace of educational spending in Atlanta during the decade, but the city's school budget nonetheless grew at an historic pace in part due to businessmen's political activism. In Philadelphia, business leaders struggled to overcome their own internal differences and to forge ties with local political bosses. In Detroit, the commercial and industrial elite's main challenge was holding onto elected office itself. In 1920s Atlanta, it was the unpredictable politics of the ballot initiative that posed the greatest obstacle to businessmen's ongoing sally for a civic welfare state.

Postwar Defeats and a Strategic Shift

Just as Coca-Cola's Samuel Candler Dobbs and his colleagues at the Atlanta Chamber of Commerce were debating "What's the Matter with Atlanta," Atlanta's business leaders were being reminded just how hard funding new public improvements in the city could be. In early 1919, city officials voted to hold a referendum on a modest set of bond issues, worth $1 million in all, to fund an assortment of projects, from improving the local water system to providing supplemental funding for the fire department. In an exceptional move for Atlanta, local officials also resolved to ask voters to approve a small property-tax hike, from $1.25 to $1.50 per $100 in assessed valuation, the proceeds of which would go to the city's underfunded school system. The chamber of commerce joined a number of other local organizations in championing these measures, including the Atlanta Federation of Trades, the Atlanta Federation of Women's Clubs, and the socioeconomically elite, all-male, and all-white President's Club. As the election approached, the city's newly elected mayor, James L. Key, moved to rally support. He called for a half-day holiday on election day and named a special committee composed of "a strong man from each ward" to help publicize the bond issue and to get voters to the polls.[3]

But the efforts of the mayor, his special committee, and such a varied array of local organizations fell short. On March 5, 1919, the bond proposals passed by a two-thirds majority, but far from enough registered voters had cast ballots to legally approve the measures. Meanwhile, the proposed tax hike failed to win even a simple majority of the small number of Atlantans who had gone to the polls.[4]

Stunned by the defeat, leading proponents of the bond and tax referenda went searching for scapegoats. Abysmal turnout among white voters had primarily caused the loss. But leading white newspapers immediately pointed their fingers at the small number of African American voters in the city who had unanimously opposed the ballot measures. In 1908, following a pattern established by other southern states, Georgia had passed legislation that sharply curtailed African Americans' ability to vote. Barred outright from participating in Democratic primaries, some African American men nonetheless managed to overcome other tactics, like poll taxes, meant to curb the registration of African American voters. In turn, loopholes in state laws allowed these men to participate in special elections, such as referenda on bond issues and tax increases.[5]

In the aftermath of the election, editorials in local white newspapers patronizingly blamed African American opposition on a "misapprehension" in the African American community and furthermore cited "a subtle and adroit canvass" that had "misled" local African Americans "into assuming an attitude of hostility against a measure of vital importance to them."[6] In reality, African American resistance had grown from the deliberate efforts of local African American leaders who hoped to use black Atlantans' limited franchise to improve city services in the city's African American neighborhoods.

For years, African Americans in Atlanta had lobbied local officials for better government services in their communities but to little avail. The city's leading African American newspaper, the *Atlanta Independent*, calculated in the spring of 1919 that local officials had built twenty new schools for the city's white children in the previous thirty years but only one for African American students. The salaries of the most veteran black teachers were lower than those of rookie white educators. The newspaper also noted that the city allocated disproportionately small sums for police and fire protection in African American neighborhoods, a trend mirrored to varying degrees in all city services. Until the early 1920s, for instance, African Americans could not visit a single public library or public park in the city.[7]

African Americans had long objected to such neglect, but when the proposed ballot initiatives of 1919 included no provisions for the city's African American neighborhoods, they embraced a new strategy. Led by African American ministers, club women, the *Atlanta Independent* and its editor Benjamin Davis, and the local branch of the NAACP, prominent black Atlantans organized vigorously to register all eligible African American men and to convince them to help defeat the ballot proposals either by going to the polls and voting "no" or at least by registering and simply staying home on election day. The blame that white leaders hurled on African American voters in the aftermath of the election suggested that the roughly 1,200 African American men who were registered to vote at the time had succeeded in gaining recognition of their electoral power. Many whites' immediate reaction, however, was to point to African Americans' part in swinging the election and argue that the city should therefore nullify the results. Just after the votes had been tallied that March, Atlanta's city council scheduled another referendum for April 23 to consider precisely the same proposals.[8]

But local African Americans simply organized again. This time African American women in particular redoubled their efforts to get African American men registered to vote. In so doing, black female activists built upon an organizational structure that they had created over the preceding decade through Atlanta's premier African American social service organization, the Neighborhood Union.

The Neighborhood Union was founded by Lugenia Burns Hope, an experienced social worker who had started out in the emerging profession laboring alongside Jane Addams at Chicago's Hull House. In 1898, Hope moved to Atlanta with her husband, John, who eventually became the president of Morehouse College. Once in Atlanta, Hope threw herself into the political and charitable efforts of the city's existing African American women's groups. In 1908, she resolved to expand the services available to African Americans in the city after a local African American woman died from an illness that her neighbors had failed to notice in time. Hope pledged to mobilize African American women to ensure that no one else would suffer a similar fate and to improve living conditions in Atlanta's African American neighborhoods more generally. Over the years that followed, Hope and her collaborators built a robust organization that stretched throughout Atlanta's African American areas. They divided up the city and put women in charge of meeting the needs of every African American household in their respective districts. This structure not only allowed the Neighborhood Union to provide services effectively. It also gave the organization great potential in grassroots politics.[9]

Figure 15. Lugenia Burns Hope, founder of the Neighborhood Union, with her husband, John Hope, the first African American president of Morehouse College. The Neighborhood Union was arguably the most robust grassroots organization in Atlanta in the early twentieth century. *Lugenia Burns Hope and John Hope, undated, Neighborhood Union Collection, Atlanta University Center Robert W. Woodruff Library.*

In the run-up to the bond election of April 1919, Hope assumed leadership of a newly formed Women's Registration Committee and proclaimed that African American women, many of them associated with the Neighborhood Union, would push eligible men to register for the election "from the rostrums of every service, sacred and secular, fraternal or social there is to be from now until the [registration] books close."[10] Within a month, the efforts of Hope, the Neighborhood Union, and other African American men and women had added another 500 African Americans to the voter rolls, bringing the total to over 1,700. Wholly misconstruing the intent of African American activists, the *Atlanta Constitution* (white Atlanta's leading newspaper) reported that African American women had held "a mass meeting" a week before the election to encourage African American men to register and took this "to mean that they will begin an active campaign in favor of the . . . propositions." With particular condescension, the newspaper praised "the colored people" for becoming "better informed as to the present needs of their schools and the necessity for improvement."[11]

As the April contest neared, Mayor Key pursued strategies similar to those he had utilized during the March election, including putting a committee of "strong men" in charge of the campaign. This time, however, Key also reached out to African American voters by inviting a contingent of African American leaders to city hall to discuss the upcoming contest. Other white proponents of the ballot measures, by contrast, focused exclusively on gathering more white votes, often by turning to racist appeals. One chastised whites for having "allowed the Negro to hinder our progress" and argued, "if we withhold our means . . . we are starving the minds of all white children concerned."[12] Despite such dire warnings, in the month and a half separating the two elections, white opposition to the referenda actually grew thanks in part to a new white organization, the Atlanta Tax Payers League, an ephemeral group formed to fight the proposed tax increase and bond issues. Overall, the efforts of white leaders for and against the proposals increased white registration by four thousand voters compared to the March election—a mixed blessing in a contest that demanded the participation of an exceptionally large portion of the registered electorate. When the votes were counted, the combination of higher registration rates, African American resistance, and heightened white opposition had brought yet another defeat for the ballot initiatives' proponents. Low voter turnout was also to blame. Once again not enough Atlantans had gone to the polls to make the results count. Those who did rejected all but one of the measures.[13]

In the months that followed, developments suggested that white business leaders were committed to overcoming such obstacles in the future. Beginning in the fall of 1919, leading members of the Atlanta Chamber of Commerce took a number of steps to increase the organization's influence over local affairs and to lay the groundwork for rallying public support in future elections. Chamber leaders initiated an ambitious membership drive and moved to tighten the organization's links with city officials, no doubt in part to erase lingering perceptions from the prewar period that the chamber was an opponent of city hall. The chamber revised its bylaws to make the head of Fulton County's board of commissioners and Atlanta's mayor ex officio members of its board of directors. The chamber of commerce also opened its ranks to women for the first time. In justifying its decision to admit female members, chamber leaders explained how women could assist in furthering projects that the organization strongly favored but that "essentially belong to women's sphere," such as "beautifying the yards and the public spaces of the city . . . in short, all the housekeeping and home-making matters." After women gained the right to vote a year later, however, elite businessmen began to view them not only as "municipal housekeepers" but also as a crucial electoral bloc that could help further their policy goals.[14]

Chamber of commerce leaders also moved to link their agenda of government expansion to what they hoped would become a broadly popular new front in their ongoing effort to attract more businesses to the city. That December, the chamber of commerce's subcommittee on industrial promotion began discussing the prospects of increasing the city's population to five hundred thousand by 1930—up from about two hundred thousand in 1920—by "securing the location of hundreds of new enterprises."[15] Just after the New Year, one of the newest members of the chamber's board of directors, Mayor Key, took up the cause. In his annual address to the city council, Key called for the adoption "of a definite and scientific plan to meet the demands for a city of not less than 500,000 inhabitants" and urged that this plan "comprehend every line of public improvements and development." He advocated "the construction and expansion of a modern school system; the development and construction of crosstown thoroughfares, viaducts and bridges; widening and paving of streets . . . expansion of the parks of the city . . . and public comforts for the downtown district." Having just learned that achieving these objectives might demand African American support, Key also urged the construction of the first municipal library for African American use.[16]

The campaign for a half million Atlantans picked up steam as the year progressed. In March 1920, the chamber of commerce circulated a mailing throughout the city entitled "Atlanta—500,000 in Ten Years." According to a local newspaper, the flyer made "the argument that if Atlanta really expects to be a city of half a million in ten years, it ought to begin to prepare now for the additional thousands."[17] But the biggest push that year came when Key—along with elite white businessmen and the leaders of some of the city's most prominent white women's associations—organized a Fourth of July festival to rally support for the cause. At least in terms of attendance, their efforts were a success. Close to thirty thousand Atlantans reportedly gathered at Lakewood Park on Independence Day. The festivities included "magnificent pyrotechnical displays, athletic contests, horse races and speed demonstrations by dare-devil motorcyclists." The city also unveiled a new granite monument to commemorate the start of its campaign for a half million inhabitants.[18]

State Senator Ivan E. Allen Sr. (a wealthy furniture and office supply dealer and former president of the Atlanta Chamber of Commerce) introduced the event's three main speakers: the governor, the mayor, and Eugene R. Black, who had succeeded Samuel Candler Dobbs as president of the chamber of commerce earlier that year. A lawyer by training, Black became president of the Atlanta Trust Company in 1921. Married to the daughter of Henry Grady—postbellum Atlanta's most famous booster—Black would later serve as governor of the Atlanta Federal Reserve Bank and, in the early 1930s, as head of the U.S. Federal Reserve.[19] In his speech, Mayor Key admonished the crowd, "Improve the educational system, improve the public utilities. If you do not continually improve the city, then we are not worth a population of 500,000 and we had better stop striving."[20] Newspapers did not record the speech that Black gave that day, but soon after his election to the chamber of commerce presidency in December 1919, he expressed similar convictions, emphasizing "the paramount importance of attaining co-operation from every Atlantan, and arousing their enthusiasm for the movements that must be made to achieve the success Atlanta deserves, is acquiring, and must provide for with added facilities and resources."[21]

Whether or not Black discussed the same issues when he spoke from the dais at the Independence Day celebration, the event itself spoke to white business elites' understanding of the type of popular politics that they needed to embrace to achieve their agenda. The chamber of commerce's drive to gain female members had already suggested that it would be a politics that crossed gender lines. As a business-initiated bond campaign would soon attest, it would also be a politics that could traverse the boundaries of Jim Crow.

Race Versus Civic Disgrace

For the remainder of the summer and fall of 1920, federal, state, and local elections seemed to put white business leaders' and local officials' burgeoning pro-growth agenda on hold. Soon thereafter, however, disagreements surfaced about how best to fund the expansion of city services. As Mayor Key and the incoming city council began to hammer out a new budget in January 1921, Key expressed skepticism about the chances of gaining popular approval for another bond issue. Instead, he came out in favor of levying an emergency tax, as opposed to debt spending, to help the city fund new public improvements, a move that in part entailed pursuing government expansion on a significantly smaller scale. As Key complained, passing bonds "seems almost a hopeless task."[22]

Key had also pushed for an emergency tax in 1919 and 1920 to help the city meet additional expenses in the absence of available bonds. In those years, the city council had gone along with Key, even as a number of local groups had opposed the emergency taxes. In the fall of 1919, for instance, the Atlanta Federation of Trades had come out against an emergency tax proposal that city council had recently passed. The union also began to organize on behalf of a $3 million bond issue for the city's schools. One of the most influential elite white women's associations in the city, the Atlanta Woman's Club, immediately joined forces with the union, while editors of the *Atlanta Constitution* also expressed their support. Later that year, the superintendent of Atlanta's schools, W. F. Dykes, argued that $5 million was needed to remedy educational shortcomings in the city.[23]

Yet it was not until the January 1921 budget negotiations, when white business leaders came out against Key's call for yet another emergency tax, that the movement for debt spending gained traction. After Key announced his proposal, objections from business interests seemed to roll in. The board of directors of the Atlanta Food Retail Association was the first to decry Key's emergency tax and instead proposed a bond issue somewhere in the range of $8 million to $10 million. Leading banker and former mayor Robert Maddox testified against the emergency levy and told city council's finance committee that the time was ripe for issuing bonds. The first member of the city council to publicly oppose Key's proposal and instead advocate debt spending was E. Harry Goodhart, a close political ally of some of the most economically successful men in the city. Just months before, in fact, a number of business leaders had drafted Goodhart to run against Mayor Key in his bid for reelection. Their ranks included "300 of Atlanta's most prominent businessmen," including the well-known banker William Lawson Peel and chamber of commerce president Eugene Black. Key had won the election handily, but Goodhart retained his seat as an alderman from the city's Eighth Ward. Thereafter, Goodhart led the fight in city hall to place a bond issue of unprecedented scope on the local ballot.[24]

On January 21, 1921, city officials resolved to put a proposal for $8.85 million in bonds to the voters, including $4 million for the city's schools, $2.85 million for its water system, $1.25 million for sewers, and $750,000 to build the so-called Spring Street viaduct, a bridge designed to cross a wide stretch of railroad tracks obstructing automobile traffic in the downtown section of the city. Alderman Goodhart cast the only dissenting vote but only because he wanted even more bonds for the city's schools. As it had in 1919, the city council proposed a small property-tax increase (again from $1.25 to $1.50 per $100 of assessed value), this time to finance the proposed debt. Soon after these measures were approved, Mayor Key dropped his opposition and instead did his part to organize support on their behalf.[25]

The ensuing campaign contrasted sharply with those of 1919. From the beginning the effort was rooted in an alliance between men and women led by some of the city's wealthiest and most famous citizens. Frank M. Inman, son of the wealthy cotton trader Samuel Inman, chaired the committee that took charge of organizing the effort. Unlike in 1919, when Key named an all-male committee to rally support, this time a well-known and widely respected past president of the Atlanta Federation of Women's Clubs, Katherine Lumpkin, served as the campaign's associate chair. The bond campaign took on an even more elite hue when Mayor Key, following the advice of the chamber of commerce and other groups, named a special commission to oversee the expenditure of the bond revenues should the ballot initiatives pass. Key named sixteen members to the new body, one from each of the city's eleven wards plus five members from the city at large. He appointed the head of the Atlanta Federation of Trades, the general chairman of the Order of Railroad Conductors, and a former head of the Atlanta Board of Education, as well as three women, including Lumpkin.[26]

But the remaining ten members of the new commission were all white male business executives. They included bank presidents and vice presidents, wealthy cotton and cattle traders, the owner of a chain of four stores, the Atlanta Chamber of Commerce's new president Lee Ashcraft, and a former secretary of the chamber. The ordinance creating the commission vested the body "with all of the legal authority that could be delegated it by city council under the charter of Atlanta." City officials could not strip themselves of the ultimate power to allocate public funds. Nonetheless, the new law stipulated that, if approved, none of the bond money could be spent without the new commission's first offering its recommendation.[27]

With this business-dominated commission in place, leaders of the bond campaign set out to ensure that the new body would, in fact, have money to spend. With the defeats of 1919 fresh in their minds, one of their first moves was to reach out to African American voters. According to some accounts, Mayor Key and Frank Inman promised that a third of the $4 million in bonds allocated for schools would go to the city's African American community. Key and Inman reportedly listed specific African American schools that would be slated for renovation as well as new schools that would be constructed, including the city's first African American high school. Inman later denied that he or any other white leader had made specific promises. Still, at a mass meeting at a leading African American church, Inman assured attendees that African American neighborhoods would be "treated properly and fairly." Key echoed Inman's pledge, emphasizing that city officials would allocate the proceeds of the bond issue based on "justice and fair play."[28]

Lumpkin, Key, and other white leaders especially sought to win the support of African American women. Women were eligible to participate in their first special election that year thanks to the newly enacted Nineteenth Amendment. Lumpkin appointed a "negro bond committee" consisting of "twenty-two colored women designated as leaders by members of their own race," including Lugenia Burns Hope.[29] Soon thereafter, Hope and the rest of the committee were invited to city hall for a special meeting with Lumpkin, the mayor, and the superintendent of schools, who promised, according to an African American woman in attendance, that "colored men and women would decide the kind of High School we would get." Before the meeting adjourned, Hope and the rest of the committee wholeheartedly endorsed the bonds.[30]

Lumpkin and other white leaders' outreach to African American women was just one part of an elaborate effort to organize all female voters in the city. Soon after her appointment, local newspapers reported that Lumpkin had already enlisted between 450 and 500 female volunteers to assist in the campaign. These and other women organized on a ward-by-ward basis and canvassed local neighborhoods by going door to door. Lumpkin urged female church groups to join the effort and reached out to women in neighborhood parent-teacher associations, who in turn organized rallies and worked to register female voters. The Atlanta Federation of Women's Clubs endorsed the cause and encouraged its member organizations to get out the vote.[31]

Leaders of the bond campaign supplemented such grassroots organizing with countless speeches and a flurry of advertisements and flyers. In arguing their position, they turned to an apocalyptic rhetoric that warned of the imminent decline of both the city and its citizenry if voters did not approve the proposed spending. In combining boosterish appeals to improve the economic health of their city with calls to save the local citizenry, campaign leaders gave voice to the two main concerns that motivated businessmen's attempt to build a civic welfare state. Without the much-needed money, they warned, Atlanta would descend into "stagnation, disintegration, and civic disgrace."[32] One advertisement in a local newspaper proclaimed, "Bonds, Only, Can Save Atlanta's Commercial and Civic Life" and further admonished, "If this warning is not heeded there is an impending danger that we may awake one of these fine mornings and find Atlanta—our great city of the South—in the very throes of death."[33] Campaign materials often bemoaned the impact of the city's deficient sewer and water systems on public health and argued that Atlanta was a "very sick city."[34] At the same time, campaign leaders underscored the need for school bonds by arguing that education "completely determines the social, economic, and civic outlook of [the city's] future citizenry."[35]

When the referendum took place on March 8, 1921, turnout was extensive. Only five hundred or so Atlantans voted against the ballot initiative, and over twenty thousand voted for it. An unprecedented number of African American voters reportedly participated in the contest. Over forty local organizations had endorsed the proposal, including the chamber of commerce, the Atlanta Real Estate Board, and the Atlanta Federation of Trades. Initiated by elite business interests and passed by an alliance that cut across race, gender, and class lines, the bond issue was the largest that Atlantans passed before the Great Depression. It was also the first to win the electorate's approval since 1910. Later that summer, voters overwhelmingly approved the tax hike that the city council had originally proposed to help finance the bonds—the only tax increase put before voters for the remainder of the decade.[36]

Figure 16. A cartoon from a local Atlanta newspaper depicting a plucky professional man (perhaps a businessman) explaining why he supported the $8.85 million bond issue that voters were asked to approve in March 1921. Atlanta Constitution, *February 13, 1921.*

In the end, the new, business-dominated bond commission funneled a sizable amount of bond revenue toward educational facilities in African American neighborhoods. But white officials did not allocate a full third of the $4 million that voters had approved for the city's schools to Atlanta's African American community, as Mayor Key and Frank Inman had reportedly promised and as would have been proportionate to the number of African Americans in the city. Instead, they appropriated less than a fourth, but the $990,000 that black schools received was still a lump sum of record size. The city used the bonds to build eight elementary schools, three junior high schools, and two senior high schools for Atlanta's white students along with three new elementary schools, one junior high school, and the promised senior high school for African American schoolchildren. Leading black entrepreneur Heman E. Perry won the $212,000 contract to build the African American high school. The school was eventually named after Booker T. Washington and still serves students on Atlanta's West Side.[37]

By using the vote to gain concessions from the city's white leadership, African Americans in Atlanta had scored a major political victory. Of course, the 1919 and 1921 bond campaigns also underscored that Atlanta's white business elite and other leading white Atlantans would abet spending public funds for the benefit of African American neighborhoods only begrudgingly. The city's white business leadership (and doubtless most white Atlantans) refused to see African Americans as citizens and thus did not envision them as beneficiaries of the civic welfare state that they hoped to build. Instead, white leaders conceived of African Americans as their political subjects: almost

Figure 17. A postcard depicting Booker T. Washington High School, Atlanta's first high school serving African American students. *Courtesy of the Kenan Research Center at the Atlanta History Center.*

completely barred from voting, excluded from most publicly run facilities, and deserving of public funds only insofar as they served white interests.

Indeed, for the next several years, African Americans in Atlanta returned to enduring a relentless combination of effrontery and neglect from white officials. First, in early 1922, the city's business-dominated city planning commission implemented Atlanta's first citywide zoning ordinance, a measure that legislated residential segregation as part of a familiar project central to businessmen's vision of a civic welfare state: building a decentralized city of homeowners—in Atlanta's case, one designed explicitly for whites. Later that year, the local branch of the Ku Klux Klan reached the height of its political power and placed one of its members in the mayor's chair. These developments coincided with—although they did not completely cause—a multiyear drought in white business leaders' ability to win bonds for further civic improvements. Only later in the decade would public spending again truly rise, not coincidentally thanks to resurgent boosterism among white business elites that again prodded them to solicit African American support.

The Lines of Race Redrawn

The public entity that authored Atlanta's segregationist zoning ordinance—the city planning commission—grew out of the first meeting of the Atlanta Chamber of Commerce's board of directors after the body's reorganization in 1919. As a newly appointed ex officio member of the board, Mayor Key had attended that gathering and had quickly signed on to chamber leaders' proposal to create an official body "capable of planning every phase of the developments that the city requires."[38] The new commission was originally designed to have twenty-four members: eight appointed by the mayor, eight by the board of county commissioners, and eight by the chamber of commerce. After the city council endorsed the idea, a commission was named along these lines. Not surprisingly, the chamber of commerce drew from its own ranks for its share of appointments. But Key and the county commissioners also tapped chamber of commerce men. In all, fifteen out of the twenty-four members of Atlanta's original city planning commission were chamber of commerce leaders.[39]

In time, public officials, along with members of the city planning commission themselves, moved to streamline the new board. Instead of twenty-four members, the commission would now feature only six, all of them appointed by the mayor. This change merely intensified businessmen's dominance of the body. After its reorganization, and up through the passage of the 1922 zoning ordinance, the city's planning board consisted of Frank Pittman, the head of a successful construction company; real-estate developer Robert R. Otis; wealthy railroad executive C. A. Wickersham; Joel Hurt, one of the city's wealthiest and most famous entrepreneurs; a token representative of organized labor; and U.S. senator Hoke Smith, a successful lawyer, newspaper publisher, hotel owner, and when he was governor, leader of the 1908 movement to disfranchise black Georgians.[40]

The city planning commission was initially designed to oversee an array of public initiatives, even those not commonly associated with city planning, suggesting that white business leaders had originally hoped to use the body to influence nearly all aspects of local affairs. One of the commission's first meetings took on the question of merging the city and county school systems, while early subcommittees included one on local history and others dedicated to tackling housing and public welfare, recreation, arts, and music, as well as finance and taxation, transportation, and building regulations.[41]

Eventually the powers of the new commission were drawn more sharply. After consulting with city planning experts throughout the country, Atlanta's commissioners took their advice not to "put too many irons in the fire." They dropped "questions of school government," intellectual development, and the arts as not "strictly city planning." Instead, they limited their purview to "plans for laying out, widening . . . and locating of streets . . . the relief of traffic congestion [and] the development of housing and sanitation conditions," among other duties.[42] They also hired a consultant to guide them: Robert Whitten, a Cleveland city planner who urged the commission to adopt a wide-ranging zoning ordinance to shape Atlanta's future development.[43]

In championing zoning, Whitten emphasized its potential to increase property values and the city's tax revenues and also promote homeownership, a project that he associated with fostering specific civic goals. He decried the "enormous waste of haphazard building" and claimed that a half billion dollars were squandered each year across the country because of the preventable depreciation of property.[44] Along with staving off economic loss, "on the human side," Whitten promised that zoning would bring "about an increase in health, comfort and happiness for the people."[45] During an Atlanta Chamber of Commerce luncheon, Whitten argued that the city's "industrial commercial and residential sections should be separated; the white and colored residential sections should be segregated; apartment houses should be set in a separate district from the family home district; buildings should be limited in their height . . . and plans to make the city suitable to take care of a population five times its present population and to beautify it should be taken."[46]

Whitten also urged the city planning commission to set aside plenty of land for single- or two-family homes instead of apartment buildings. "Apartments are good enough for adults," he argued, "but residences should be encouraged for the good of our future citizens. A child has no place in an apartment house for his full and satisfactory development."[47] Whitten later claimed that by stabilizing property values and setting aside space for the construction of "proper" housing, "zoning protects the home sections, promotes home ownership and good citizenship."[48] In Atlanta, segregation became an especially central part of this project. Many white leaders believed that the threat of black encroachment on white territory—especially its potential for lowering the value of white-owned property within the city's racist real estate market—was deterring white Atlantans from buying homes. The U.S. Supreme Court ruled racial zoning ordinances unconstitutional in the middle of World War I. Nonetheless, in early 1922, Atlanta's business-dominated planning commission embraced Whitten's arguments and unveiled a new zoning plan with residential segregation as one of its main components. The measure faced resistance from a small group of real estate developers, but most leading civic organizations backed the plan. The Atlanta Chamber of Commerce, the Atlanta Real Estate Board, the Atlanta Woman's Club, and the Atlanta Federation of Trades all gave it their hearty endorsement.[49]

In its final form, Atlanta's 1922 zoning measure not only legally delineated which sections of the city would be African American and which would be white. It also made clear that African Americans would be left out of the decentralized city of family-owned homes that Whitten and the businessmen on the city planning commission hoped to develop. The zoning ordinance restricted black settlement to the core of the city while reserving every single neighborhood on the outskirts of Atlanta for whites. As the city council considered the measure, the planning commission explained that the zoning plan would further a goal dear to business leaders in Atlanta (as well as in Philadelphia and Detroit): the prevention of residential congestion. In the city's African American neighborhoods, however, the city's new zoning ordinance would virtually guarantee overcrowding. In 1924, Georgia's state supreme court ruled the racial restrictions in Atlanta's zoning ordinance unconstitutional after a white property owner, Annie Bowen, brought suit against the city. Bowen owned an investment property that abutted an African American neighborhood. The property was officially zoned "white," but Bowen claimed that she could not find a white buyer for the property. Bowen complained that Atlanta's zoning ordinance violated her right to sell to whomever she saw fit, including an African American. Georgia's supreme court agreed. Even so, Atlanta officials continued to use the zoning plan to guide the city's growth. By 1930, roughly 60 percent of Atlanta's eighty-five thousand African Americans would live in just three of the city's wards. Those three were also the city's most populous.[50]

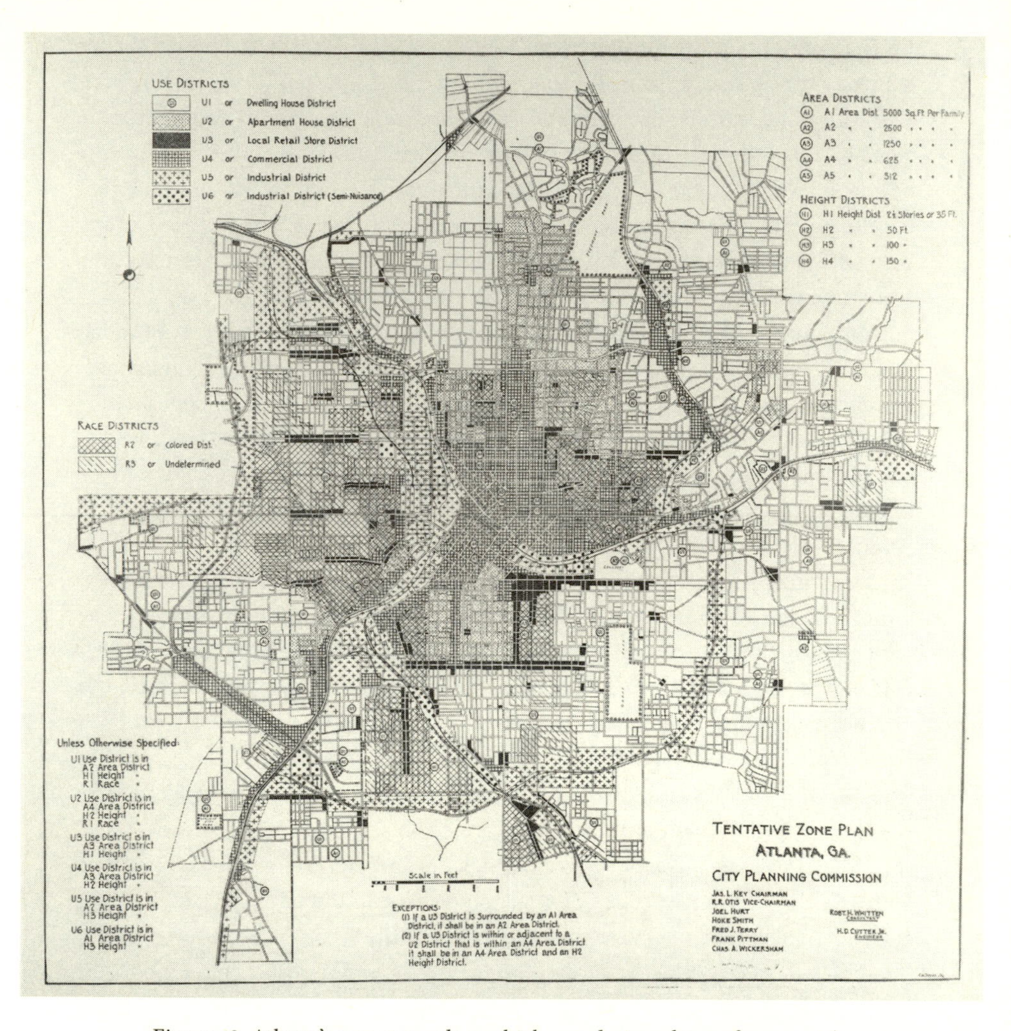

Figure 18. Atlanta's 1922 zone plan, which was designed to enforce racial segregation and to promote residential decentralization, at least for the city's white residents. Note the key on the left side of the map indicating "Race Districts." *Edward M. Bassett Papers, #2708, Division of Rare and Manuscript Collections, Cornell University Library.*

Soon after public officials passed the new zoning ordinance, the city's voters elected a well-known member of the Ku Klux Klan, Walter A. Sims, as their next mayor. Founded in 1915 just miles outside of Atlanta, the Second Ku Klux Klan established a particularly strong presence in its hometown. According to one historian, "Tens of thousands of white Atlantans from all walks of life belonged to the Klan in the early twenties."[51] Another scholar gives a lower estimate of "at least 15,000 in 1923."[52] Whatever the actual count, in the mayoral election of 1922, it proved enough to put the Klan's candidate into office.

From time to time, the local Klan's publication, the *Searchlight*, sounded the antielitist, populist notes that historians have recently associated with the Ku Klux Klan in the 1920s South. Indeed, *Searchlight* editorials more than once railed against corporate power in the city, decrying Atlanta's "well-organized commercial clubs" and "the autocratic chamber of commerce," a pattern that one historian has taken to suggest that members of Atlanta's KKK were primarily "lower middle class."[53] Perhaps so, but Sims's election did not bring a sea change in local politics. In the 1922 mayoral race, along with his proclamation for Klan-style "one hundred percent Americanism," Sims called for an agenda that closely mirrored what Atlanta's white business elite was advocating at the time. As the *Atlanta Constitution* reported, Sims called for the continuation of the city's "rapid expansion program" so that Atlanta could "eventually become one of the largest and best cities in the country."[54] Moreover, he urged public officials to prepare for "a city of a half million people" through improving the city's water, sewer, and school systems, and he endorsed the continued expenditure of the 1921 bond issue "in exact accord with the conditions under which it was voted by the people."[55] Sims also pledged to keep the business-dominated bond commission intact. The Sims administration rarely coupled the Klan's anti-Catholic, anti-black, and anti-Semitic stances with attacks on local capitalists, although in at least one speech Sims did denounce downtown real estate owners for not paying their fair share of local taxes. Meanwhile, the elite leadership of the Atlanta Chamber of Commerce seemed largely enamored of Sims, eventually praising his tenure as one of "the best administration's Atlanta has ever had."[56]

More than any Klan-inspired populist insurgency, white business leaders' main challenge in furthering their pro-growth agenda in the mid-1920s remained winning the right to fund its core components through debt spending. Doubtless Sims's affiliation with the Klan made this project all the more difficult. Until 1926, the strategy of reaching across racial lines to win bond elections went unused.

That said, in the first bond election held after Sims took office, winning African American support would have been nearly impossible anyway. Moreover, forces other than African American opposition ushered in defeat. In 1923, leading business groups moved to combine an effort to push poor, African American residents from the downtown section of the city with an attempt to build a central park following the spirit, if not the scale, of New York City's. As originally proposed, the park was designed to encompass 126 acres and sit just a few blocks from the city's main thoroughfare, Peachtree Street, "within easy walking distance of the business center," just east of where Centennial Olympic Park sits in Atlanta today.[57] The initial design for the park included a large public stadium and room for a golf course, baseball diamond, and tennis courts, as well as a lake and a swimming pool. Some of the project's supporters also hoped that the park would feature a new municipal art gallery along with other museums.[58] In addition to providing such amenities, however, the new park was intended to erase a downtown neighborhood "now largely occupied by negro tenements," a section of the city that the white editors of the *Atlanta Constitution* described as "an unsightly zone of depression and shacks . . . destined to become a typical 'sleepy hollow' in the very midst of the city's activities."[59]

Downtown real estate developer M. C. Kiser first proposed the idea of the new park, but the Atlanta Real Estate Board soon became the organizational leader of the campaign. The chamber of commerce, the Atlanta Woman's Club, and Mayor Sims all joined the cause. At first, proponents called for a $2 million bond issue exclusively for funding the downtown park. But protests from owners of adjacent properties and from Atlantans in other parts of the city brought changes to that plan. White residents who lived near the proposed park argued that it would destroy many blocks that were "rapidly becoming business sections" and should therefore be spared the city's sledgehammers.[60] Atlantans who lived in neighborhoods other than downtown pushed to have some of the new bond money spent to build parks closer to them. In the end, the city council agreed to put a measure on the ballot for $2 million in bonds, as originally planned, but reserved only $900,000 for a scaled-down version of the central park—eighty acres in size—and pledged the remaining $1.1 million to fund new neighborhood parks in each of the city's wards. The Atlanta Real Estate Board and other leading civic groups endorsed the amended proposal, as did the businessmen on the city planning commission, which by law had to place its stamp of approval on the plan.[61]

Public officials scheduled the referendum on the park bonds for

September 5, 1923. Newspapers described a "whirlwind campaign" preceding the election, funded in part through donations from the chamber of commerce and the Atlanta Real Estate Board and executed with the help of local white women's associations.[62] Advocates of the proposal called the city's lack of adequate park space "a real emergency" and emphasized that "more adequate playground and recreation space is essential to the full and complete growth of Atlanta." Real estate developer M. C. Kiser, the originator of the central park idea, sounded a similar note of alarm, proposing that "more and better parks and recreation centers must be established near the center of the city if Atlanta expected to hold her topmost place among the cities of the South." Kiser also viewed the new central park as a way to create "a beautiful place in which leisure hours might be spent under the most uplifting surroundings" and to allow "poor people who have a right to enjoy parks and recreation centers" the opportunity "to give their children the advantage of such places."[63]

African American leaders predictably opposed the plan, which constituted an early instance of the "slum clearance" and "negro removal" that would become commonplace in American cities after World War II. African American newspaper editor Benjamin Davis decried the park proposal on the front page of the *Atlanta Independent*. "If the bond proposition carries—which it ought not for a thousand sound and sane reasons—seventy-five acres of territory will be taken from the residential space that Negroes now occupy in the city." Noting that the recent zoning ordinance had already drastically curtailed where African American Atlantans could live, Davis asked, "Where is this great concourse of people to go, when they are denied this space if the bonds carry? Where are they to find housing?" Implying that there was little room left in Atlanta's already densely populated African American neighborhoods, Davis concluded that displaced African Americans' only choice would be to "migrate east, north and west, where they can find something to do, thereby . . . entailing to our city a great economic loss."[64]

In the end, however, it was factors other than African American opposition that brought the defeat of the park bonds. Just two weeks before the September referendum, accusations surfaced that the commission in charge of the 1921 bond issue had misallocated funds for the city's schools by overpaying for land. Whether or not these claims were true, the commission no longer had enough money to complete new buildings for Atlanta's all-white technical high school or for its all-white Girls' High, as the commission had originally promised. The same officials were slated to oversee the park bonds if they were approved. Opposition to the park initiative quickly grew. The Atlanta Federation of Trades even rescinded its endorsement of the plan. The main upshot of the controversy, however, was to suppress voter turnout. Only about a third of registered voters bothered to cast a ballot. Those who did voted against the bonds 4,418 to 2,360.[65]

African American voters played only a minor role in the ill-fated park referendum. But in the next bond election, the city's small African American electorate captured the attention of white elites once again. In early 1925, Mayor Sims called for another $2 million bond issue to construct a new twenty-story city hall. Leaders of the Atlanta Chamber of Commerce and the Atlanta Real Estate Board backed the plan, which promised to promote development in the city's downtown.[66] By contrast, a front-page editorial in the *Atlanta Independent* argued: "There is no town in the south where the Negro is so brazenly discriminated against industrially and economically as in Atlanta. The spending of the two million dollars, if authorized, will in no way help the negro. Every job will be given to the white man and a white man will receive every dollar spent in the erection of this building. Why should we be interested in shouldering a two million dollar debt to furnish employment for white men to the exclusion of ourselves?"[67]

Voters approved the $2 million bond issue 6,323 to 1,226. But with 13,926 registered voters, another 641 votes were necessary to push the number of supporters over the legal threshold that governed Atlanta's bond elections. It is unclear how many African Americans were registered at the time, but at least 1,200 were registered in every other bond election held between 1919 and 1929. If that many African Americans had voted as a bloc in favor of the referendum, their numbers could have easily put the total over the top. Of course, better voter turnout among white voters also could have changed the result. Even so, the 1925 bond election again suggested how the small number of eligible African American voters in Atlanta could influence the outcome of pivotal contests.[68]

Members of Atlanta's white commercial and industrial elite were particularly disturbed by the failure of the city hall referendum. Just that fall, leading businessmen had initiated an effort to raise a quarter million dollars to fund a nationwide advertising campaign to bring new business to the city. In the mid-1920s, Atlanta's economy began to suffer from a boom in nearby Florida. Not only were firms bypassing Atlanta for points south, but local businesses were also moving across the state border. As the national economy soared in the middle of the decade, Atlanta's economy began to sour. To stave off further decline, white business leaders formed the Forward Atlanta Commission, charged with raising money for and executing a campaign of unprecedented scope to boost the city's profile.[69] The defeat of the city hall bonds threatened to undercut the commission's work. As one local newspaper explained, "other Southern cities have taken occasion, since the recent failure of the Atlanta people to vote for the bond issue, to make unpleasant thrusts at this city, and to insinuate that Atlanta is taking backward steps."[70] Atlanta's white business leaders resolved to prove these detractors wrong—both by resubmitting the city hall plan for voter approval and by coupling it with another far-reaching bond issue similar to the one that had passed in 1921. As the chairman of the Forward Atlanta Commission and wealthy white businessman Ivan Allen Sr. explained, "When we get ready to advertise, we are going to have to tell what advantages we have in schools, in sewer and water improvements, in civic building and general progress. . . . We must first provide these schools and improvements before we can advertise them."[71] Meeting Allen's call demanded floating bonds since leaders of the Forward Atlanta campaign remained committed to advertising a city that had an exceptionally low tax rate. As it had earlier in the decade, this dual commitment to urban boosterism and debt-financed public spending brought another aggressive push to get voters to the polls.

An Interracial Reprise

By 1926, when the next major bond vote was held, Atlanta's KKK was already in decline. Just months after Walter Sims's election as mayor in 1922, the Dallas Klansman Hiram Wesley Evans had managed to displace the national organization's reigning Imperial Wizard—Atlanta's own William J. Simmons. Many Klansmen in Atlanta remained loyal to the native son and refused to recognize the organization's new official head. Tensions began to build in the spring of 1923. Evans sought to debilitate Simmons's supporters and eventually suspended the charter of Atlanta's main Klan lodge. Finally, in 1925, Evans moved the KKK's national headquarters from Atlanta to Washington, D.C. Amid all of this turmoil, most Atlanta Klansmen "simply ceased to pay their dues or attend meetings." Just a few years after its choice for mayor had captured city hall, Atlanta's Klan was no longer a significant, organized political force.[72]

The CITY BUILDER

December

43 MILLION

Messages

During 1926 there have been placed in the hands of the people ofthe United States 43,280,303 messages "selling" Atlanta.

Try to picture what that means,—the force, the power represented by such a deluge of advertisements. Think of the Atlanta story thus placed in the hands of important business men in all parts of the country; men with money to invest, men at the heads of concerns whose branches should be in Atlanta. And you will realize why this great campaign has contributed so materially to the growth of Atlanta during the past year.

The leading article in this issue tells the full story. The figures are laid before you. How Atlanta has developed because of the advertising campaign is expressed in terms of actual visible growth,—as reported by competent observers in each particular field of Atlanta activity.

Here is proof that the Forward Atlanta Campaign has brought profit to you, personally—and to every phase of Atlanta in which you are interested.

THE EDITORS

Figure 19. The cover of the December 1926 issue of the Atlanta Chamber of Commerce's publication, the *City Builder*, depicts a collection of advertisements that were circulated across the nation as part of the Forward Atlanta Commission's campaign to attract new firms to the city. *Courtesy of the Kenan Research Center at the Atlanta History Center.*

Perhaps thanks to this development, in early 1926, onetime Klan candidate Mayor Sims could be found making a speech on behalf of an $8 million bond issue at a mass gathering of African Americans. An editorial in the *Independent* described Sims's address as "a splendid presentation from an official standpoint" and said that Sims had "argued well for the City." Unlike in 1921, there were no reports of white officials making specific promises to African American voters about how the bond money would be spent. The *Independent* suggested that such promises would have been "misleading, unwarranted and impossible of belief" anyway. Even so, the African American newspaper argued, "We have nothing to gain by defeat of the Bonds, and all to gain if they go over."[73]

Taking Sims's appeal at face value, the *Independent*, the NAACP, and a collection of male and female African American activists organized another drive to get African American voters registered and out to the polls.[74] According to one observer, nearly all of the African Americans registered at the time "voted practically one hundred per cent solid for the entire program," which included $3.5 million in bonds for the city's school system, $2 million for sewer construction, $1 million for a new city hall, $500,000 for the water department, and another $1 million to build two additional bridges across an awkward "gulch" of railroad tracks in the downtown section of the city.[75] According to the city's comptroller, $8 million was the most that the city could afford without entailing a tax increase to finance the new debt. A familiar cast of white organizations offered their endorsements: the Atlanta Chamber of Commerce, the Atlanta Real Estate Board, and the city's elite women's clubs. Members of a new conglomerate of downtown commercial and real estate interests—the Atlanta Improvement Association—played an especially prominent role in the campaign. By contrast, the Atlanta Federation of Labor, protesting that the city's schools deserved a greater appropriation, made the exceptional move of not backing the bonds.[76]

In building support for the initiative, local leaders pursued a strategy similar to the one that they had employed during the successful campaign of 1921: a combination of rallies, parades, and grassroots organizing, especially by the city's female activists. Like Mayor Key before him, Mayor Sims put a well-known business leader in charge of the campaign: Fred Wilson, a leader of the new business-focused Atlanta Improvement Association. Sims also appointed William Candler—a leader of the Forward Atlanta advertising movement and a son of Coca-Cola's founder—to chair a new bond commission that Sims named to oversee the expenditure of the proposed funds.[77] On election day "shrieking sirens of the fire and police departments, clanging bells and whistles of every large manufacturing plant in the city," and a "telephone barrage" were all mustered to get voters to the polls. Around eleven thousand out of fifteen thousand registered Atlantans showed up to vote. Together they ratified the new set of bond proposals by wide margins.[78]

Reacting to the victory, Mayor Sims exhibited a boosterish spirit similar to the one that had driven the push for the new windfall in the first place. "By passage of this bond issue," Sims proclaimed, "Atlanta put the world on notice that it is bidding for big new industrial enterprises and that it is preparing for the greatest era of development in the annals of the city."[79] Insofar as the new funding was part of a broader attempt to bring new firms to Atlanta, it served a winning cause. Scores of new businesses relocated to the city in the late 1920s. As local business leaders like William Candler, head of the Forward Atlanta advertising campaign, had hoped, Atlanta had avoided "more taxes" but nonetheless—and perhaps thereby—had gained "more taxpayers." The price that Candler and his white colleagues paid African American voters for their help in this endeavor turned out to be predictably low. Out of the $3.5 million in new bonds for education that voters approved in 1926, schools serving African American children received just $250,000.[80]

As in previous contests, during the bond campaign of 1926—the decade's last—white business leaders faced little trouble enlisting the support of city officials to further their cause. Throughout the 1920s, politicians happily placed most bond measures backed by local business leaders on the ballot, and the mayor and many other public officials usually stumped enthusiastically in support of them. But wealthy Atlantans did not always face such an easy path negotiating with local officeholders.

For instance, as World War I came to a close, a small group of white elites were busy agitating for a public art museum. In 1918, Mayor Asa Candler created the city's first art commission. Around the same time, the city also promised a tract of land in Alanta's Piedmont Park as a site for the museum. By the mid-1920s, however, progress on the effort had stalled. By that point wealthy furniture dealer and art collector J. J. Haverty, the Atlanta Chamber of Commerce, the Atlanta Woman's Club, and the well-off membership of the Atlanta Art Association, including its best-known member, Mrs. Samuel Inman, were at the forefront of the movement for a public gallery.[81] In arguing for the cause, Haverty exhibited a familiar boosterism, warning that "every city of importance in America [has] an art gallery," including many of

Atlanta's New South competitors, such as Memphis, Charleston, Houston, and New Orleans.[82] Chamber of commerce president Paul Norcross called for a new gallery to make Atlanta "the art center of the south."[83] Inman justified the proposal using a similar tone but also suggested that the museum promised particular benefits for the city's children. "The last school census showed Atlanta to have more than 50,000 school children," Mrs. Inman explained. "To make available to these children a museum in which they may see beauty and harmony in outline and color will be stimulated in them forces that will reach, in another generation, decidedly higher standards than we have today. . . . Its influence will be felt in more artistic homes and grounds, more beautiful streets and public buildings, more elevated thoughts and desires, and a better citizenship."[84]

Despite the wealth and political prominence of the art museum's main backers, however, city officials never allocated money for the project. In October 1925, the city council considered asking voters for permission to float bonds to fund a new museum, but nothing came of its deliberations. Atlanta's government may have eventually bent to the will of the museum's rich proponents, but the issue became moot in 1926. In May of that year, Harriet H. W. High—wife of the late department store owner Joseph Madison High—donated her family's mansion near the intersection of Peachtree and Fifteenth Streets to serve as Atlanta's first art museum.[85]

Similarly, white businessmen battled repeatedly with the city's board of education over school finances. Unlike in Detroit and Philadelphia, Atlanta's city charter set the school budget as a fixed percentage of the city's total revenue. Just after the war, school finances were capped at 22 percent of Atlanta's total budget. A few years later, the proportion was raised to 26 percent. Segments of the white business community, including leaders of the chamber of commerce, tried to raise this percentage to 30 percent early in the decade. But their call for higher educational spending was tied to a push for a new, smaller school board elected from the city at large—an idea intended to increase elite Atlantans' influence over school politics, much like similar proposals in Detroit and Philadelphia. Atlanta's electorate rejected the notion in favor of ward-based representation.[86]

Yet even as business leaders hoped for more school funding, they also remained committed to ensuring that Atlanta's board of education lived within its annual allotment and functioned following strict "business principles." For school officials, this proved an almost impossible task. On nearly an annual basis, Atlanta's school system ran short of funds, often threatening an early end to the school year or a temporary suspension of teachers' salaries. Pleading poverty and citing the city charter, the mayor and city council usually refused to fill the gap. Faced with a standoff between the school board and other city officials, leading members of the local business community were often asked to loan money to the board of education to keep the schools open and teachers paid.

In 1923, for instance, the board of education declared that it did not have the money to pay teachers that November and December. With Mayor Sims and the council failing to step forward, bankers from Citizens and Southern National Bank loaned the school board over $300,000 at 4.5 percent interest to tide the district over. School officials faced a similar shortfall the next year. This time, however, the city's bankers—distraught over the board's financial practices and worried that they would not be repaid—were reluctant to step in. After Mayor Sims rounded up nearly forty wealthy Atlantans to guarantee loans made to the board of education, local banks once again floated the school system funds. Atlanta's school board soon moved to improve its prospects by lobbying for the power to raise an annual tax dedicated to the schools. By that point, however, local business leaders had completely lost faith in the school board's ability to manage the district's budget. White business elites spearheaded the opposition to the board of education's proposal, which quickly died.[87]

When the school board again ran out of funding in 1926, local business leaders used the opportunity to try to gain control of the board other than through implementing at-large elections. After school officials requested an additional $500,000 from the city to cover salaries for the rest of the year, Mayor Sims and the city council instead issued certificates of credit to the city's teachers. But local banks refused to honor them. Instead, a consortium of businessmen, led by Frank Neely, president of Rich's, one of Atlanta's premier department stores, pledged to lend the board the necessary funds only if school officials allowed five businessmen—a so-called Citizens Advisory Committee—to oversee the city's educational budget. With no alternative, the board accepted the offer. After studying the school system's finances, the advisory committee mandated a series of cuts to keep the school budget within the 26 percent of municipal revenue allotted by the city charter. Members of the board of education acquiesced, but only for a time. After teachers protested the Citizens Advisory Committee's cancellation of their automatic salary increase, the school board broke with its businessmen advisers and reinstated the annual raises. Soon thereafter, the city attorney ruled that the

Citizens Advisory Committee "had no legal standing and that the Board's obligation to it was moral only." For the remainder of the decade, despite their attempts to abolish the ward-based board of education and, short of that, to control its fiscal practices, Atlanta's business leaders had to live with a school board they could not control.[88]

Still, the disputes between businessmen and public officials over school finances and the art museum were exceptions rather than the rule. Instead, it was a combination of strict laws governing bond elections, voter apathy, and the activism of African American voters that proved the main hurdles to white business elites' expansionist agenda, not resistance from local officials. Out of six bond elections held in the decade after World War I, white business leaders and their allies won only two. Nonetheless, the nearly $17 million in bonds that voters approved in those contests were enough to drive social spending in the city to new heights and to do so at a pace unrivaled in the city's history up to that point.

To be sure, the boosterish emphasis that white business leaders and their allies in public office placed on keeping taxes low—along with the challenges of winning the right to incur debt—dampened the scale of government expansion in 1920s Atlanta. Municipal spending per capita in Atlanta was 60 percent higher in 1929 than it had been before World War I, adjusted for inflation. Still, Atlanta spent only 73 percent as much per person as Philadelphia did in 1929 and merely half as much as Detroit.[89]

Of course, the low-tax consensus among elite Atlantans and the challenges of the popular politics surrounding ballot initiatives explain only part of this discrepancy. Despite African Americans' extensive and generally under-recognized use of the ballot to improve city services in Atlanta's African American neighborhoods, black activism hardly made a dent in the vast inequalities that plagued Atlanta's public sector. More than any other political factor, the gulf that separated the scale of public sector expansion in Atlanta, Philadelphia, and Detroit was rooted in one trend: Atlanta's systematic neglect of nearly a third of its population based on race. Indeed, amid all of the drama, successes, failures, alliances, and strange bedfellows that accompanied businessmen's campaign for government expansion in 1920s Atlanta, Jim Crow let white business leaders pursue their vision of a civic welfare state on the cheap.

CHAPTER 5

Businessmen's Social Politics Beyond the Civic Welfare State

Unemployment, poverty, sickness, destitution in old age: these were risks that haunted every working-class laborer in the United States in the early twentieth century. But the civic welfare state that businessmen moved to build in cities like Atlanta, Philadelphia, and Detroit was not intended to address such issues. Rather, businessmen's campaign for a civic welfare state primarily sought to reform the behavior and outlook of local citizens and to foster economic growth. Urban business elites rarely if ever contended that programs like public schooling, parks, playgrounds, or other constituent parts of the civic welfare state that they hoped to construct would help alleviate poverty or provide working-class Americans with the financial stability that they so sorely lacked in the early twentieth century—an era when periodic bouts of unemployment were commonplace and the illness or death of a family member often brought financial ruin. This is not to say that business interests simply ignored these issues. As historians have described at length, a relatively small but highly visible group of employers in the 1920s intensified their experiments with what in the American context is often called welfare capitalism, or the provision of fringe benefits like pensions, stock options, sick pay, and other programs in the private sector that in part promised to increase workers' economic security. Indeed, most histories that examine businessmen's social politics per se during the 1920s do so through the lens of welfare capitalism. Perhaps the main exception is the handful of accounts that underscore businessmen's leadership of a movement to reorganize private charities into community chests. Early precursors to institutions like the United Way, community chests aimed to bring local charities under a common umbrella in order to streamline charitable giving and increase the efficiency of charitable work.[1]

The preceding chapters have already made clear that the social politics of American businessmen in the 1920s focused on far more than just private initiatives. Still, the oversights of existing accounts go further.

First, when a major epidemic of unemployment engulfed the nation early in the decade, business leaders in cities across the country helped spearhead efforts to aid the unemployed through a combination of private and government action. In so doing, businessmen embraced a set of practices that had long but underappreciated roots in the American past. By the early 1920s, these tactics offered employers an alternative both to government-sponsored unemployment compensation and to providing unemployment benefits to their employees on their own, which virtually no employers believed to be in their interest.

Next, even during more stable economic times, businessmen in some cities, including Detroit, viewed public assistance distributed at the local level—not just private charity coordinated by community chests—as an important mechanism for aiding the indigent and especially the unemployed.

Finally, by examining employers' private-sector experiments with welfare capitalism independent of businessmen's broader public agenda, historians have yet to fully appreciate how a number of the welfare capitalist programs that employers implemented in the private sector complemented social initiatives that business leaders were simultaneously seeking to pursue through government.

It is best to conceive of businessmen's social politics in the early twentieth century as an opportunistic amalgam—a mixture that melded private and public action in sometimes mutually reinforcing ways to serve business interests' varied political, social, and economic goals.

Businessmen and Emergency Unemployment Relief

The 1920s began with a short but sharp economic downturn. Unemployment started to spread in 1920 as the wartime economy began to contract—an inevitability that a number of factors had delayed for a time after the armistice, from a continuation of wartime contracts in certain industries to a $2 billion loan to Europe that flowed back into the American economy through trade. By June 1921, officials estimated that roughly 4 million Americans were unemployed. At the end of that summer, the Secretary of Labor suggested that the number had risen to over 5.7 million.[2]

Local communities were the first to mobilize to aid the growing number of unemployed. They did so through a combination of both public and private programs that tended to prioritize offering the jobless temporary work, including on public improvement projects, rather than simply giving them money, food, coal, or other basic goods. Most of these programs targeted men and only secondarily women—an attempt to uphold a patriarchal, male-breadwinner ideal even during difficult economic times. Together these initiatives built on a tradition whose history stretched back to the antebellum period and whose full trajectory has for the most part been forgotten. Fully understanding businessmen's involvement in campaigns against mass unemployment in the early 1920s merits a brief sojourn into this largely overlooked past.

Even before the Civil War, a number of cities were in the habit of increasing funding for outdoor relief whenever the economy spiraled downward. A few communities also placed unemployed men in jobs on public projects. During the Panic of 1857, the mayor of New York, Fernando Wood, implemented a program that put a thousand men to work improving Central Park and sought to give other men employment constructing roads. In Philadelphia, after workers staged a protest in Independence Square, the city started a similar albeit smaller effort.[3]

Critiques of outdoor relief intensified during the depression of the 1870s. Opponents charged that just giving food, coal, or money to the unemployed promoted long-term dependence and sapped recipients' work ethic. As unemployment rose, a number of cities heightened their attempts to link public assistance to some form of work, including on public construction projects, which offered jobs exclusively to men, whether in the 1870s or in later periods.[4]

Cities pursued similar strategies amid the dire economy of the 1890s, a moment when local relief efforts reached new heights. Many cities established centralized committees, including some that were run by chambers of commerce. Elsewhere, local charities or a collection of community notables coordinated local efforts. Cities also created or expanded publicly and privately funded work-relief programs to supplement employment on major public improvements. Unemployed men seeking aid might have found themselves shoveling snow, whitewashing tenements, or chopping wood. Some women gained temporary employment in special workrooms and laundries that generally gave preference to single women who had recently lost their jobs. Married women were offered aid from time to time, but most programs resisted doing so unless a woman's husband was unemployed and had failed to find public employment or work relief of his own.[5]

Similar tactics continued to evolve after the turn of the twentieth century. According to a survey by the American Association for Labor Legislation (AALL)—one of the foremost authorities on unemployment issues at the time—nearly fifty cities formed emergency committees to aid the unemployed in the winter of 1914–15, when the American economy temporarily suffered after World War I broke out in Europe. The AALL found that nearly 100 cities in twenty-nine different states had accelerated public projects to create jobs during the crisis. Nearly all of the 115 cities surveyed had utilized public or private funding to start work-relief programs that offered jobs on tasks other than permanent public improvements. Work relief was available to women in some cases, but men remained the primary targets of local campaigns. A number of cities undertook special fund drives to help local welfare

Figure 20. During the 1914–1915 economic downturn, men crafted toys and other items out of wood in a makeshift workshop for the unemployed run by the mayor's emergency committee in New York City. Business leaders in cities across the country would encourage similar efforts during the economic downturn of the early 1920s. *Reprinted from* American Labor Legislation Review *3 (November 1915), plate between pages 512 and 513.*

agencies cope with heightened demand, while publicly and privately run employment bureaus grew increasingly common.[6]

Federal involvement in unemployment relief began after World War I. Soon after the collapse of the Central Powers, a number of federal officials, including President Woodrow Wilson, called for federal spending to provide jobs to returning military personnel and to workers displaced from their wartime posts. With many legislators intent on cutting the federal budget back to prewar levels, Congress rejected nearly all of these proposals. Lawmakers even slashed funding for the U.S. Employment Service, the federal agency best equipped to match soldiers and workers in war industries with peacetime jobs. Still, President Wilson and members of Congress managed to rally around a more indirect form of aid: $200 million in matching grants to the states for road construction, a measure that historians of the postwar moment have largely failed to note.[7]

The funding came tucked into a routine appropriations bill for the nation's postal service. The Senate Committee on Post Offices and Post Roads inserted the highway money into the act in late January 1919. In justifying the initiative, members of the committee cited its potential for creating jobs and stimulating an array of industries related to road construction, from the production of "motor trucks" to the manufacture of "cement, paving brick, crushed stone and gravel." To maximize "opportunities for continuous employment," members of the committee contended, "public improvement of all sorts should be vigorously pushed at this time."[8]

The committee proposed breaking down the $200 million into increments that Washington would allocate over three years: $50 million in 1919 and $75 million in 1920 and again in 1921. In addition to these funds, the committee cited $70 million in federal and state money that remained unspent from a similar highway act—the first of its kind—that Congress had passed in 1916. If states stepped up to match federal funds, altogether the 1919 bill promised to set in motion $475 million in expenditures over the ensuing three years, $170 million of which could be spent in 1919 alone. (In 2015 dollars, this translates into roughly $6.5 billion and $2.3 billion, respectively.)[9]

The House of Representatives debated the proposal in February 1919. With federal legislators increasingly bent on retrenchment, advocates of the measure argued that road construction offered a fiscally responsible way to address unemployment and to stimulate commerce. Representative John A. Moon, a Democrat from Tennessee, attacked federal profligacy even as he advocated the bill's passage. "We ought to destroy two thirds of these commissions that are in operation to-day under government. . . . It may be we ought to consolidate even Cabinet positions in the interest of economy." While proclaiming "let us have as simple a Government as we can," Moon nonetheless pushed hard for roads, arguing that internal improvements could encourage trade and increase federal revenues to pay off war debts.[10] Wisconsin representative Edward Everts Browne declared, "We know there will be millions of men out of employment when war industries and the Army are demobilized. Various public works have been suggested to give employment to these men, but I think none of them is as practical as road work."[11]

A number of congressmen were less sanguine. New York congressman Fiorello LaGuardia scoffed that the roads program boiled down to giving war-weary soldiers the reward of "a job with a pick and a shovel."[12] One outraged Republican asked if his fellow congressmen had "gone absolutely stark mad in a desire to spend money."[13] Even so, the measure passed by an overwhelming majority. The Senate concurred, and President Wilson gave his signature within the week.[14]

States across the country used this funding to begin constructing over seven thousand miles of roads in 1919, more than six times what they had built using federal grants in previous years. In 1920, states initiated construction of another thirteen thousand miles of roads. Justified as a palliative for unemployment, a stimulus to industry, and a means for improving the nation's transportation infrastructure, the 1919 bill put the federal government and the states in the road-building business as never before.[15]

Congress passed a smaller, $75 million highway bill during the economic downturn of the early 1920s for similar reasons. Moreover, President Warren Harding, prodded by his secretary of commerce, Herbert Hoover, convened a federal meeting—the 1921 President's Conference on Unemployment—to try to galvanize a national response to widespread joblessness. But Hoover, Harding, and members of the 1921 president's conference made clear from the start that they thought that local communities, not Washington, should be at the front of the fight. "The problem of meeting the emergency of unemployment is primarily a community problem," the conference's final report declared before listing a series of best practices that conference members hoped communities would follow when running local relief campaigns. Most of the report's recommendations drew on what cities had done in the past. They especially emphasized the importance of providing work over simply distributing charity and endorsed the practice of forming centralized committees appointed by mayors to coordinate local efforts. Historians have generally portrayed Herbert Hoover's approach to unemployment relief in the early 1920s as exemplifying his innovative emphasis on building what scholars have called an "associative state," or a form of government that relies heavily on private entities to achieve a wide range of goals. In reality, however, the tactics that Hoover and the president's conference embraced were hardly novel. They derived directly from a set of customs whose history was already generations old.[16]

After the president's conference on unemployment had adjourned, Hoover created a temporary federal committee to encourage local efforts and appointed a man named Arthur Woods as its head. Woods had been New York City's police commissioner before the war. More importantly, he had led the federal government's attempt to find work for returning soldiers and sailors in the year following the armistice. As he had in 1919, Woods acted primarily as a cheerleader in the months following the 1921 president's conference, urging city halls, local welfare agencies, and even statehouses to take action.[17]

It is difficult to gauge the degree to which the president's conference or Woods's efforts influenced local emergency campaigns. Numerous communities had begun to take action well before the president's conference met. Months before the meeting was announced, public welfare agencies and private charities throughout urban America had reported that they were spending three to four times as much as they had in prior years to cope with unprecedented demand. A number of communities had already expanded employment on public projects, and some had set up emergency committees to oversee local initiatives. No matter the conference's impact, however, it is clear that the nation mobilized during the economic crisis of the early 1920s as never before.[18]

Indeed, within two months after the president's conference, Arthur Woods issued a press release announcing that 209 out of 327 cities with populations over twenty thousand had organized emergency relief efforts that more or less paralleled the conference's recommendations. By January, that number had inched up to 225. Woods based his estimates on the mail that poured into his office from cities across the country in response to his pleas that communities take action. Fort Smith, Arkansas, sent word that it had established a rock pile "where men break big stones into little ones, to be mixed with cement and sand to improve local streets." In Pittsfield, Massachusetts, a "flying shovel squadron" composed of otherwise jobless men rushed to clear off snowy sidewalks whenever they were called. State and municipal bond sales broke records in the months following the conference, an indication that public entities throughout the nation were moving to fund an onslaught of public improvements. Officials in Baltimore claimed that roughly half of the unemployed who had registered with local officials had been put to work on municipal jobs. Cities across the country reported that they were pursuing public works during the winter, when public construction projects were often put on hold. Boston signed sewer contracts and stipulated that work begin immediately. Jobless men in North Dakota were busy laying roads despite the blistering cold.[19]

Business interests had been involved in emergency unemployment campaigns earlier in U.S. history, but their leadership was particularly pronounced in the early 1920s. Aiding the unemployed promised to prevent the jobless from moving elsewhere, thus saving employers the cost of retraining workers once the economy rebounded. With memories of the Red Scare still fresh, many business leaders hoped that providing relief would curb the threat of working-class radicalism amid widespread economic distress. Meanwhile, very few companies offered unemployment benefits at the time. As we will see, doing so would have run contrary to the logic that prodded most employers to offer fringe benefits to their workers in the first place. Most businessmen also opposed the still fledgling movement for government-sponsored unemployment insurance. Emergency unemployment relief offered employers a low-cost alternative to private benefit schemes and allowed them to push some of the burden of addressing mass unemployment onto government entities. Finally, by resurrecting America's long-standing custom of accelerating public works as a way of aiding the unemployed, local business leaders hoped to speed the completion of the public projects that they had pushed for in cities like Detroit, Philadelphia, and Atlanta since the end of the war.

The businessmen at the helm of Detroit's government mobilized especially quickly as unemployment began to spread. In the fall of 1920, the city's multimillionaire mayor, James Couzens, wrote an open letter to local employers asking them to trim workers' hours as a way of avoiding layoffs. The city also established a new employment bureau. Approximately thirty-eight thousand Detroiters registered with the new agency in its first year, sixteen thousand of whom were placed in jobs. Detroit's business-dominated city council also expanded funding for public assistance beginning in late 1920. Within months, city officials appropriated an extra $1,750,000 for relief.[20]

Detroit's department of public welfare followed a strict procedure when distributing this aid. Upon application, the destitute might receive some immediate help if necessary but soon thereafter they came under greater scrutiny. The department sent out investigators to gather information on each applicant's home conditions and family needs. If the investigators deemed applicants deserving, public officials first tried to get them a job with their former employers. If this failed, department officials referred applicants to the city's public employment bureau. If applicants still could not find work in the private sector or on a city job, then the department of public welfare would offer them temporary relief: food, shoes, clothing, fuel, and rent if eviction was imminent. The department put relief recipients to work on odd jobs in exchange for aid whenever possible. By the fall of 1921, the city's welfare department reported that it had helped twenty-two thousand families out of thirty-two thousand that had applied. Department officials managed to place a number of the unemployed in jobs on public projects. Thanks to business leaders' push for public spending in the wake of the armistice, Detroit had a staggering $90 million worth of funding on hand for public works as the unemployment epidemic took hold. In a normal year, the city employed roughly eleven thousand residents on public projects. By October 1921, that number had risen to about twenty-five thousand.[21]

In fact, Detroit's early attempts to fight unemployment were so extensive that they won Mayor Couzens an invitation to the 1921 president's conference. Upon returning, he opened up a new front in Detroit's campaign. In accordance with the conference's guidelines, Couzens summoned a group of local leaders in the fall of 1921 to form an emergency committee under his command. Business elites dominated the group, which also included the leaders of major local charities. Three members of the Detroit Federation of Labor were invited to join, but they declined out of protest, complaining that three labor delegates among so many businessmen could hardly influence the committee's deliberations.[22]

Detroit's emergency committee prioritized registering the unemployed and encouraging private employers to take on more workers. The Oakland Motor Car Corporation and the Jackson Automobile Company both pledged to increase production. Continental Motors promised to add 1,500 to 2,000 new jobs at its factory in Muskegon. The emergency committee especially sought to aid men with dependents and therefore urged local employers to dismiss married women whose husbands had jobs. A number of firms followed this directive. Some companies fired women whose sisters worked in the same establishment. Out of solidarity with local businesses, Couzens asked all married women with city jobs to resign. Female employees whose jobs were protected by Detroit's civil service law had a right to a termination hearing, but articles in the local press intimated that women who resisted the mayor's mandate would have their jobs cut by city council.[23]

Most of the additional work that Detroit's employers provided during the crisis was only part-time. Moreover, as a winter of low sales wore on, manufacturers increasingly put their bottom lines over their workers' livelihood despite the mayor and the emergency committee's pleas. With the participation of private employers waning, the efforts of Detroit's emergency committee did as well.[24]

Nonetheless, Couzens and Detroit's business-dominated city council continued to spend heavily on public improvements. All told, Detroit spent $63 million on public works projects during the downturn. Couzens later claimed that local officials had "padded the Street Cleaning Department" so thoroughly that the city had become "disgracefully clean."[25] Some populations received far more municipal jobs than others, however. Even amid the depression, the city's department of public works largely adhered to its practice of hiring African Americans for only a limited number of low-level positions. Not surprisingly, this bias was part of a broader pattern of discrimination in local emergency campaigns across the country. In cities with large Mexican populations, for instance, local officials frequently urged repatriation instead of offering relief.[26]

Along with expanding the city's payroll, Couzens sought the cooperation of state agencies in putting single, unemployed men to work clearing three hundred thousand acres of land in rural Michigan. A few hundred men from Detroit were sent to the countryside, but the plan fell short of its goals. The state proved more helpful when it came to establishing an employment bureau, which it did for the first time in the fall of 1921. The city, meanwhile, sponsored an odd jobs campaign that Couzens claimed provided work for between five hundred and one thousand men. As the unemployment epidemic continued, however, and with public employment at a maximum, local officials found it difficult to stipulate that jobless Detroiters perform some kind of labor in exchange for assistance. The department of public welfare increasingly began offering relief without demanding work in return.[27]

A similar cohort of elite businessmen and public officials steered efforts in Philadelphia. Ernest Trigg, former president of the Philadelphia Chamber of Commerce and a leader of the movement for the sesquicentennial celebration, attended the 1921 President's Conference on Unemployment. Pennsylvania's employment office estimated that there were 127,000 unemployed men and women in Philadelphia at the time. After returning from the president's conference, Trigg convinced the city's mayor, J. Hampton Moore, to implement its suggestions.[28]

In a rare instance of collaboration between the fickle mayor and the city's business leaders, Moore agreed to invite seventy-five local businessmen to city hall to organize a collective response. Not a single representative of organized labor was in attendance when the group met in early October 1921. The guest list was determined, not by the mayor, but by the Philadelphia Chamber of Commerce's Industrial Relations Committee, which had already begun organizing to address unemployment in the city.[29]

Moore began the meeting with a lengthy speech, proclaiming, "It is not a charity movement which is here contemplated, but a sensible forward-looking business movement." He emphasized that only those willing to work should receive aid and explained that this was the policy that the city's department of public welfare already followed. Perhaps because Moore considered the campaign a business movement, he announced that he would hand off most of the responsibility for its planning and execution to the chamber of commerce.[30]

By the time the meeting in Moore's office had concluded, the businessmen in attendance had formulated a basic plan. They resolved to divide the city into districts and form district committees overseen by a central citywide board selected by Trigg. District committees were to act as ad hoc employment bureaus and organize local employers in the hopes of creating more jobs.[31]

Within two weeks, district committees had been formed across the city and the central committee had obtained the U.S. Postmaster's permission to mail three hundred thousand blank unemployment registration cards to the city's residents free of charge. It had also secured the right to use police stations throughout Philadelphia for district committee meetings. The central committee called on the unemployed through the local press to mail their information immediately to their local police stations. Any requests for employment that district committees could not directly fulfill were to be sent to the local bureau of the state employment office. Soon thereafter, the central committee called on homeowners to hire jobless men to perform any repairs that they might have otherwise postponed. The committee sent out questionnaires to gather information on potential odd jobs in private residences throughout the city. In addition, local volunteers walked the city's neighborhoods to note any improvements that might be made. By late December, the committee had planned another initiative to employ four thousand unemployed men as night watchmen with local residents footing the bill by donating fifteen cents each. Meanwhile, according to Trigg, local employers "adopted various methods for keeping a maximum number of employees on at least part-time work."[32]

As was true in many cities, a number of private organizations supplemented the work of Philadelphia's business-run emergency committee. Philadelphia's largest charitable organization, the Society for Organizing Charity, created a work-relief program funded by a special $25,000 donation. A local business school ordered all of its students to dedicate part of each day to registering the unemployed. Employees in some local factories pitched in to prevent further layoffs by voting for wage cuts—doubtless their only reasonable choice among dismal alternatives. There were also a number of smaller, more scattered efforts in the city, such as one local Bible class that doubled as an employment agency. The Bible class arranged with local employers to honor its endorsement of candidates when making hiring decisions. By the end of January, the class had placed 271 of its 299 members in jobs.[33]

Compared to Philadelphia and Detroit, Atlanta's unemployment campaign was relatively lackluster, in part because unemployment was not nearly as severe in Atlanta as it was in many cities. Still, a handful of local groups organized to offer assistance to the five or six thousand Atlantans who were out of work. Here, too, private employers helped lead the way. Local business leaders established an employment exchange and elicited pledges from its members to take on approximately a thousand additional workers. Religious organizations throughout the city supplemented this effort. The city's Christian Council set up a community workroom for destitute women, while the Young Men's Christian Association (YMCA) and Young Women's Christian Association (YWCA) ran temporary employment bureaus. The city's mayor, James Key, pledged to expand employment opportunities in the city by pursuing as many public construction projects as possible—a promise that the large bond issue that the city had approved in the spring of 1921 helped make feasible. Key also took steps to form an emergency committee, as the president's conference had recommended. For the most part, however, Key left the city's business and religious leaders to organize Atlanta's response on their own.[34]

Businessmen dominated relief campaigns in other cities as well, at least according to the mail that flooded Arthur Woods's office. The letters that Woods received from a nationally known social worker at the Russell Sage Foundation, Mary Van Kleeck, particularly attest to this pattern. Van Kleeck wrote to Woods repeatedly during the economic crisis, primarily to complain about how local efforts had taken shape. She was especially frustrated that communities had not made local emergency committees "truly representative." Instead, Van Kleeck's sources suggested that local officials across the country were "leaving out both labor and social workers" and instead were "appointing business men."[35] Woods's response seemed to confirm that this was the national trend. Neither Woods nor members of the president's conference had taken significant steps to shape the composition of local emergency committees. Still, Woods granted that businessmen had frequently been put in charge of them. Moreover, he defended the pattern, arguing that it made sense for employers to take the lead since they could do the most to increase employment. Considering how frequently business interests dominated local efforts, mayors throughout the nation seemed to agree.[36]

As had been the case throughout American history, local emergency campaigns in the early 1920s were extremely porous. They aided only some of the jobless and did so fleetingly at best. Nonetheless, thanks in part to business leaders' heightened involvement, the nation had mobilized to aid the jobless to an unprecedented degree. That said, local campaigns did not have to last long. By the spring of 1922, prosperity was on the horizon.

Mixing Public and Private in Good Economic Times

Prosperity's return found a number of employers continuing and in many cases expanding their prewar experiments with welfare capitalism, which one leading scholar has defined as the provision of services "for the comfort or improvement of employees" that are neither "a necessity of the industry nor required by law."[37]

If one were to have surveyed the management practices of American companies in 1900, one would have found that most major corporations relied on the so-called drive system, or fostering worker productivity and workplace efficiency "not by rewarding merit, not by seeking to interest men in their work . . . but by putting pressure on them to turn out a large output" often through threat of dismissal.[38] Over time, however, the specter of unionization, the problem of extensive labor turnover, and sharp public criticism of prevailing employment practices encouraged an increasing number of employers to search for other ways to motivate their employees and to increase worker loyalty, especially over and above any fealty that workers may have had to local unions. In 1914, one survey found that over twenty-five hundred U.S. firms had implemented various measures that fit the developing welfare capitalist model, "from cafeterias, gardens, and profit-sharing plans to company housing, magazines, and athletic facilities."[39]

World War I and its aftermath were turning points in the history of welfare capitalism, much as they were in the history of elite businessmen's social politics more generally. During the war, the Council of National Defense established a Committee on Welfare Work as part of its efforts to minimize labor conflicts and to maximize production. According to the body's chairman, the committee's objective was "to bring home to employers, in the most forceful way, the necessity of establishing correct standards" to ensure the highest level of productivity possible while "at the same time conserv[ing] the health and efficiency" of the nation's workforce. The committee was composed primarily of corporate leaders who had experimented with welfare capitalist initiatives in the past and who wanted to spread the gospel. Other federal agencies promoted similar practices. The U.S. Department of Labor, for instance, took various steps to pressure employers to improve working conditions in the hopes of minimizing "labor disturbances," illness, and injury.[40]

Postwar trends further encouraged welfare capitalism's spread. Indeed, welfare capitalist methods seemed all the more attractive to employers amid the upheaval that followed the armistice, especially the rash of strikes that businessmen—fearing the spread of communism—tended to view through a red lens. Historians have debated the precise extent to which welfare capitalism flourished in the 1920s, but most agree that it did so as never before. Still, it is important not to exaggerate welfare capitalism's reach even as the movement hit a new high-water mark. It was primarily large, highly profitable firms that offered welfare capitalist programs in the 1920s, although some smaller enterprises did as well. According to one study, only 6.5 percent of companies employing between 500 and 2,000 workers had industrial relations departments at the tail end of the decade—one indicator of a firm's commitment to the welfare capitalist enterprise. Fifty percent of businesses employing over 2,000 workers had established one. In 1929, the National

Industrial Conference Board (NICB), an employer-sponsored research organization, surveyed roughly 4,400 firms with 250 or fewer employees and found that only 4.6 percent of them offered some sort of pension program. By contrast, 26.4 percent of firms with 251 or more employees offered pensions to at least some of their workers—a proportion that nonetheless underscores that pensions were far from widespread even among larger corporations. Other programs were more prevalent. The NICB found that over 70 percent of the firms that it had surveyed offered some form of group insurance on the eve of the Great Depression, while over 90 percent had implemented initiatives to promote worker safety. Of course, these figures mask how greatly programs varied from company to company. As much as it is important not to exaggerate welfare capitalism's reach, it is just as crucial not to underestimate the shoddiness of the services that some employers actually provided.[41]

Even so, the adoption of welfare capitalist methods was a significant trend, enough to convince not only employers but also many academics, pundits, and politicians that welfare capitalism was ushering in a new industrial age. The movement managed to appeal both to employers who cared only about their bottom lines as well as to the handful of executives who genuinely sought more enlightened and humane management techniques that would relegate the "drive system" to history's dustbin.[42] For instance, the president of one of Philadelphia's largest employers confessed that his company tried "to make the place attractive to men . . . for a very selfish reason." "There is no philanthropic thing in it at all," he admitted.[43] By contrast, Charles Schwab of Bethlehem Steel contended, "Our primary job is to make steel" but also to do so "under a system which must be justified. If . . . this system does not enable men to live on an increasingly higher plane, if it does not allow them to fulfill their desires and satisfy their reasonable wants, then . . . the system itself should fail."[44] According to Schwab, workers had every right to expect that companies strive to offer "steady employment, a voice in the regulation of their working conditions, opportunity to save and to own stock, and some guarantee of security in old age," albeit only "as far as conditions permit."[45]

Whatever employers' motivations, however, welfare capitalism promised a great deal from management's perspective. Employers at large firms implemented a host of new welfare capitalist programs to try to convince employees that management was taking workers' views into account. Whether employers did so through the creation of company unions or by establishing other platforms that enabled some degree of employee representation, their goals were often the same: to smooth over points of friction between labor and management, and especially to prevent the formation of unions that employers might find far more difficult to control. Employers also tinkered with a host of policies that aimed to curb labor turnover and to foster workers' interest in promoting a given firm's success. Pensions, stock option plans, group life insurance, sick pay: many of these programs demanded continuous, long-term employment—not to mention a firm's continued profitability—for a worker to receive benefits. In factories that employed large numbers of immigrants, offering such programs also promised to bind foreign-born workers to their bosses more than to their ethnic communities at a time when immigrants in American cities commonly formed mutual benefit societies—organizations in which members pooled their resources to aid one another in the event of temporary unemployment, sickness, or the death of a loved one. Some employers tried to increase workers' commitment to the job simply by raising wages, both in general and through bonuses. The pay of manufacturing workers rose in the 1920s, although only slightly.[46]

Employers involved in welfare capitalism often supplemented monetary benefits with an array of programs designed to make work a more attractive, even fun place to be. Some factories began a range of sports teams; constructed running tracks, gyms, and even stadiums; screened movies; and organized dances. Such efforts sought to blur the boundary between work and leisure and to make the workplace increasingly central to workers' lives. Athletic events promised to promote solidarity and company pride. Dances and other social activities might encourage employees to forge friendships that might make work more pleasant. Employers also hoped that offering leisure activities at the factory might prevent workers from spending their free time carousing and showing up to work haggard or hungover.[47]

This focus on recreation was one of the main ways that the content and goals of welfare capitalism overlapped with a broader portion of the business community's simultaneous campaign for a civic welfare state. Employers deeply involved in welfare capitalism knew that they could not control every hour of their employees' lives. They needed to offer edifying recreational opportunities not only at work but throughout the city. Having government pay for parks, libraries, the construction of stadiums, and other recreational activities that working-class urbanites could potentially utilize during their off hours allowed business leaders—both those who did and those who did not run welfare capitalist programs—to socialize the costs of trying to shape how employees used their free time.[48]

Companies that employed a large number of immigrants frequently complemented other welfare capitalist policies with "Americanization" programs. Such firms offered English-language classes as well as instruction in supposedly "American" customs, which often boiled down to attempting to reform practices that offended employers' notions of good hygiene, whether it was immigrants' "doing their laundry in rivers and streams" or "eating from a common dish." From business leaders' point of view, Americanization classes in the workplace promised to reinforce efforts to promote public health through local government programs and to do for foreign-born adults what pillars of the civic welfare state like playgrounds and public education promised to do for immigrant children: mold them to fit employers' ideal conception of the culturally homogenized citizen-worker. Immigrant adults could not be compelled by law to endure Americanization efforts like children in public schools, but pressure from management could make them undergo a similar regimen in the workplace. All of this said, many employers began to wind down their Americanization efforts as the 1920s progressed. The war and a series of federal laws, culminating in the Johnson-Reed Act of 1924, dramatically stemmed the flow of immigrants into the United States during the decade. Millions of immigrants remained in the country, but by the end of the 1920s, most of them had been in the United States for years, many of them had learned English, and thus employers increasingly began funneling their resources elsewhere.[49]

Of course, whether in the case of Americanization or other programs, welfare capitalist initiatives did not always go as employers planned. At firms that offered stock options, employees often sold when prices were high rather than hold on to their stocks over the long haul, thus undermining employers' attempt to use stock options to deepen workers' commitment to their company's long-term fate. Company unions and other employee representation plans helped to resolve small-scale disputes, but workers involved in them—seeing a rare opportunity to press for better wages and working conditions—often refused to behave as docilely as employers desired. Employees in other firms, meanwhile, resisted accepting employer-created entities like company unions as meaningful alternatives to worker-run labor organizations in the first place. Throughout the 1920s, employers found that they still had to resort to hiring spies and other classic union-busting techniques to hamper workers' attempts to organize on their own terms.[50]

As these patterns begin to suggest, welfare capitalist programs largely failed to garner workers' loyalty over the long term. When it came to factories, most remained deeply unpleasant places to work. Conditions continued to be unhealthy, hours could be exceedingly long, and pay was usually too meager to meet workers' needs. Moreover, the promise of fringe benefits often failed to live up to employees' expectations. Instead of creating new bonds between managers and workers, benefit schemes often bred new forms of resentment among employees who felt that their bosses were not following through on their promises. For instance, employers frequently doled out bonuses in ways that employees found unfair or confusing. One worker equated the bonus system at his factory with "playing the horses." Others complained that working hard enough to get a bonus just encouraged management to raise its expectations. "If we turn out a job in two hours," one worker explained regarding the bonus system, "next week" the goal for producing the same amount "will be cut to one and a quarter hours." Meanwhile, employers who offered group insurance programs sometimes forced their employees to keep up their contributions even in hard times when workers' hours were cut rather than making up at least part of the difference using company funds.[51] Finally, among other stipulations, private pension programs often demanded that workers remain with the same firm for an extremely lengthy period in order to receive benefits. One worker caricatured the array of obstacles that could stand between employees and their pensions: "If you remain with this company throughout your productive lifetime; if you do not die before the retirement age; if you are not discharged, or laid off for an extended period; if you are not refused a pension as a matter of discipline; if the company is in business; and if the company does not decide to abandon the plan, you will receive a pension . . . subject to the contingency of its discontinuance or reduction after it has been entered upon." Workers' skepticism of welfare capitalist policies was all the greater since employers remained just as willing as ever to lay off workers whenever they felt the need to cut labor costs.[52]

Indeed, the threat of unemployment and the destitution that often went with it remained a constant for many working-class Americans in the 1920s, especially since almost no companies included unemployment benefits in their arsenal of welfare capitalist practices. The NICB found that 0.3 percent of firms with fewer than 250 employees offered unemployment benefits in 1929, while only 0.8 percent of firms with 251 or more employees did so. From management's perspective, offering unemployment insurance threatened to undercut other welfare capitalist efforts to increase workers' time on the job. More important, most employers saw little upside to having an ongoing obligation to an employee whom they had fired.[53]

Urban business leaders did take modest steps to aid the jobless even after the unemployment epidemic of the early 1920s had subsided. But their efforts were relatively indirect in most cities and stemmed from their involvement with local charities more generally. Chambers of commerce in cities across the country were at the forefront of a major movement to reorganize private charities in the years following the war. Urban businessmen had long complained about the number of solicitations that they had to field from charity workers and about how difficult it was to evaluate the relative merits of individual organizations seeking their support. In the opening years of the century, chambers of commerce in a number of locales had begun to endorse charitable organizations in order to help businessmen decide where to direct their contributions. During World War I, however, the massive Red Cross and war chest fund drives convinced an increasing number of businessmen that federating local charities into an overarching organization would best address such concerns. Before the 1920s, roughly a dozen cities had formed community chests, as the federations came to be known. That number exploded as the decade continued and as local chambers of commerce grew increasingly enamored with the idea. By 1929, there were over three hundred community chests scattered across the country.[54]

Along with streamlining charitable giving, community chests promised to accomplish a number of goals in business leaders' opinion. Federation might prevent the unnecessary replication of services, thus limiting waste. A consolidated pot of funds could also be used as leverage to promote certain charitable practices while discouraging others. As one of the leaders of Philadelphia's community chest movement explained, "The community chest plan is calculated to improve the efficiency of the work done. . . . Each agency's books are carefully audited, its program of work studied thoroughly." Through federation, the author continued, "better standards of work can be insisted upon." Finally, organizing community chests tended to heighten elite businessmen's influence over local charities more generally, especially since many community chests received the majority of their donations from a small group of wealthy donors. In Philadelphia, 440 donors gave nearly half the contributions that the city's chest received in 1923. In Detroit, 341 contributors provided nearly 60 percent of its community chest's funds. Data from cities as diverse as Nashville, Cleveland, Milwaukee, and Youngstown suggest that donations in many places followed a similar pattern. Leading donors, in turn, often ended up on the boards of local chests.[55]

Of course, business leaders' involvement in creating and directing community chests did not necessarily mean that they contributed to private charities with newfound generosity or enthusiasm. Welfare workers across the country complained that many businessmen resisted giving even in communities that had established chests. Fund-raisers especially bemoaned the parsimony of corporations, which charities had increasingly begun to solicit for donations by the 1920s. Corporate contributions made up nearly a quarter of the donations to Atlanta's community chest by the end of the decade. Chests in cities like New Orleans, Milwaukee, and Portland, Oregon, received a similar proportion of their funding from corporations. In some cities, including Seattle, the figure was a good deal higher. Even so, many corporations resisted giving. Companies that employed largely white-collar workers who were less likely to utilize the services of local charities than working-class laborers frequently refused to contribute in meaningful amounts. Corporations with branches in a given community often shied away from donating since doing so might have set a precedent that companies would then have to repeat at all of their branch locations. Some executives questioned whether corporate giving was even legal, considering companies' obligations to maximize profits on behalf of their stockholders—an objection that charity workers tended to view as an empty excuse meant to shoo them away. Other executives complained that corporate donations were not tax deductible. Tax deductions for charitable contributions by individuals had been written into the tax code during World War I. Executives in communities across the country pressed charity officials to lobby Congress for a similar loophole for their firms. If employers were going to support their local community chest, they wanted to make sure that their companies would benefit in return.[56]

It is important to emphasize that businessmen's involvement in the community chest movement—which, again, focused on private charities—did not preclude business leaders in some cities from supporting certain forms of publicly sponsored aid to the poor. In fact, in Detroit it was the municipal government, not private charities, that offered the vast majority of assistance to the indigent in the 1920s. By one count the city provided 97 percent of aid to the poor distributed in the city in 1929.[57] It is difficult to link this trend directly to corporate desires. But Detroit's business leaders enjoyed exceptional power during the decade. They certainly could have tried to push the city's charitable methods in a different direction had they wanted to, but there is little evidence that they did so. Business leaders' overarching silence on the matter perhaps suggests the tacit approval of a practice that had clear benefits for the city's leading industry. Seasonal layoffs remained commonplace in auto manufacturing throughout the 1920s, especially when car companies retired certain models and prepared their factories to roll out new ones. Just as they did during the economic crisis of the early 1920s, firms in the auto industry had a vested interest in finding ways to tide over the unemployed during temporary closures as a way of avoiding the costs of training new workers once factories reopened. Private charity offered at best a highly unpredictable mechanism for doing so. Each major batch of layoffs would have demanded a whirlwind campaign for private donations to help keep the jobless afloat. In addition, the owners and managers of local companies likely would have had to pony up large sums themselves to ensure that the unemployed received aid. Increasing public relief avoided the hassle of making countless solicitations to potential donors and also meant that all taxpaying citizens—rather than primarily business leaders themselves—would foot the bill.[58]

Expenditures by Detroit's department of public welfare (DPW) tracked closely with employment trends in the city. In 1925, which the department described "as the most prosperous year industrially as well as commercially in the history of Detroit," officials claimed that the DPW's employment bureau nonetheless registered over 10,000 jobless Detroiters and placed about 8,000 of them in jobs.[59] Most found work in private establishments. About 700 were put to work on public projects and another 450 on odd jobs. The largest category of Detroiters to gain aid from the DPW in 1925 did so because of illness, but the next largest group to garner relief was the unemployed, followed by families who had fallen on hard times due to a father's desertion. Overall, department officials distributed slightly more than $700,000 in outdoor relief in 1925.[60]

In 1927, by contrast, when Detroit experienced "a serious industrial depression" in part because Ford closed shop to prepare for a new model, the city offered over $1.7 million in public assistance, and aiding the unemployed became the department's number one priority.[61] Out of about 11,000 total relief cases handled by the department in 1927, just over 6,000 were categorized as due to unemployment. Only 1,500 were considered related to illness and just 845 to desertion.[62] As was true earlier in the decade, the jobless received public aid only after rigorous investigation—inquiries that could delve into the most personal facets of the lives of the unemployed, leading to all sorts of judgments by DPW workers. Take the case of David L., who according to DPW officials, "had a natural disinclination for work and had always felt that his family interfered with his stage career. For a time after his wife's death he worked intermittently and then, in discouragement, gave up the pretense. His mother, a proud little English Woman, begged and pleaded with him. Finally, in desperation, she came to the [DPW] at the suggestion of friends. Feeling the pressure of outside influence, David started back to work and the [DPW] assisted until he drew pay."[63] DPW officials did not always chalk up unemployment to laziness or misplaced priorities, however. For instance, Joseph S.

> had worked in the automobile industry for fifteen years. He had been married for ten and had three sturdy children. . . . Two years before he came to the Department, Mrs. S. had become ill and the savings had gone for doctor and hospital bills. Eleven months before, when Joseph was forty-three, he was laid off at the factory but felt that he would be called back within a short time as he had always been before. Four months went by and he was not re-employed. He found another job that lasted for five months. Two months more of idleness, Mrs. S. still ill, the savings gone, payments on the contract overdue, the children in need of clothing and more nourishing food. Joseph made the rounds of the factories every day and came home at night weary and discouraged. His brother had helped but he was also out of work. The Visitor [from the DPW] referred Mrs. S. to the clinic for medical attention and the Division provided food, rent, milk and clothing. None of this would have been necessary, "if" as Joseph Jr. expressed it in a letter to the Visitor, "my Daddy could only get a job."[64]

In contrast to Detroit, business leaders in other cities were far more resistant to government officials' offering financial assistance to the poor. In Philadelphia, the city charter that business leaders helped to author in 1919 created Philadelphia's first department of public welfare, but the new department was not designed to offer financial aid to the indigent. Instead, the creation of Philadelphia's department of public welfare (DPW) was primarily a bureaucratic reform. Earlier in the century, the city had a single department of public health and charities. The new charter separated the old department into two entities. The new DPW included a bureau of recreation and a bureau of legal aid and was designed to act as a clearinghouse that directed the needy to appropriate private charities. Department officials were also responsible for placing orphaned and neglected children into homes and institutions. The department oversaw the local mental hospital as well as the city's remaining almshouses, which primarily housed the elderly. A handful of widowed and single mothers received aid from a Mother's Assistance Fund. But most of Philadelphia's poor, including the unemployed, had to turn to private organizations for relief. The business leaders who led the effort to redesign Philadelphia's charter still strongly opposed boss rule when they did so. At the time, they likely wanted to prevent machine politicians from using public assistance as a mechanism for building loyalty among poor voters. Yet even after most businessmen in Philadelphia had made peace with the political machine in the 1920s, there is little evidence to suggest that they attempted to strike a new balance between public and private charity in the city.[65]

Business leaders in Atlanta barely weighed in on the issue other than through the contributions that they made to the city's community chest. As in most southern cities, local officials in Atlanta offered virtually no aid to the poor. According to one study, public authorities provided only 3 percent of relief distributed in Atlanta in the first quarter of 1929. Private organizations provided the rest.[66]

No matter what balance they favored between public and private assistance, however, most business leaders in 1920s America viewed poverty and unemployment as issues to be managed through small-scale payments. They hardly conceived of poverty and chronic unemployment as problems that it was in their interest to solve. Business leaders mobilized to aid the unemployed during the downturn of the early 1920s to an exceptional degree, but in stable economic times, joblessness and the poverty that often accompanied it were indications of surplus in the labor market, a trend that helped employers keep wages low.

Businessmen's experiments with welfare capitalism likewise sought to turn workers' economic vulnerabilities to employers' advantage. Most welfare capitalists attempted to leverage economic insecurity and convert it into a management tool, one that would make workers more dependent on and hopefully more loyal to their employers and more committed to the success of their firms. The development of a social welfare state that would address the economic vulnerabilities of the working class through government programs like public pensions for the elderly, health insurance, and unemployment compensation was therefore a possibility that most employers hoped to stave off. Business interests had little trouble doing so until the Great Depression. But the legacy of urban business leaders' political activism in the 1920s would make that task much harder in the decade that followed.

EPILOGUE

The 1930s and After

Not long into the Great Depression, local governments began to buckle under the enormous debt they had accumulated in the 1920s. Detroit's debt was roughly $345 million in 1929, up from $41 million in 1919. The amount that Philadelphia and Atlanta each owed had more than tripled during the same period. The political activism of urban business leaders was not responsible for all of this growth. But business elites had pressed hard for debt spending in all three cities. Now local officials faced the challenge of meeting their debt obligations at a moment when tax revenues were plummeting and demand for public assistance was on the rise.[1]

At first, cities drew on past practices in attempting to aid the unemployed. Detroit remained exceptional in the amount of public relief that it offered. Local officials in Philadelphia and Atlanta continued to resist providing public charity, although in both cases they offered more in the 1930s than they had in earlier years. But the fact that all three cities were at risk of defaulting on their debts placed sharp limits on what public officials were willing to spend on aid.

Federal officials infamously failed to fill the breach in the early years of the Depression. Instead, Herbert Hoover, now president, looked back at the emergency campaigns that businessmen had helped to lead in the early 1920s and mistook them for an effective way of tackling mass joblessness even during an economic downturn that was far worse than the one that had followed World War I. As Hoover wanted, communities across the country supplemented any public relief that they offered with a number of other initiatives as they had in earlier periods. But again, fiscal crises in cities like Detroit, Atlanta, and Philadelphia limited what governments could contribute to local emergency campaigns, especially their ability to put the unemployed to work on public improvement projects as they had in the past. At the same time, private charities saw their budgets plunge, a pattern that further hampered emergency efforts in cities across the country.

Meanwhile, most employers who offered fringe benefit programs slashed them as a way of cutting costs. Welfare capitalism had in part hinged on a leap of faith: that the economy would remain robust enough to keep benefit programs afloat over the long term. Any loyalties that welfare capitalists had succeeded in garnering from workers in earlier years increasingly dissolved amid the Great Depression.

All of these patterns helped usher in the New Deal. And all of them had roots in the social politics that businessmen had embraced earlier in the century.

Government revenue in Detroit dwindled in the early years of the Great Depression as the value of real estate plummeted and more and more people lost their homes or prioritized feeding their families over paying their taxes. In the late 1920s, Detroit's government had spent less than 20 percent of the revenue that it collected from property taxes to finance its debt. By 1933, that proportion had risen to a catastrophic 66 percent. Detroit's mayor at the time, Frank Murphy, attempted to meet the needs of the jobless nonetheless. Murphy had been elected in the fall of 1930 with widespread working-class support thanks to his pledge to do everything in his power to help the unemployed. By the start of 1931, nearly a third of Detroit's workers lacked a job. A year later, an official in Detroit's department of public welfare suggested that there were nearly 350,000 Detroiters without full-time work.[2]

As had been true earlier in the century, Detroit's government—not private charities—remained the main source of relief in the city. Local officials rapidly expanded funding for public assistance early in Murphy's term. For a time, Detroit appropriated an average of $2 million a month to aid the needy—a good deal more than it had spent in an entire year during the 1920s, even during moments when the local economy had been weak. But the city eventually had to cut back. "This load of relief," the mayor attested, "is one that cannot be shouldered indefinitely by any city, without bringing in its wake financial ruin."[3] Mayor Murphy's observation was especially true in Detroit's case since power players in New York City's all-important market for municipal bonds demanded that Detroit officials cut government spending, including on public assistance. Meanwhile, local business leaders made clear that there were sharp limits on the amount of aid distributed by the city that they were willing to tolerate. In a turnaround from the 1920s, members of Detroit's business elite began to decry the city's welfare practices as the Depression continued. One leader of the Detroit Board of Commerce complained in March 1931 that Detroit's comparatively generous welfare policy was making it "sap city of America." Another argued that the dole had lured "derelicts from all parts of America" who hoped to leech off the generosity of Detroit's public officials.[4]

But more than businessmen's complaints, it was the struggle to maintain the city's fiscal solvency that limited the amount of public assistance that Detroit could provide. In the summer of 1931, the city reduced its appropriation for relief to $7 million for the approaching fiscal year—still far higher than what local officials had spent in the 1920s but less than half of what they had made available the previous year. The department of public welfare was forced to slash the city's welfare load. Aid to everyone from single adults to families with fewer than three children was put on the chopping block. The department pushed fifteen thousand people off of its rolls in just ten days. Department officials then resolved to reinvestigate remaining welfare cases in the hopes of cutting thousands more. By the end of the summer, there was "actual starvation in Detroit," according to the mayor.[5]

And yet offering relief through the DPW was just one of many ways that Detroiters mobilized to aid the unemployed. Echoing steps taken a decade earlier, Murphy established an emergency body, the Mayor's Unemployment Committee (MUC), in the fall of 1930 to lead a community-wide campaign. The MUC of the 1930s was much more representative of local interests than the corporate-run body that the city had established in the early 1920s. Murphy's MUC included a prominent local pastor and representatives of organized labor. But local business leaders also remained involved. The secretary of the board of commerce's industrial committee, E. E. Kramp, served as the MUC's executive secretary, and the committee's treasurer was the president of a major local bank.[6]

Detroit's MUC pursued an array of initiatives that paralleled the ones that local communities had undertaken during earlier economic downturns. It embarked on a massive drive to register the unemployed and encouraged employers to spread out workers' hours to keep more people on the job. It collected and distributed clothing, tried to drum up odd jobs, and sought to find ways to shelter the homeless. The MUC raised funds from private donations and used them to offer free lunches to the city's school children and to help families whom the city's welfare department had cut from its rolls. As they had in earlier periods, city officials attempted to supplement these efforts by putting men to work on public projects, but this proved difficult given the city's budget crisis. Appropriations to Detroit's department of public works fell dramatically in the opening years of the Depression. In 1932, the department spent $4.8 million, down from $25.5 million just two years earlier. Funding for other city services was slashed as well, but none of these cuts made much of a difference. The debt that the city had accumulated in the 1920s was simply too high for Detroit to stay afloat. In 1933, the city lapsed into default.[7]

Both Philadelphia and Atlanta managed to avoid a similar fate but only by resorting to draconian extremes. By 1931, Philadelphia was on the edge of default as well, a crisis that ushered in a reign of austerity under a familiar political character, J. Hampton Moore, the supercilious mayor who had served in the early 1920s. Like many of the city's independent reformers, Moore had abandoned the antimachine cause by the early years of the Great Depression when he won the mayor's seat once again, this time thanks to the backing of local political bosses. To help the city avoid default, Moore slashed 3,500 municipal jobs, staggered hours for a number of other city employees, reduced pay, and forced policemen and firemen to go on furlough. Moreover, he curtailed spending on public improvements, including by halting work on projects that were already under way.[8]

Moore also resisted appropriating public funds to aid the unemployed. On this front, he remained as politically tone-deaf as ever. Moore tended to blame the unemployed for their own fate and denied the extent of suffering in the city. After touring one of Philadelphia's poorest neighborhoods, Moore claimed that he had seen "little of poverty." Rather, he attested, "I have counted automobiles and watched them pass at a given point. Rich and poor, white and colored, alien and native born, all riding by. . . . There is no starvation in Philadelphia."[9]

Moore's delusions were not widely shared. In November 1930, over two hundred of the city's leading businessmen and professionals gathered for lunch at one of the city's fanciest hotels, the Bellevue-Stratford, and decided to form the Committee for Unemployment Relief under the leadership of Horatio Gates Lloyd, a partner at one of the city's preeminent banks, Drexel and Company, the local subsidiary of the Morgan banking empire. The Lloyd Committee, as the body came to be known, mixed public and private action in familiar ways. It raised millions in private donations and won a municipal appropriation of $3 million for relief before the parsimonious Mayor Moore took office. It was Lloyd, however, not public officials, who supervised distribution of these funds. Lloyd even set up shop in the city's department of public welfare and oversaw both public and private relief efforts from an office there. The Lloyd Committee sought to create a variety of makeshift work, offer loans to the unemployed, find shelter for the homeless, and provide meals to needy children in their schools. In 1932, Lloyd and his collaborators initiated a fund-raising drive that reportedly gathered more than any other charitable campaign in Philadelphia's history. Demand for aid in the city was so high, however, that the committee ran through its share of the funds in just three months. With Mayor Moore committed to a policy of extreme frugality and the city struggling to avoid default, public officials offered little additional help. Worried that its mere existence was giving false hope to the destitute, the Lloyd Committee disbanded soon thereafter.[10]

Atlanta's attempt to avoid default included the city paying teachers and other municipal employees in scrip instead of cash. City workers could hypothetically use the makeshift currency at local stores, but the reality often proved different. One Atlanta policeman later recalled, "If you wanted to buy a ton of coal or pay your utility bill," a storeowner might refuse the scrip. Other local vendors made customers pay a surcharge when using the stand-in money. At least one local department store (Rich's) allowed teachers and other municipal workers to cash their scrip even if they did not purchase anything. This was one of many examples of local businesses loaning the city funds. In 1932, the city borrowed nearly $2 million from local banks just to stay afloat.[11]

Atlanta had virtually no history of offering public aid to the destitute. The Depression changed that, but only to a degree. Instead, it was the Atlanta Community Chest, its member organizations, and a newly formed Emergency Relief Committee that carried most of the burden. The Salvation Army provided food, shelter, and clothing. A community employment service registered the jobless. A new "Penny Club" collected one-cent donations at stores and restaurants throughout the city and used a portion of them to pay unemployed men to perform odd jobs two days per week. African Americans were eligible to receive aid, but the Penny Club paid them $1.25 compared to $2.00 for white beneficiaries. The Atlanta Chamber of Commerce concocted an elaborate plan to transport poor white families out of the city and resettle them on abandoned farms in the Georgia countryside. The chamber of commerce managed to enlist only forty-five families after a year of effort. Thereafter, it canceled the program due to a dearth of interest and funds.[12]

Similar shortages riddled private relief efforts throughout the city. The Emergency Relief Committee and the Atlanta Community Chest fell far below their fund-raising goals year after year. City and county officials pitched in but only modestly. The city set up an emergency relief center in Atlanta's municipal auditorium, which served more or less as a soup kitchen, and Fulton County offered cash assistance. For the most part, however, local officials avoided tackling unemployment head-on. Even by 1932, prominent Atlantans were still trying to deny that there was significant suffering in the city.[13]

Historians used to attribute a similar degree of denial and indifference to Herbert Hoover during his presidency in the early 1930s. In fact, Hoover was much more aggressive in attempting to address the Great Depression than any of his predecessors had been during earlier economic downturns. In an attempt to stimulate the economy, the Hoover administration spent more on public works than the federal government had during the previous thirty years combined. Under Hoover, federal officials initiated work on over 800 buildings and encouraged the construction of over 37,000 miles of roads through matching grants to the states. When Hoover took office in 1929, there were 180,000 workers employed on federal improvement projects. By 1931, that number had risen to 760,000 and would hit 860,000 by the time Hoover left the White House in March 1933.[14]

The problem was that millions of Americans were out of work at the time. Hoover proved far less innovative when it came to aiding the overwhelming majority of them. Instead, he primarily turned to the nation's long-standing custom of tackling mass unemployment through local initiatives. The emergency relief efforts of the early 1920s convinced the president that similar campaigns could alleviate the misery of the Great Depression. He even tapped the same man, Arthur Woods, to lead the federal government's campaign. Hoover put Woods in charge of the newly formed President's Emergency Committee on Employment (PECE) in the fall of 1930. The body was designed to serve virtually the same role as the task force that Woods had led in the early 1920s. As Woods explained, "The principal part of our work is co-operating with local organizations. . . . The best that we can do is to let various places know what others are doing as a guide for their own efforts."[15] Woods quickly realized that the federal government needed to do much more and resigned once Hoover made clear that he disagreed.

Yet instead of shifting tacks, Hoover simply replaced Woods with a man more amenable to his philosophy of relief and put him in charge of a new committee: the President's Organization for Unemployment Relief (POUR), a body that had a similar mission to the now defunct PECE. With public and congressional pressure mounting, however, Hoover finally expanded federal aid during his last year in office, pledging $1.5 billion in federal loans to the states to finance public works along with $300 million to help states offer direct relief to the jobless. But even at that late date, Hoover hoped to keep aiding the unemployed primarily a local rather than a federal responsibility over the long term. Especially in the case of the new relief funds, Hoover wanted Americans to view federal aid as a last resort, so he and the agency in charge of distributing the money—the Reconstruction Finance Corporation (RFC)—waited to confirm that cities and states had already exhausted their resources before offering help. Otherwise, Hoover and RFC leaders feared, the nation's long history of providing relief primarily at the local level would come to a permanent close, replaced by an ever-growing national system. In the end, however, the RFC's delays had the opposite effect. By adding to the growing perception that Hoover was indifferent to the plight of the unemployed, the RFC's dallying merely whetted many Americans' appetites for a much more aggressive government response.[16]

If working-class Americans could not turn to the federal government for meaningful aid in the early years of the Great Depression, neither could they rely on the welfare capitalist programs that employers had implemented in previous years. Only a minority of employees in the United States had come into contact with welfare capitalism in the first place, but most of those who had saw their benefits disappear as the Great Depression deepened. Stock options and profit-sharing plans quickly lost their value. Companies that had implemented recreational and educational initiatives cut them to save money. Some employers attempted to stagger workers' schedules in order to keep as many people employed as possible, but most companies did so only temporarily, and it was hardly enough amid an unprecedented wave of layoffs. Workers who had accumulated pensions before the Depression lost them when they lost their jobs. A handful of firms managed to keep some of their benefit programs running, including Du Pont, AT&T, and Procter & Gamble—in most cases large corporations in sectors that the Depression hit less hard than it did others. But most workers in firms with welfare capitalist programs saw the promises that employers had made in earlier years evaporate in the 1930s.[17]

As the Depression persisted, of course, federal officials implemented a set of permanent social programs that provided a degree of economic security for working-class Americans that welfare capitalism never had. Through landmark legislation like the Social Security Act of 1935 and the Fair Labor Standards Act of 1938, Franklin Delano Roosevelt's New Deal included a number of the very social policies that most American businessmen had rejected in earlier years, including government-funded unemployment compensation, public pensions for the elderly, and a federal minimum wage. These policies have constituted pillars of America's social welfare state ever since—again with the social welfare state defined as a collection of programs that generally do one of two things: either stipulate how employers must treat, compensate, and otherwise provide for their employees, or that lessen the degree to which certain categories of the economically vulnerable, such as the elderly or unemployed, have to depend on the labor market in order to survive.[18]

A small group of employers collaborated with the Roosevelt administration in designing some of the new social policies that took root during the New Deal, especially the unemployment and old-age pension programs created through the Social Security Act of 1935. They included executives of exceptionally large firms like Gerard Swope of General Electric, Morris Leeds of Leeds and Northrup, and Walter Teagle of Standard Oil of New Jersey. Along with Marion Folsom of Eastman Kodak and Sam Lewisohn of Miami Copper, these men were tapped by President Roosevelt to serve on an advisory board to the body charged with authoring the Social Security Act. Scholars have debated the role that these moguls played in the eventual design of the bill. Evidence suggests that their influence was limited at best. Moreover, even if these executives had extensively influenced the act, the fact remains that they did not represent the sentiments of the overwhelming majority of businessmen at the time, most of whom had turned against Roosevelt's New Deal by 1935 in general and also opposed the Social Security Act specifically. One of the Roosevelt administration's handpicked corporate advisers, Marion Folsom, later attested that "only five percent of employers" were supportive of legislation "along the lines" of the Social Security Act.[19]

It is an oddity of both historical scholarship and popular memory that the social welfare state that was created during the New Deal is rarely depicted as a landmark in the history of *urban* social policy, but it was, especially at the time of its inception. The benefits of legislation like the Social Security Act and the Fair Labor Standards Act—not to mention the National Labor Relations Act, which put in place federal protections for workers attempting to unionize—flowed primarily toward industrial workers who disproportionately resided in urban America. Agricultural and domestic workers were initially left out of many of these programs, a concession to white southerners in Congress who wanted to prevent the large number of African Americans employed in those sectors in the South from receiving benefits.[20]

In short, the New Deal was in part a repudiation of urban business leaders' conviction that the problems of urban America could be solved solely through education and attempting to change how urban Americans lived and spent their leisure time. New Dealers believed that urban Americans needed more than just parks, playgrounds, museums, libraries, and certain forms of city planning. Of course, the Roosevelt administration hardly renounced such initiatives. New Deal employment programs like the Works Progress Administration left countless new or remodeled schools and recreational outlets in their wake as well as a dizzying amount of new infrastructure—sewers, water mains, and roads—that helped further the project of urban decentralization. Even so, the social politics that sat at the heart of the New Deal were importantly different from what had come before, above all because they were rooted in the conviction that local social programs like schooling or building parks might be necessary for building good cities but were by no means sufficient for doing so.[21]

It would be decades before Americans would confront the problems of urban America with anything approaching the intensity that their predecessors had possessed in the opening decades of the twentieth century. But when they did so in the 1960s, a similar conviction still prevailed. The political left has lambasted the War on Poverty of the 1960s for focusing too much on reforming the supposedly problematic culture of the poor through education, job training, and empowerment rather than treating the problem of poverty as a symptom of the maldistribution of jobs and economic resources. The political right, by contrast, has criticized the War on Poverty and President Lyndon B. Johnson's Great Society initiatives more generally for offering too many handouts and thus encouraging a problematic dependence on government. This debate in itself is illustrative of the War on Poverty and the Great Society's multifaceted approach to urban social problems. On one hand, the War on Poverty and Great Society entailed the expansion of immediate financial benefits to the urban poor by increasing the availability of government-subsidized housing, expanding Social Security benefits, and providing subsidized medical care through programs like Medicare and Medicaid. On the other, the Johnson administration was convinced that a permanent solution to the problem of poverty lay in preparing the urban poor for sustained employment. Thus, the War on Poverty and the broader Great Society combined the expansion of programs offering direct financial benefits to the poor with a host of programs that sought to foster the cultural attitudes and vocational skills that federal policymakers believed were necessary to prepare the poor for stable careers.[22]

In explaining the reconfiguration of urban social policy in more recent decades, scholars and pundits tend to appeal to familiar tropes like the intensification of antigovernment sentiment, the spread of free market ideology, and the devolution of government authority away from Washington and toward statehouses and city halls. But other trends merit attention. Among the most important is the degree to which the nation's overarching approach to urban social issues has lapsed back toward an exclusive focus on attempting to reform the behavior and attitudes of supposedly problematic urban populations. This pattern has run through a number of the most formative developments in urban social policy in recent years, including the war on dependence that intensified in the 1980s under Ronald Reagan—an effort that blamed a host of urban problems on the poor's supposed overreliance on government benefits, particularly welfare. By the 1990s, this fight had become remarkably bipartisan, culminating in the passage of the welfare reform act of 1996, which placed sharp limits on how long welfare recipients could receive aid. Of course, the federal government did not retreat completely from offering financial assistance to the poor. Most notably, the Earned Income Tax Credit (EITC) —a direct tax subsidy for the working poor and an indirect one for the corporations that pay them low wages—has expanded markedly since the mid-1990s. Still, the EITC must in part be seen as the soft underside of a much more aggressive attack against the supposedly degenerative influence of welfare without work.[23]

Or take another, similarly bipartisan effort. Even as government authority has devolved toward state and local government in certain policy areas, federal involvement in public education has grown precipitously since the 1980s, culminating in the passage of No Child Left Behind in 2001 and the Race to the Top initiative under President Barack Obama. To be sure, urban schools are often targets of criticism, but education per se is frequently cited—from presidential speeches to exceptionally successful documentary films—as a uniquely potent antidote to an array of urban social problems, from poverty to crime. In the case of urban education, this effort has entailed more than simply giving students the knowledge that they need to thrive in the contemporary economy. Rather, it has frequently included an emphasis on reforming the behavior and attitudes of low-income children, especially by conditioning them to reject the supposed pathologies of their parents, families, and neighbors, whether crime, drug use, or failing to embrace middle-class ambitions—an approach that one observer has dubbed the "new paternalism" in urban education.[24]

Or consider another signature urban policy of recent decades: the move to tear down aging high-rise public housing projects and replace them with suburbanesque, mixed-income communities through yet another exceptionally bipartisan effort, Hope VI. Adopted in the 1990s, the Hope VI program was in part designed to address the social problems that many policymakers associated with life in high-rise projects, from violent crime to drug abuse. Changing the manner in which the urban poor lived, so the argument went, would help them overcome the supposed cultural repercussions of urban impoverishment while resurrecting urban neighborhoods. Only some residents of old high-rise projects ended up finding homes in the new, smaller developments created through Hope VI. The rest were given vouchers to help them find housing elsewhere in the city. This trend, too, underscores one of the main thrusts of the Hope VI program: to break up the supposedly degenerative communities that the old projects had helped to foster.[25]

The federal government has remained involved in some urban issues through initiatives like Hope VI and federal education policy, but it has of course retreated from many others. This fact—combined with heightened capital mobility—has encouraged another definitive trend in American urban policy in recent years: a surging emphasis on local boosterism as a mode of urban development. Tax breaks are often the main mechanisms that cities use to lure new businesses and wealthier residents, but such incentives are frequently coupled with select spending by state and especially local governments on basic infrastructure, downtown beautification, improving public schooling (at least in certain neighborhoods), and on big ticket attractions like museums, stadiums, and parks that are intended to lure investors, entrepreneurs, and well-off residents while expanding the local tourist industry.

There are Americans who might endorse these trends because they think that the federal government should be smaller or because they believe that it might be appropriate for the government to subsidize basic education but not to ensure economic security over the long term. What is more sobering, however, is the degree to which politicians and activists who are outwardly committed to fostering a degree of economic security for all Americans and who are open to utilizing government as part of that project have come to speak of policies like education, knocking down high-rise public housing, and luring new businesses and residents to cities through select public expenditures on museums or other downtown attractions as if such policies by themselves were capable of fostering significantly greater degrees of economic fairness and stability for vulnerable and often impoverished urban populations.

Urban business leaders in the early twentieth century supported extensive government spending on a host of local social programs, including public schooling, libraries, museums, parks, playgrounds, and promoting public health. But they favored such policies because they believed those programs would address a host of urban social problems without compromising employers' power to determine wages, the distribution of jobs, and the conditions of work. They embraced government-sponsored social policy alongside steep economic inequality. They viewed widespread urban poverty as an issue that they might need to manage from time to time but that they had no intention to solve. They promoted urban development, including by spending heavily on certain social programs, because expanding the local market for goods and real estate promised to line their pockets, not because they believed that the benefits of economic expansion would trickle down to make all urban residents financially better off. Such a leap of faith would have been as unwarranted nearly a century ago—when employers frequently paid their workers poverty wages—as it is today, when working poverty remains prevalent.

Activists and policymakers who care deeply about the fate of American cities and the large numbers of economically insecure and poor people who reside in them might benefit from keeping this history in mind. Its lessons are clear. We need to link movements for better schools, better housing, more robust cultural institutions, and more livable cities directly to a struggle to alter the distribution of jobs and wages in metropolitan America—a fight to promote economic security on a group rather than an individual basis and to provide meaningful support to the large number of urban Americans trapped on the outskirts of the labor market or on its lowest rungs. Otherwise, we risk mimicking the inegalitarian politics of early twentieth-century capitalists despite hoping for egalitarian ends.

NOTES

Introduction

1. On federal experiments with economic planning, see Ellis W. Hawley, "Herbert Hoover, the Commerce Secretariat, and the Vision of an 'Associative State,' 1921–1928," *Journal of American History* 61 (June 1974), 116–40; Ellis W. Hawley, *The Great War and the Search for a Modern Order: A History of the American People and Their Institutions, 1917–1933* (New York: St. Martin's Press, 1979); William J. Barber, *From New Era to New Deal: Herbert Hoover, the Economists, and American Economic Policy, 1921–1933* (New York: Cambridge University Press, 1985); Robert F. Himmelberg, *The Origins of the National Recovery Administration: Business, Government, and the Trade Association Issue, 1921–1933* (New York: Fordham University Press, 1993 [1976]); Marc Allen Eisner, *From Warfare State to Welfare State: World War I, Compensatory State Building, and the Limits of the Modern Order* (University Park: Pennsylvania State University Press, 2000). On Prohibition and government expansion, see James A. Morone, *Hellfire Nation: The Politics of Sin in American History* (New Haven, CT: Yale University Press, 2003). Scholars studying individual public policies like public schooling and public health have noted the growth of such programs during the 1920s, but they have rarely depicted those patterns as part of a broader trend. Indeed, despite the contributions of Hawley, Morone, and others, portraits of the 1920s as a relatively antigovernment moment have persisted. For instance, see Lynn Dumenil, *The Modern Temper: American Culture and Society in the 1920s* (New York: Hill and Wang, 1995). Lizabeth Cohen's influential study of business and labor in the interwar period—which includes discussions of workers' and employers' attitudes toward government—likewise reinforces this view of the decade, among other reasons because it pays scant attention to Chicago's rapidly expanding public sector in the 1920s aside from discussing public assistance to the poor—a minor facet of municipal spending in the early twentieth century. Lizabeth Cohen, *Making a New Deal: Industrial Workers in Chicago, 1919–1939* (New York: Cambridge University Press, 1990). Cohen also tends to portray employers as simply opposed to government and does little to explore employers' attitudes toward municipal, as opposed to state or federal, social programs. See, for instance, Cohen, *Making a New Deal*, 181–83. On public spending in Chicago, see Table 1 of this book.

While the pages that follow focus primarily on trends in American cities, state governments also grew markedly in the years following World War I, a pattern that is ripe for further scrutiny. See, for example, R. Rudy Higgens-Evenson, *The Price of Progress: Public Services, Taxation, and the American Corporate State, 1877–1929* (Baltimore: Johns Hopkins University Press, 2002). George B. Tindall has highlighted this trend at the state level in the South and also linked it to business interests, albeit primarily through the lens of business-friendly governors. George B. Tindall, "Business Progressivism: Southern Politics in the 1920s," *South Atlantic Quarterly* 62 (Winter 1963), 92–106.

2. Daniel Rodgers has detailed the dynamics of this transatlantic exchange of policy ideas in the late nineteenth and early twentieth centuries. Daniel T. Rodgers, *Atlantic Crossings: Social Politics in a Progressive Age* (Cambridge, MA: Belknap Press of Harvard University Press, 1998). On the development of American social policy in earlier periods, see, for example, William J. Novak, *The People's Welfare: Law and Regulation in Nineteenth Century America* (Chapel Hill: University of North Carolina Press, 1996); David J. Rothman, *The Discovery of the Asylum: Social Order and Disorder in the New Republic* (Boston: Little, Brown, 1971); Michael B. Katz, "The Origins of the Institutional State," *Marxist Perspectives* 1 (Winter 1978), 6–22; Carl F. Kaestle, *Pillars of the Republic: Common Schools and American Society, 1760–1860* (New York: Hill and Wang, 1983); William J. Reese, *The Origins of the American High School* (New Haven, CT: Yale University Press, 1999); Roy Rosenzweig and Elizabeth Blackmar, *The Park and the People: A History of Central Park* (Ithaca, NY: Cornell University Press, 1992); Charles Rosenberg, *The Cholera Years: The United States in 1832, 1849, and 1866* (Chicago: University of Chicago Press, 1987 [1962]).

3. As discussed further in the text and notes of Chapter 5, historians have extensively examined the development of fringe benefit programs in the early twentieth century (or what is often called "welfare capitalism" in the American context). Indeed, most histories written in recent years that focus intensively on the social politics of American businessmen in the early twentieth century have done so in three main ways: through the lens of welfare capitalism; by underscoring business interests' overarching resistance to the rise of a social welfare state; or by tracing the ideas and activism of the small group of corporate moguls who did in fact participate to some degree in the process of designing the social welfare state that eventually took shape during the New Deal. The social politics of the urban business elites discussed in this book were far more encompassing that these accounts suggest. For an older work that offers a more wide-ranging examination of businessmen's political attitudes than many pieces of scholarship, see Robert Wiebe, *Businessmen and Reform: A Study of the Progressive Movement* (Cambridge, MA: Harvard University Press, 1962). Wiebe pays only passing attention to businessmen's political activism on the local stage, however. Meanwhile, scholars interested in specific policy areas like schooling, the promotion of public health, or various forms of city planning have noted that business interests at times supported such programs, but they have rarely woven these patterns into a more encompassing account of corporate social politics per se.

4. Throughout this book, I utilize Gøsta Esping-Andersen's definition of the social

welfare state as government policies that to some degree "decommodify" human labor. For instance, in the case of government-sponsored social insurance or public assistance, such programs lessen, to varying extents, the degree to which eligible recipients must rely solely on the labor market—on the commodification of their labor—to gain a living. In cases like maximum-hour and minimum-wage laws, such measures set limits on the degree and the price at which people can sell themselves or be utilized as commodities in the labor market. Through these types of programs, governments assert a level of human worth beyond a person's value as a labor commodity and thus they, too, decommodify. Gøsta Esping-Andersen, *The Three Worlds of Welfare Capitalism* (Princeton, NJ: Princeton University Press, 1990), ch. 1. While explicit definitions of the social welfare state are difficult to find in many historical works, this or a similar conception runs through historical scholarship written from a variety of perspectives. See, for instance, Theda Skocpol, *Protecting Soldiers and Mothers: The Political Origins of Social Policy in the United States* (Belknap Press of Harvard University Press, 1992); Margaret Weir, Ann Shola Orloff, and Theda Skocpol, eds., *The Politics of Social Policy in the United States* (Princeton, NJ: Princeton University Press, 1988); Seth Koven and Sonya Michel, eds., *Mothers of a New World: Maternalist Politics and the Origins of Welfare States* (New York: Routledge, 1993); Michael B. Katz, *In the Shadow of the Poorhouse: A Social History of Welfare in America*, 10th anniversary ed. (New York: Basic Books, 1996); James T. Patterson, *America's Struggle Against Poverty, 1900–1980* (Cambridge, MA: Harvard University Press, 1981); Roy Lubove, *The Struggle for Social Security, 1900–1935* (Cambridge, MA: Harvard University Press, 1968). Daniel T. Rodgers uses the concept of decommodification more explicitly than most although also more broadly. Rodgers, *Atlantic Crossings*, 29–30.

5. On workmen's compensation, see James Weinstein, *The Corporate Ideal in the Liberal State* (Boston: Beacon Press, 1968), ch. 2; Skocpol, *Protecting Soldiers and Mothers*, 285–98; John Fabian Witt, *The Accidental Republic: Crippled Workingmen, Destitute Widows, and the Remaking of American Law* (Cambridge, MA: Harvard University Press, 2004). Historians have debated the precise extent of employers' involvement and support of workmen's compensation legislation. See, for example, David A. Moss, *Socializing Security: Progressive-Era Economists and the Origins of American Social Policy* (Cambridge, MA: Harvard University Press, 1996), 129–31. On examples of business support for old-age pensions in the late 1920s, see, for example, Jill Quadagno, *The Transformation of Old Age Security: Class and Politics in the American Welfare State* (Chicago: University of Chicago Press, 1988), 102–03; Christopher J. Cyphers, *The National Civic Federation and the Making of a New Liberalism, 1900–1915* (Westport, CT: Praeger, 2002), conclusion. On the handful of corporate executives who participated to some degree in crafting federal social legislation during the New Deal, particularly the Social Security Act of 1935, see, for example, Edward Berkowitz and Kim McQuaid, *Creating the Welfare State: The Political Economy of Twentieth-Century Reform*, 2nd ed. (New York: Praeger, 1988), 115–26; Sanford M. Jacoby, "Employers and the Welfare State: The Role of Marion B. Folsom," *Journal of American History* 80 (Sept. 1993), 527–44. Scholars have debated at length the degree to which these executives actually influenced

New Deal social legislation. For an astute review and evaluation of this literature, see Jacob S. Hacker and Paul Pierson, "Business Power and Social Policy: Employers and the Formation of the American Welfare State," *Politics and Society* 30 (June 2002), 277–325, esp., 298–315. As Hacker and Pierson discuss, Peter Swenson has taken a different approach to this debate by contending that members of Congress and the Roosevelt administration attempted to anticipate employers' interests when crafting the Social Security Act of 1935 and other New Deal social legislation in the hopes of building a robust consensus around those policies over the long term. Peter A. Swenson, *Capitalists against Markets: The Making of Labor Markets and Welfare States in the United States and Sweden* (New York: Oxford University Press, 2002), esp. chs. 9–10. See also Peter A. Swenson, "Varieties of Capitalist Interests: Power, Institutions, and the Regulatory Welfare State in the United States and Sweden," *Studies in American Political Development* 18 (Spring 2004), 1–29; Jacob S. Hacker and Paul Pierson, "Varieties of Capitalist Interests and Capitalist Power: A Response to Swenson," *Studies in American Political Development* 18 (Fall 2004), 186–95. For a more recent work that revisits these debates, see G. William Domhoff and Michael J. Webber, *Class and Power in the New Deal: Corporate Moderates, Southern Democrats, and the Liberal-Labor Coalition* (Stanford, CA: Stanford University Press, 2011), which attempts to move beyond focusing exclusively on a small number of corporate actors in directly shaping New Deal social legislation toward an examination of the research that wealthy benefactors helped to fund and that, in turn, may have influenced the New Deal.

6. For a discussion of business interests' varying attitudes toward Prohibition, including an overview of the pertinent literature, see Ranjit S. Dighe, "The U.S. Business Press and Prohibition," *Social History of Alcohol and Drugs* 22 (Spring 2008), 228–42. On the battle over prostitution in Atlanta, see Chapter 1 of this book.

7. I measure against a prewar baseline because municipal spending plummeted during the war for a number of reasons, including a federal mandate that local governments halt all but the most essential public improvements. If one were to measure spending at the end of the 1920s against a 1919 baseline, the rate of growth of municipal spending in most cases would be significantly higher.

8. The population of Detroit grew 179 percent between 1916 and 1929. Philadelphia's grew 16 percent and Atlanta's 46 percent.

Unless otherwise indicated, the figures presented in this introduction are drawn from a data set compiled using the U.S. Bureau of the Census' *Financial Statistics of Cities Having a Population of over 30,000*. (In the case of Detroit, Philadelphia, and Atlanta, I have confirmed the trends outlined here in pertinent annual reports for those cities.)

Specifically, the figures for government spending are based on net payments for governmental costs (which the census bureau defined as payments "on account of operation and maintenance, interest, and outlays") minus payments for interest. For net governmental cost payments in 1929, see Table VIII on p. 32 of that year's report. For 1916, see Table VI on p. 52. Net (as opposed to gross) governmental payments simply exclude payments made from one governmental department or entity to another.

As explained below, in addition to excluding payments for interest, the figures presented here do not include the money that local governments spent to retire their debts, which the census bureau categorized as "nongovernmental costs." For definitions of governmental versus nongovernmental costs, see, for instance, pp. 37–38 in the 1916 report and p. 13 in the 1929 report. In earlier reports, governmental costs were referred to as "corporate payments," which likewise excluded funds used to pay off municipal debts. See, for instance, the definitions for corporate and temporary payments on pp. 7 and 9 of the 1904 report. The section on corporate payments and debt in the discussion of Table 4 on p. 9 offers important clarification of the definition of corporate payments given on p. 7 in the 1904 report. Comparable to later periods, the 1904 figures used here are net payments; in other words, they exclude so-called transfer payments—or internal payments by departments or other government entities to one another.

9. The figures for debt presented in this paragraph compare gross indebtedness in 1919 and 1929 and have not been adjusted for inflation.

10. The number of people living in cities with populations over three hundred thousand rose 49 percent. The figures in this paragraph include costs for government operations and maintenance as well as for outlays (e.g., public construction and purchasing property). Categories for social spending are the census bureau's. Spending in cities with populations between one hundred thousand and three hundred thousand followed a similar trajectory. In those cities, spending per capita adjusted for inflation declined by 1 percent between 1904 and 1916 and grew by 46 percent between 1916 and 1928. Spending per person on schooling in those cities was 67 percent higher in 1929 than in 1916; on recreational programs, 50 percent; on libraries, 47 percent; on hospitals, 6 percent; on sewer systems, 39 percent; and on other facets of public health, 54 percent. During the same period, the number of people living in cities with populations between one hundred thousand and three hundred thousand rose 52 percent. U.S. Census Bureau, *Financial Statistics of Cities*.

Figures for overall growth in local government spending offered here differ from those provided in the landmark *Recent Social Trends in the United States: Report of the President's Research Committee on Social Trends* (New York: McGraw-Hill, 1933) because key data provided in that report include only expenditures for operation and maintenance, not outlays for public construction, which are, of course, crucial to take into account. See Carroll H. Wooddy, "The Growth of Governmental Functions," in *Recent Social Trends*, vol. 2, 1312.

11. Key works include Theda Skocpol and John Ikenberry, "The Political Formation of the American Welfare State in Historical and Comparative Perspective," *Comparative Social Research* 6 (1983), 87–148; Margaret Weir and Theda Skocpol, "State Structures and the Possibilities for 'Keynesian' Responses to the Great Depression in Sweden, Britain, and the United States," in *Bringing the State Back In*, ed. Peter Evans, Dietrich Rueschemeyer, and Theda Skocpol (New York: Cambridge University Press, 1985); Ann Shola Orloff, "The Political Origins of America's Belated Welfare State," in *The Politics of Social Policy in the United States*, ed. Margaret Weir, Ann Shola Orloff, and Theda

Skocpol (Princeton, NJ: Princeton University Press, 1988); Skocpol, *Protecting Soldiers and Mothers.*

12. For one of the few pieces of scholarship that has tried to move beyond most "state-centered" or "institutionalist" scholars' focus on the social welfare state when it comes to the development of American social policy in the early twentieth century, see Tracy L. Steffes, *School, Society, and State: A New Education to Govern Modern America, 1890–1940* (Chicago: University of Chicago Press, 2012).

13. Rodgers, *Atlantic Crossings,* 7, quotation. On the struggle to define progressives and progressivism and debates over the utility of those terms, see especially Daniel T. Rodgers, "In Search of Progressivism," *Reviews in American History* 10 (Dec. 1982), 113–32. See also Glenda Elizabeth Gilmore, *Who Were the Progressives?* (New York: Bedford/St. Martin's, 2002). For a leading piece that argues for the abandonment of the concepts altogether, see Peter G. Filene, "An Obituary for the 'Progressive Movement,'" *American Quarterly* 22 (1970), 20–34. For examples of major works that have tried to define progressivism from various angles and especially to link progressivism to different social classes, see Samuel P. Hays, *American Political History as Social Analysis* (Knoxville: University of Tennessee Press, 1980); Richard Hofstadter, *Age of Reform: From Bryan to FDR* (New York: Knopf, 1955); Robert H. Wiebe, *The Search for Order, 1877–1920* (New York: Hill and Wang, 1967); J. Joseph Huthmacher, "Urban Liberalism in the Age of Reform," *Mississippi Valley Historical Review* 49 (Sept. 1962), 231–41; John Buenker, *Urban Liberalism and Progressive Reform* (New York: Scribner, 1973); Michael McGerr, *A Fierce Discontent: The Rise and Fall of the Progressive Movement in America, 1870–1920* (New York: Free Press, 2003). These are just a handful of examples drawn from an enormous literature that explores the reformist spirit that marked the period. Other key overviews of the era include Nell Irvin Painter, *Standing at Armageddon: The United States, 1877–1919* (New York: Norton, 1987); Robyn Muncy, *Creating a Female Dominion in American Reform, 1890–1935* (New York: Oxford University Press, 1991); Alan Dawley, *Struggles for Justice: Social Responsibility and the Liberal State* (Cambridge, MA: Belknap Press of Harvard University Press, 1991); James T. Kloppenberg, *Uncertain Victory: Social Democracy and Progressivism in European and American Thought, 1870–1920* (New York: Oxford University Press, 1986); Rodgers, *Atlantic Crossings*; Jackson Lears, *Rebirth of a Nation: The Making of Modern America, 1877–1920* (New York: HarperCollins, 2009). Given the centrality of the decade following World War I to this book, it is worth noting how many of the works just listed end just after the war.

14. Like "progressivism," the term "corporate liberalism" has been used in a variety of ways. For example, compare Weinstein, *The Corporate Ideal in the Liberal State,* and Ellis W. Hawley, "The Discovery and Study of a 'Corporate Liberalism,'" *Business History Review* 52 (Autumn 1978), 309–20. On Hawley's usage of the term, see also Rodgers, "In Search of Progressivism," 129n27. The corporate liberal framework has been helpful in explaining the rise of a number of the economic regulations and regulatory institutions that took root in the early years of the twentieth century, such as the Federal Reserve Bank. But the concept has proven far less effective in explaining the rise of major pieces

of New Deal social legislation like the Social Security Act of 1935. On corporate liberalism and the rise of various economic regulations and institutions, see, for example, Weinstein, *The Corporate Ideal in the Liberal State*; Martin J. Sklar, *The Corporate Reconstruction of American Capitalism, 1890–1916* (New York: Cambridge University Press, 1988); James Livingston, *Origins of the Federal Reserve System: Money, Class, and Corporate Capitalism, 1890–1913* (Ithaca, NY: Cornell University Press, 1986). See also Gabriel Kolko, *The Triumph of Conservatism: A Re-interpretation of American History, 1900–1916* (New York: Free Press, 1963). On scholarship examining corporate influence on New Deal social legislation, see the discussion in note 5 above.

15. Richard Hofstadter titled the section of his *Age of Reform* "Entre'Acte," or intermission. Hofstadter, *Age of Reform*, 280. It is an image of the decade that has been challenged on a number of fronts, albeit from different angles than this book's focus on the political activism of business interests and on the expansion of urban government. For example, see Arthur S. Link, "What Happened to the Progressive Movement in the 1920s?" *American Historical Review* 64 (July 1959), 833–51; William E. Leuchtenberg, *The Perils of Prosperity, 1914–1932* (Chicago: University of Chicago Press, 1993), ch. 7; Howard Zinn, *LaGuardia in Congress* (Ithaca, NY: Cornell University Press, 1959); Clarke A. Chambers, *Seedtime of Reform: American Social Service and Social Action, 1918–1933* (Minneapolis: University of Minnesota Press, 1963); Tindall, "Business Progressivism." The work of Ellis Hawley cited above has been especially influential in challenging this vision of the decade. Hawley's examination of federal economic planning under Herbert Hoover during his time as U.S. Secretary of Commerce underscores how a business-friendly reformism of a different kind flourished at the federal level.

Chapter 1. At Cross Purposes

1. On municipal reform see, for example, Samuel P. Hays, "The Politics of Reform in Municipal Government in the Progressive Era," *Pacific Northwest Quarterly* 55 (Oct. 1964), 157–69; Weinstein, *The Corporate Ideal in the Liberal State*, ch. 4; Martin J. Schiesl, *The Politics of Efficiency: Municipal Administration and Reform in America, 1880–1920* (Berkeley: University of California Press, 1977); Michael Ebner and Eugene Tobin, eds., *The Age of Urban Reform: New Perspectives on the Progressive Era* (Port Washington, NY: Kennikat Press, 1977); Kenneth Finegold, *Experts and Politicians: Reform Challenges to Machine Politics in New York, Cleveland, and Chicago* (Princeton, NJ: Princeton University Press, 1995); Amy Bridges, *Morning Glories: Municipal Reform in the Southwest* (Princeton, NJ: Princeton University Press, 1997); Jessica Trounstine, *Political Monopolies in American Cities: The Rise and Fall of Bosses and Reformers* (Chicago: University of Chicago Press, 2008).

2. Melvin G. Holli, "The Impact of Automobile Manufacturing upon Detroit," *Detroit in Perspective* 2 (Spring 1976), 179–80; Sidney Glazer, *Detroit: A Study in Urban Development* (New York: Bookman Associates, 1965), 86; Melvin G. Holli, ed., *Detroit* (New York: New Viewpoints, 1976), 60, 117–19; Olivier Zunz, *The Changing Face of*

Inequality: Urbanization, Industrial Development and Immigrants in Detroit, 1880–1920 (Chicago: University of Chicago Press, 1982), esp. parts 2–4.

3. For a discussion of early investment in Detroit's automotive firms and a description of this process of class consolidation, see Donald Finlay Davis, *Conspicuous Production: Automobiles and Elites in Detroit, 1899–1933* (Philadelphia: Temple University Press, 1988), chs. 2–4.

4. Davis, *Conspicuous Production*, 61–63, 125–37. Davis depicts James Couzens as similarly alienated from the city's corporate elite. But as the next chapter explains, when it came to social politics on the local level, this was true in some respects but not in many others. For Davis's discussion of Couzens, see, for example, *Conspicuous Production*, 11–12, 132–35, 137–43.

5. Davis, *Conspicuous Production*, 101–3.

6. Davis, *Conspicuous Production*, 63, 65–66, 103; John B. Rae, *American Automobile Manufacturers: The First Forty Years* (New York: Chilton, 1959), 34–35; Raymond R. Fragnoli, *The Transformation of Reform, Progressivism in Detroit—and After, 1912–1933* (New York: Garland, 1982), 20–21.

7. Jake D. Elenbaas, "The Boss of the Better Class: Henry Leland and the Detroit Citizens League, 1912–1924," *Michigan History* 54 (Summer 1974), 132, 135–36; Fragnoli, *Transformation of Reform*, 21–22.

8. Holli, *Detroit*, 121; Holli, "The Impact of Automobile Manufacturing," 182; Glazer, *Detroit*, 79; Zunz, *The Changing Face of Inequality*, 106.

9. Fragnoli, *Transformation of Reform*, 11, 39–41.

10. Fragnoli, *Transformation of Reform*, 22–26, 151; Raymond R. Fragnoli, "Progressive Coalitions and Municipal Reform: Charter Revision in Detroit, 1912–1918," *Detroit in Perspective* 4 (Spring 1980), 125; Elenbaas, "The Boss of the Better Class," 138–39.

11. Elenbaas, "The Boss of the Better Class," 132–33.

12. Fragnoli, *Transformation of Reform*, 9–10.

13. Rodgers, *Atlantic Crossings*, 166–69; William H. Wilson, *The City Beautiful Movement* (Baltimore: Johns Hopkins University Press, 1989), chs. 1–3; Peter Hall, *Cities of Tomorrow: An Intellectual History of Urban Planning and Design in the Twentieth Century*, 3rd ed. (Malden, MA: Blackwell Publishing, 2002), 189–91. See also Jon A. Peterson, *The Birth of City Planning in the United States, 1840–1917* (Baltimore: Johns Hopkins University Press, 2003). On the City Beautiful movement and the cultural center in early twentieth-century Detroit, see Daniel M. Bluestone, "Detroit's City Beautiful and the Problem of Commerce," *Journal of the Society of Architectural Historians* 47 (Sept. 1988), 245–62. See also Jon C. Teaford, *Cities of the Heartland: The Rise and Fall of the Industrial Midwest* (Bloomington: Indiana University Press, 1993), 145.

14. Rodgers, *Atlantic Crossings*, 169–73; Hall, *Cities of Tomorrow*, 191–97; Alison Isenberg, *Downtown America: A History of the Place and the People Who Made It* (Chicago: University of Chicago Press, 2004), ch. 1; Mansel Blackford, *The Lost Dream: Businessmen and City Planning on the Pacific Coast, 1890–1920* (Columbus: Ohio State University Press, 1993); Teaford, *Cities of the Heartland*, 138–46; Carl Smith, *The Plan of*

Chicago: Daniel Burnham and the Remaking of the American City (Chicago: University of Chicago Press, 2006). Morgenthau is quoted in Hall, *Cities of Tomorrow*, 190.

15. Bluestone, "Detroit's City Beautiful and the Problem of Commerce," 257–58.

16. "How the Board Helped Secure the New Library," *Detroiter*, Mar. 19, 1921, 9; Frank B. Woodford, *Parnassus on Main Street: A History of the Detroit Public Library* (Detroit: Wayne State University Press, 1965), ch. 11, quotations on pp. 179, 184. On Andrew Carnegie's role in the development of public libraries more generally, see George S. Bobinski, *Carnegie Libraries: Their History and Impact on American Public Library Development* (Chicago: American Library Association, 1969); Abigail Van Slyck, *Free to All: Carnegie Libraries and American Culture, 1890–1920* (Chicago: University of Chicago Press, 1995); Theodore Jones, *Carnegie Libraries Across America: A Public Legacy* (New York: Wiley, 1997).

17. "How the Board Helped Secure the New Library," 9–10; Woodford, *Parnassus on Main Street*, 187–90; Fragnoli, *Transformation of Reform*, 10, 107.

18. Woodford, *Parnassus on Main Street*, 219–23, quotation on 221.

19. Jeffrey Abt, *A Museum on the Verge: A Socioeconomic History of the Detroit Institute of Arts, 1882–2000* (Detroit: Wayne State University Press, 2001), chs. 1–2, quotation on 68.

20. Abt, *A Museum on the Verge*, 81–97; Bluestone, "Detroit's City Beautiful and the Problem of Commerce," 249.

21. "The Child: An Unfinished Product," *Detroiter*, Nov. 1913, 11, 21; Paul Boyer, *Urban Masses and the Moral Order in America, 1820–1920* (Cambridge, MA: Harvard University Press, 1978), 242–51, quotation on 245. See also Dominick Cavallo, *Muscles and Morals: Organized Playgrounds and Moral Reform* (Philadelphia: University of Pennsylvania Press, 1981); Peterson, *Birth of City Planning*, 166–70.

22. "Detroit Needs Playgrounds," *Detroiter*, Dec. 1913, 25; "The Child: An Unfinished Product," 21, includes quotation.

23. "Splendid Recreation System Is Assured," *Detroiter*, May 3, 1915, 1; "The Child: An Unfinished Product"; "We Must Provide More Places for Recreation," *Detroiter*, Mar. 29, 1915, 5; "The Recreation and Survey Commission," *Detroiter*, July 10, 1922, 19.

24. William P. Lovett, *Detroit Rules Itself* (Boston: Gorham Press, 1930), 140–41; Fragnoli, *Transformation of Reform*, 127–28, 143, 159–60, 166–67.

25. Fragnoli, *Transformation of Reform*, 107, 150; Abt, *Museum on the Verge*, 103–4. For a discussion of the composition of the city council after charter reform, see the following chapter.

26. Jeffrey Mirel, *The Rise and Fall of an Urban School System: Detroit, 1907–81* (Ann Arbor: University of Michigan Press, 1993), 1, 4–5, 7, 10–12, 20–26.

27. Lincoln Steffens, "Philadelphia: Corrupt and Contended," *McClure's*, July 1903; Lloyd M. Abernethy, "Insurgency in Philadelphia, 1905," *Pennsylvania Magazine of History and Biography* 87 (Jan. 1963), 3–20; Abernethy, "Progressivism, 1905–1919," in *Philadelphia: A 300-Year History*, ed. Russell F. Weigley (New York: W. W. Norton, 1982), 537–43, 550–53, 561–64; Bonnie R. Fox, "The Philadelphia Progressives: A Test of the

Hofstadter-Hays Thesis," *Pennsylvania History* 34 (Oct. 1967), 372–94; Committee of Seventy, *The Charter: A History* (Philadelphia: Committee of Seventy, 1980). The best treatment of Philadelphia's political machine in the early twentieth century and of the independent municipal reform movement is Peter McCaffery, *When Bosses Ruled Philadelphia: The Emergence of the Republican Machine, 1867–1933* (University Park: Pennsylvania State University Press, 1993).

28. McCaffery, *When Bosses Ruled Philadelphia*, ch. 7; Domenic Vitiello, "Machine Building and City Building: Urban Planning and Industrial Restructuring in Philadelphia, 1894–1928," *Journal of Urban History* 34 (Mar. 2008), 403–4; Charles W. Cheape, *Moving the Masses: Urban Public Transit in New York, Boston, and Philadelphia, 1880–1912* (Cambridge, MA: Harvard University Press, 1980), 162–80.

29. For a discussion of this process of party consolidation, see McCaffery, *When Bosses Ruled Philadelphia*, 82–95.

30. McCaffery, *When Bosses Ruled Philadelphia*, 87.

31. On the Vares, see Abernethy, "Progressivism," 545; McCaffery, *When Bosses Ruled Philadelphia*, 102, 104; John T. Salter, *The People's Choice: Philadelphia's William S. Vare* (New York: Exposition Press, 1971). On rifts within the machine, see, for example, Abernethy, "Progressivism," 551–52, 561–64; McCaffery, *When Bosses Ruled Philadelphia*, 179–80, 184–85; Donald W. Disbrow, "Reform in Philadelphia under Mayor Blankenburg, 1912–1916," *Pennsylvania History* 27 (Oct. 1960), 380–81; Robert Edward Drayer, "J. Hampton Moore: An Old Fashioned Republican" (Ph.D. diss., University of Pennsylvania, 1961), 89–90.

32. McCaffery, *When Bosses Ruled Philadelphia*, ch. 7. On electoral fraud and other illegal tactics in the pre-World War I period, see, for instance, McCaffery, *When Bosses Ruled Philadelphia*, 137, 139; Abernethy, "Progressivism," 539.

33. Philip Scranton, "Large Firms and Industrial Restructuring: The Philadelphia Region, 1900–1980," *Pennsylvania Magazine of History and Biography* 96 (Oct. 1992), 419, 424–446; Philip Scranton, *Endless Novelty: Specialty Production and American Industrialization, 1865–1925* (Princeton, NJ: Princeton University Press, 1997), ch. 11.

34. For the composition of the original Committee of Seventy, see McCaffery, *When Bosses Ruled Philadelphia*, 172–75. On the composition of Blankenburg's campaign committee, see Fox, "The Philadelphia Progressives," 383. On the leaders of the charter reform effort, see Philadelphia Charter Committee, *Report of the Sub-Committee on the Charter* (Philadelphia, 1919); *Boyd's Philadelphia City Business Directory*, 1918; *Philadelphia Social Register*, 1918. For Blankenburg's occupation, see Abernethy, "Progressivism," 551. On Ernest Trigg, see, for instance, "Organization Perfected," *New York Times*, Aug. 4, 1918.

35. David Brownlee, *Building the City Beautiful: The Benjamin Franklin Parkway and the Philadelphia Museum of Art* (Philadelphia: Philadelphia Museum of Art, 1989), chs. 2–4; Vitiello, "Machine Building and City Building," 412–16; Jonathan E. Farnham, "A Bridge Game: Constructing a Co-operative Commonwealth in Philadelphia, 1900–1926" (Ph.D. diss., Princeton University, 2000), 278–99. For the early membership of OAACPS, see City Parks Association of Philadelphia, *Seventeenth and Eighteenth*

Annual Reports, 1905–1906, 5–10. The Merchants and Manufacturers Association and the Philadelphia Chamber of Commerce are listed under their earlier names, the Merchants and Travelers Association and the Trades League, respectively.

36. City Parks Association of Philadelphia, *Seventeenth and Eighteenth Annual Reports, 1905–1906*, 7; Drayer, "J. Hampton Moore," 120; Brownlee, *Building the City Beautiful*, 22, 72; Vitiello, "Machine Building and City Building," 412–19.

37. Farnham, "A Bridge Game," 185–87, 278–90; City Planning Association of Philadelphia, *Fifteenth Annual Report of the City Planning Association of Philadelphia*. This annual report consisted of three volumes outlining Crawford's and Day's plan.

38. In contrast to the bulk of OAACPS's plans, the Northeastern Boulevard project sparked a good deal of controversy. Some opponents were against the plan itself, but most objections concerned how the roadway was built, a dynamic described briefly later in this chapter.

39. Abernethy, "Progressivism," 540–41; Farnham, "A Bridge Game," 221–22; McCaffery, *When Bosses Ruled Philadelphia*, 158.

40. Farnham, "A Bridge Game," 222–26; Abernethy, "Progressivism," 541–42.

41. Brownlee, *Building the City Beautiful*, 21–28; Farnham, "A Bridge Game," 323, 329–30; McCaffery, *When Bosses Ruled Philadelphia*, 91–93.

42. Abernethy, "Progressivism," 550–53, 555; Disbrow, "Reform in Philadelphia under Mayor Blankenburg," 380–81, 382, 386–88; McCaffery, *When Bosses Ruled Philadelphia*, 183; Vitiello, "Machine Building and City Building," 417–18; Brownlee, *Building the City Beautiful*, 28, 50–51, 73.

43. Brownlee, *Building the City Beautiful*, 29–30; Farnham, "A Bridge Game," 329–32; Abernethy, "Progressivism," 563; Vitiello, "Machine Building and City Building," 418.

44. Drayer, "J. Hampton Moore," 89–90; Abernethy, "Progressivism," 561–62.

45. "Penrose Calls for New City Charter to Kill Boss Rule," *Philadelphia Inquirer*, Nov. 18, 1918; "Move to Eliminate City Charter Evils Will Start Today," *Philadelphia Inquirer*, Nov. 20, 1918; Drayer, "J. Hampton Moore," 93–94; Abernethy, "Progressivism," 562–64; Committee of Seventy, *The Charter*, 3.

46. "Dinner Crystallizes Demand for Phila. Charter's Revision," *Philadelphia Inquirer*, Dec. 11, 1918; "Charter Committee for Council of 19 and $5000 Salary," *Philadelphia Inquirer*, Jan. 8, 1919; "Revised City Charter Ready for Lawmakers," *Philadelphia Inquirer*, Mar. 3, 1919; Frederick P. Gruenberg, "Philadelphia Stirreth," *National Municipal Review*, Aug. 1919, 420–21; Abernethy, "Progressivism," 563; Drayer, "J. Hampton Moore," 119; Committee of Seventy, *The Charter*, 3.

47. "Sproul Predicts Charter Harmony," *Philadelphia Inquirer*, Dec. 28, 1918; "Revised City Charter Ready for Lawmakers"; Abernethy, "Progressivism," 564.

48. "Penrose Champions Charter Revisions," *Philadelphia Inquirer*, Dec. 27, 1918; "Revised City Charter Ready for Lawmakers"; Gruenberg, "Philadelphia Stirreth," 420–21; "Another Hearing on Charter Bills," *Philadelphia Inquirer*, Mar. 27, 1919; McCaffery, *When Bosses Ruled Philadelphia*, 89; Drayer, "J. Hampton Moore," 117–19; Abernethy, "Progressivism," 564; Committee of Seventy, *The Charter*, 3.

49. "Revised Charter Ready for Lawmakers;" Drayer, "J. Hampton Moore," 115–16; Gruenberg, "Philadelphia Stirreth," 421.

50. "New School Code Is Introduced in the State Senate," *Philadelphia Inquirer*, Jan. 25, 1911; "Penrose to Aid Vare in School Code Opposition," *Philadelphia Inquirer*, Mar. 21, 1911; "Education Board to Consist of 15 Named by Judges," *Philadelphia Inquirer*, Mar. 26, 1911; "Move to Eliminate City Charter Evils Will Start Today," *Philadelphia Inquirer*, Nov. 11, 1920; Drayer, "J. Hampton Moore," 120. For a general treatment of the 1911 Pennsylvania School Code, see William Issel, "The Politics of Public School Reform in Pennsylvania," *Pennsylvania Magazine of History and Biography* 102 (Jan. 1978), 59–92.

51. Abernethy, "Progressivism," 554; William H. Issel, "Modernization in Philadelphia School Reform, 1882–1905," *Pennsylvania Magazine of History and Biography* 94 (July 1970), 359, 381–83.

52. David Fort Godschalk, *Veiled Visions: The 1906 Race Riot and the Reshaping of American Race Relations* (Chapel Hill: University of North Carolina Press, 2005), 13–15; Thomas Mashburn Deaton, "The Chamber of Commerce in the Economic and Political Development of Atlanta from 1900 to 1916," *Atlanta Historical Bulletin* 19, no. 3 (1975), 19–21; Deaton, "Atlanta During the Progressive Era" (Ph.D. diss., University of Georgia, 1969), 48–51, 74, 80–82, 87, 96. See also Don H. Doyle, *New Men, New Cities, New South: Atlanta, Charleston, Nashville, Mobile, 1860–1910* (Chapel Hill: University of North Carolina Press, 1990).

53. Clifford M. Kuhn, *Contesting the New South Order: The 1914–1915 Strike at Atlanta's Fulton Mills* (Chapel Hill: University of North Carolina Press, 2001), 33–34; Godschalk, *Veiled Visions*, 13–15; John Dittmer, *Black Georgia in the Progressive Era, 1900–1920* (Urbana: University of Illinois Press, 1977), 12; Ronald H. Bayor, *Race and the Shaping of Twentieth-Century Atlanta* (Chapel Hill: University of North Carolina Press, 1996), 7.

54. Godschalk, *Veiled Visions*, 13–14, 19, 21–30, 36–52, 85–111; Tera W. Hunter, *To 'Joy My Freedom: Southern Black Women's Lives and Labor After the Civil War* (Cambridge, MA: Harvard University Press, 1997), 124–28; Dittmer, *Black Georgia in the Progressive Era*, 123–31. On the difficulties of determining an accurate count of African American fatalities related to the riot, see Godschalk, *Veiled Visions*, 105–06.

55. Godschalk, *Veiled Visions*, 86, 98, ch. 6.

56. Deaton, "Atlanta During the Progressive Era," 346; Stuart Galishoff, "Germs Know No Color Line: Black Health and Public Policy in Atlanta, 1900–1918," *Journal of the History of Medicine and Allied Sciences* 40 (Jan. 1985), 30, 33, 41; Philip N. Racine, "Atlanta's Schools: A History of the Public School System, 1869–1955" (Ph.D. diss., Emory University, 1969), 97–98; Howard L. Preston, "Parkways, Parks, and 'New South' Progressivism: Planning and Practice in Atlanta, 1880–1917," in *Olmsted South: Old South Critic/New South Planner*, ed. Dana F. White and Victor A. Kramer (Westport, CT: Greenwood Press, 1979), 231.

57. Thomas Mashburn Deaton, "James G. Woodward: The Working Man's Mayor," *Atlanta History* (Fall 1987), 11–14, 16.

58. Deaton, "James G. Woodward," 16–17; Kathryn W. Kemp, *God's Capitalist: Asa Candler of Coca-Cola* (Macon, GA: Mercer University Press, 2002), 175; "Bob Maddox Typical of Progressive Atlanta," *Atlanta Constitution*, Nov. 14, 1908. On Paxon, see Franklin M. Garrett, *Atlanta and Environs: A Chronicle of Its People and Events*, vol. 2 (Athens: University of Georgia Press, 1969), 812–13. On Kriegshaber, see Mark K. Bauman, "Victor Kriegshaber, Community Builder," *American Jewish History* 79 (Autumn 1989), 96.

59. "Maddox Says Lines Are Clearly Drawn," *Atlanta Constitution*, Nov. 20, 1908, quotation. Maddox received 7,260 votes and Woodward, 3,930. Deaton, "James G. Woodward," 17.

60. "'Greater Atlanta' by a Million Dollars in Bonds," *Atlanta Constitution*, Feb. 19, 1908.

61. "Citizens Show Their Approval of Bond Issue," *Atlanta Constitution*, Feb. 20, 1908.

62. "The City Bond Issue," *Atlanta Constitution*, Aug. 12, 1908. See also "Report Favors Big Bond Issue of $1,500,000," *Atlanta Constitution*, Mar. 28, 1908; Kemp, *God's Capitalist*, 138–39.

63. "Report Favors Big Bond Issue of $1,500,000"; Deaton, "Atlanta During the Progressive Era," 346–47; "How City Will Pay Back $3,000,000 Bond Issue," *Atlanta Constitution*, Feb. 14, 1910.

64. "$1,000,000 Bond Issue Called," *Atlanta Constitution*, Jan. 24, 1919.

65. Deaton, "Atlanta During the Progressive Era," 347–48; Kemp, *God's Capitalist*, 139; Galishoff, "Germs Know No Color Line," 29 (quotation), 34–41; "Women Workers for City Bonds," *Atlanta Constitution*, Jan. 30, 1910; "Women Work Zealously in the Bond Campaign," *Atlanta Constitution*, Feb. 3, 1910; "Prominent Atlanta Women Working Hard for Bond Issue," *Atlanta Constitution*, Feb. 6, 1910; "Bonds Indorsed by Labor Men," *Atlanta Constitution*, Feb. 10, 1910.

66. "Inaugural Speech Made by President F.J. Paxon," *Atlanta Constitution*, Dec. 17, 1909. On the establishment of the Carnegie Library, see Garrett, *Atlanta and Environs*, 375–77.

67. "Maddox Urges Forward Policy for Gate City," *Atlanta Constitution*, Jan. 5, 1909 (quotation); Preston, "Parkways, Parks, and 'New South' Progressivism," 231–34; Elizabeth A. Lyon, "Frederick Law Olmsted and Joel Hurt: Planning for Atlanta," in White and Kramer, *Olmsted South*, 182, 185–86, 189; Gail Anne D'Avino, "Atlanta Municipal Parks, 1887–1917: Urban Boosterism, Urban Reform in a New South City" (Ph.D. diss., Emory University, 1988), 112–14, 117–18, 123, 129–30, 150, 161–62.

68. "Build for Future of Atlanta, Say Business Men Indorsing Movement for Bond Issue," *Constitution*, Nov. 30, 1912; "Preachers to Aid Grady Bond Issue," *Atlanta Constitution*, Apr. 30, 1914; "Wilkerson Names Bond Committee," *Atlanta Constitution*, Jan. 20, 1915; "Favor Bond Issue to Furnish Work for Unemployed," *Atlanta Constitution*, Jan. 28, 1915; "J. M. B. Hoxsey Says Bond Issue Would Save City Money and Suffering—But!," *Atlanta Constitution*, Jan. 31, 1915; "Says Candler Is Not Working Man's Friend," *Atlanta*

Constitution, Aug. 4, 1916; "Georgia Will Help in Fight to Change the Bond Election Laws," *Atlanta Constitution*, Feb. 13, 1917; "Tax Rate Increase to $1.50 Adopted by Council," *Atlanta Constitution*, June 19, 1917; "Tax Increase Stricken From Bill," *Atlanta Constitution*, Aug. 1, 1917; "Legislators Scored by Atlanta Officials," *Atlanta Constitution*, Aug. 2, 1917.

69. On the attempt to revise Atlanta's city charter in 1911 and 1913, see Deaton, "Atlanta During the Progressive Era," 365–400; Willie Miller Bolden, "The Political Structure of Charter Revision Movements in Atlanta During the Progressive Era" (Ph.D. diss., Emory University, 1978), ch. 4. On the commission plan more generally, see Bradley Robert Rice, *Progressive Cities: The Commission Government Movement in America, 1901–1920* (Austin: University of Texas Press, 1977).

70. "Build for Future of Atlanta, Says Business Men Indorsing Movement for Bond Issue," *Atlanta Constitution*, Nov. 30, 1912; "'Growing Pains' and the Bond Cure," *Atlanta Constitution*, Dec. 1, 1912; "City Fathers Are Unanimous in Favoring Bonds," *Atlanta Constitution*, Dec. 3, 1912; "City Is Short $1,000,000 of Appropriations Asked for Maintenance in 1913," *Atlanta Constitution*, Jan. 17, 1913; "Plan Bond Issue for City's Needs," *Atlanta Constitution*, June 4, 1913; "For Bond Issue Committee Calls," *Atlanta Constitution*, June 6, 1913; "Charter Reform Will Be Issue This Fall," *Atlanta Constitution*, June 25, 1913.

71. Deaton, "Atlanta During the Progressive Era," 381.

72. "Sands Will Report on Atlanta System," *Atlanta Constitution*, Nov. 12, 1912; "Sands Tells How City Government May Be Bettered," *Atlanta Constitution*, Dec. 31, 1912.

73. Georgina Hickey, *Hope and Danger in the New South City: Working-Class Women and Urban Development in Atlanta, 1890–1940* (Athens: University of Georgia Press, 2003), 134–44; Harry G. Lefever, "Prostitution, Politics and Religion: The Crusade Against Vice in Atlanta in 1912," *Atlanta Historical Journal* 24 (Spring 1980), 7–29; Deaton, "Atlanta During the Progressive Era," 387–88, 400–404; Deaton, "James G. Woodward," 20.

74. On the recall, see the sources cited in note 73 above. On the aborted bond election, see "Urge Bonds as the Solution of Atlanta Needs," *Atlanta Constitution*, Oct. 24, 1914; "Sentiment Grows for Bond Issue," *Atlanta Constitution*, Oct. 30, 1914; "Bond Issue of $3,000,000 for Civic Improvements Recommended to Council," *Atlanta Constitution*, Dec. 15, 1914; "Election Called for September 30 to Vote on Bonds," Aug. 3, 1915; "Councilmen Favor Move to Postpone Election on Bonds," *Atlanta Constitution*, Sept. 16, 1915.

75. "Criticism Kills Bonds, Says Cooper, Secretary Chamber of Commerce," *Atlanta Constitution*, Sept. 8, 1915.

76. On charter reform in 1920s Atlanta, see Kesavan Sudheendran, "Community Structure in Atlanta: A Study in Decision Making, 1920–1939" (Ph.D. diss., Georgia State University, 1982), 305–19; Bolden, "The Political Structure of Charter Revision Movements in Atlanta During the Progressive Era," 230–42.

77. David M. Kennedy, *Over Here: The First World War and American Society (*New York: Oxford University Press, 1980), 187–89.

78. McGerr, *A Fierce Discontent*, 303–4; Dawley, *Struggles for Justice*, 234–37; Leuchtenberg, *Perils of Prosperity*, 36; Kennedy, *Over Here*, 258–70. On the upheaval that followed the armistice, see also, Painter, *Standing at Armageddon*, ch. 12; Leuchtenberg, *The Perils of Prosperity*, ch. 4; Kennedy, *Over Here*, ch. 5; Burl Noggle, *Into the Twenties: The United States from Armistice to Normalcy* (Urbana: University of Illinois Press, 1974); Beverly Gage, *The Day Wall Street Exploded: A Story of America in Its First Age of Terror* (New York: Oxford University Press, 2009).

79. Painter, *Standing at Armageddon*, 346–47, 349, 359, 361, 368–75.

80. Painter, *Standing at Armageddon* 358–60; Leuchtenberg, *Perils of Prosperity*, 71.

81. Painter, *Standing at Armageddon*, 360, 377, 381.

82. Painter, *Standing at Armageddon*, 362–64, 379.

Chapter 2. Detroit

1. Zunz, *Changing Face of Inequality*, 287–88; Fragnoli, *Transformation of Reform*, 182.

2. Fragnoli, *Transformation of Reform*, 134, 175–83; *Detroit Labor News*, Nov. 1, 1918; Aug. 23, 1918; Sept. 28, 1923, Oct. 2, 1925; Mirel, *Rise and Fall of an Urban School System*, 27–28.

3. These calculations are based on the occupations listed for candidates and the election results given in the *Civic Searchlight* from 1919 through 1929. For the Detroit Citizens League's endorsement of Ewald, see "Nine Are Indorsed by Civic League," *Detroit News*, Oct. 25, 1925, clipping, scrapbook 8, MS Detroit Citizens League [DCL], Burton Historical Collection [BHC], Detroit Public Library [DPL]; "Citizens League Issues Election List," *Detroit News*, Nov. 7, 1927, clipping, scrapbook 9, DCL, BHC, DPL; "League Silent on Mayoralty," *Detroit Times*, Oct. 27, 1929, clipping, scrapbook 10, DCL, BHC, DPL.

4. Mirel, *Rise and Fall of an Urban School System*, 53. On Frank Cody and mayoral politics, see discussion below. Information on school board members in the 1920s whose candidacies had been backed by the Detroit Citizens League is based on issues of the *Civic Searchlight* from 1919 through 1929.

5. Harry Barnard, *Independent Man: The Life of Senator James Couzens* (New York: Charles Scribner's Sons, 1958), 83–94, 96–97, 98–100, 115–16; Fragnoli, *Transformation of Reform*, 173–74; Robert Conot, *American Odyssey* (New York: Morrow, 1974), 198, 201; C. C. McGill, "Senator James Couzens," *Detroiter*, Jan. 3, 1928, 7.

6. For the council as a rubber stamp, see "Boss of Our Town," *Detroit Saturday Night*, Sept. 24, 1921, clipping, scrapbook 5, DCL, BHC, DPL. There were certainly other instances of friction between Couzens, public officials, and the city's business leaders during his term, but they proved temporary. For instance, at one point Couzens resigned from the Detroit Board of Commerce to protest its failure to support one of his

proposals, but he rejoined the following year. "Detroit Hospital Fight," *New York Times*, Mar. 21, 1921; "Mayor Couzens Quits Board of Commerce," *Detroit Labor News*, Apr. 1, 1921; "Many Board Members Attend Luncheon in Honor of Postmaster Smith," *Detroiter*, Apr. 22, 1922.

7. U.S. Bureau of the Census, *The Thirteenth Census of the United States: Abstract of the Census, 1910* (Washington, D.C., 1910), 62; *The Fourteenth Census of the United States: Population, Volume I* (Washington, D.C., 1920), 64; *The Fifteenth Census of the United States, Population, Volume 2* (Washington, D.C., 1930), 18; Conot, *American Odyssey*, 195; Mirel, *Rise and Fall of an Urban School System*, 60; Zunz, *Changing Face of Inequality*, 290–92.

8. "Money, Houses, Labor Called Detroit Needs," *Detroit News*, Oct. 17, 1919, clipping, scrapbook 3, DCL, BHC, DPL, first quotation; "Labor Is Cure for City Ills," *Detroit Free Press*, Oct. 17, 1919, clipping, scrapbook 3, DCL BHC, DPL, second quotation.

9. "Labor Is Cure for City Ills," includes quotations; Davis, *Conspicuous Production*, 103.

10. "City Administration Essays Solving Many Problems in 1920," *Detroiter*, Jan. 3, 1920, 3.

11. "Detroit, Plus Couzens, Blazes Trail for Cities," *Detroit News*, Dec. 14, 1922, clipping, scrapbook 6, DCL, BHC, DPL; "How Money Was Spent Under Couzens Regime," *Detroit News*, July 21, 1922, clipping, scrapbook 6, DCL, BHC, DPL.

12. "Couzens Asks Rent Sermon," *Detroit News*, Aug. 21, 1920, clipping, scrapbook 4, DCL, BHC, DPL.

13. For the cartoon, see the *Detroiter*, June 30, 1919, 4.

14. "Detroit Has Made Splendid Beginning on Program of Parks and Playgrounds," *Detroiter*, Aug. 13, 1919, 4.

15. "Not a Penny Spent for Parks,' *Civic Searchlight*, Jan. 1920, 1.

16. *Annual Report for the City of Detroit for the Year Ending Dec. 31, 1920*, 341, quotation; *Annual Report for the City of Detroit for the Year Ending Dec. 31, 1919*, 11. On the expenditure of funds from the $10 million bond issue for parks and playgrounds, see C. E. Brewer to Frank Doremus, May 2, 1923, Recreation Department folder, box 3, 1923, Mayors Papers, BHC, DPL.

17. David Tyack and Elisabeth Hansot, *Managers of Virtue: Public School Leadership in America, 1820–1980* (New York: Basic Books, 1982), 141, 144–52; "Mayor's Veto Perils Condon," *Detroit Free Press*, June 3, 1919, clipping, scrapbook 3, DCL, BHC, DPL; "Cody Chosen as Schools' Head; Salary $9,000," *Detroit Free Press*, June 27, 1919, scrapbook 3, DCL, BHC, DPL; "Frank Cody Named Head of Detroit's School System," *Detroiter*, Mar. 24, 1919, 2; Mirel, *Rise and Fall of an Urban School System*, 28, 29–31.

18. *Annual Report of the Detroit Public Schools . . . 1920*, 13.

19. *Annual Report of the Detroit Public Schools . . . 1920*, 12. For the overhaul of Detroit's schools in general, see Mirel, *Rise and Fall of an Urban School System*, 66–68; Arthur B. Mohelman, *Public Education in Detroit* (Bloomington, IL: Public School Publishing Co., 1925), chs. 14–15.

20. *Annual Report of the Detroit Public Schools . . . 1920*, 14.

21. *Annual Report of the Detroit Public Schools . . . 1920*, 15.

22. *Annual Report of the Detroit Public Schools . . . 1920*, 15.

23. *Annual Report of the Detroit Public Schools . . . 1923*, 50.

24. *Annual Report of the Detroit Public Schools . . . 1923*, 50; *Annual Report of the Detroit Public Schools . . . 1925*, 36; *Annual Report of the Detroit Public Schools . . . 1928*, 81; *Cardinal Principles of Secondary Education: A Report of the Commission on the Reorganization of Secondary Education, Appointed by the National Education Association* (Washington, D.C.: Department of the Interior, Bureau of Education, 1918).

25. *Annual Report of the Detroit Public Schools . . . 1914*, 104–7; *Annual Report of the Detroit Public Schools . . . 1917*, 19–21; *Annual Report of the Detroit Public Schools . . . 1921*, 20; *Annual Report of the Detroit Public Schools . . . 1926*, 56; *Annual Report of the Detroit Public Schools . . . 1929*, 84. See also Mirel, *Rise and Fall of an Urban School System*, 69.

26. *Annual Report of the Detroit Public Schools . . . 1921*, 7, 14.

27. "Schools," *Detroiter*, Sept. 10, 1923.

28. Mirel, *Rise and Fall of an Urban School System*, 65; *Annual Report of the Detroit Public Schools . . . 1920*, 10; *Annual Report of the Detroit Public Schools . . . 1929*, 17.

29. City of Detroit, *Annual Report . . . 1919*, 214, 217; *Annual Report . . . 1920*, 602; *Annual Report . . . 1929*, 284, 290; "Detroit, Plus Couzens, Blazes Trail for Cities"; Woodford, *Parnassus on Main Street*, ch. 13.

30. Fragnoli, *Transformation of Reform*, 73–74; Davis, *Conspicuous Production*, 163–69.

31. Barnard, *Independent Man*, 138.

32. "City Bond Limit Passed by 37 Million," *Detroit Free Press*, Mar. 19, 1923, clipping, scrapbook 6, DCL, BHC, DPL; "Doremus Takes Office Monday," Apr. 4, 1923, clipping, scrapbook 6, DCL, BHC, DPL; "City at Crisis, Mayor Urges Rigid Economy," May 26, 1923, clipping, scrapbook 6, DCL, BHC, DPL, quotation. Couzens perhaps saw this crisis on the horizon. In early 1922 he called on city officials to curtail unnecessary spending in the coming year. See Mayor James Couzens to the Honorable Common Council, Jan. 10, 1922, City Council folder, box 1, 1922, Mayors Papers, BHC, DPL.

33. "12 to 1," *Detroit Times*, Oct. 10, 1923, clipping, scrapbook 6, DCL, BHC, DPL.

34. Fragnoli, *Transformation of Reform*, 228–29, 294–96; Steve Babson, *Working Detroit: The Making of a Union Town* (New York: Adama Books, 1984), 49–50. For the DFL's endorsements, see *Detroit Labor News*, Nov. 2, 1923; Nov. 9, 1923.

35. "Mayor Doremus Needed," *Detroit Times*, Oct. 1, 1923, clipping, scrapbook 6, DCL, BHC, DPL; "City Tax Rate Fixed at $20.93," *Detroit Free Press*, May 23, 1924, clipping, scrapbook 7, DCL, BHC, DPL; Fragnoli, *Transformation of Reform*, 307–08.

36. "Citizens League and the City Budget," *Civic Searchlight*, Mar. 1924, quotation. Fragnoli misleadingly paints the Governmental Committee as primarily a group lobbying for lower taxes even as he also acknowledges its advocacy for schooling and recreation. See Fragnoli, *Transformation of Reform*, 296–300.

37. Fragnoli, *Transformation of Reform*, 299.

38. Kevin Boyle, *Arc of Justice: A Saga of Race, Civil Rights, and Murder in the Jazz Age* (New York: Henry Holt, 2004), 140–42; Fragnoli, *Transformation of Reform*, 308–10. For an account of the 1924 mayoral election and the Ku Klux Klan in Detroit more generally, see also Kenneth T. Jackson, *The Ku Klux Klan in the City, 1915–1930* (New York: Oxford University Press, 1967), ch. 9.

39. Fragnoli, *Transformation of Reform*, 309–311; Boyle, *Arc of Justice*, 141; "John W. Smith, New Postmaster, Joins the Board of Commerce," *Detroiter*, Apr. 8, 1922; "Many Board Members Attend Luncheon in Honor of Postmaster Smith"; "Mayor Smith," *Detroiter*, Nov. 10, 1924.

40. Boyle, *Arc of Justice*, 142; "Anti-Klan Rally Mobbed," *Detroit Free Press*, Oct. 22, 1924, clipping, scrapbook 8, BHC, DPL, DCL; *Detroit Labor News*, Aug. 22, 1924; Sept. 12, 1924; Oct. 17, 1924; Oct. 24, 1924.

41. Boyle, *Arc of Justice*, 143; Fragnoli, *Transformation of Reform*, 312, 317n44; "Smith Wins but Bowles Will Fight," *Detroit News*, Nov. 5, 1924, clipping, scrapbook 8, BHC, DPL, DCL.

42. John W. Smith, "Business Men Will Probe City's Finances," *Detroiter*, Jan. 5, 1925; "An Open Letter to Richard P. Joy," *Detroiter*, Jan. 12, 1925; "Committee on City Loan Funds," *Civic Searchlight*, Jan. 1925, 3; Davis, *Conspicuous Production*, 58, 102; John C. Lodge, "Detroit's Progress Uninterrupted," *Detroiter*, Nov. 9, 1925, quotation. For Lodge as a founding member of the Detroit Citizens League, see Fragnoli, *Transformation of Reform*, 23.

43. "444 Millions Asked for City," *Detroit News*, May 22, 1925, clipping, scrapbook 8, DCL, BHC, DPL; "Mayor's Note Balks Action on Civic Center," *Detroit Free Press*, Aug. 19, 1925, clipping, scrapbook 8, DCL, BHC, DPL; "Memorial Fight Won by Mayor," *Detroit Times*, Aug. 25, 1925, clipping, scrapbook 8, DCL, BHC, DPL.

44. Boyle, *Arc of Justice*, chs. 5–6; David Allan Levine, *Internal Combustion: The Races in Detroit, 1915–1926* (Westport, CT: Greenwood Press, 1976), 153–65; Richard W. Thomas, *Life for Us Is What We Make It: Building Black Community in Detroit, 1915–1945* (Bloomington: Indiana University Press, 1992), 136–38; Victoria W. Wolcott, *Remaking Respectability: African American Women in Interwar Detroit* (Chapel Hill, NC: University of North Carolina Press, 2001), 140–41.

45. Fragnoli, *Transformation of Reform*, 317; "The Ku Klux Klan Shows Its Strength," *Detroit Saturday Night*, Oct. 10, 1925, clipping, scrapbook 8, DCL, BHC, DPL.

46. Fragnoli, *Transformation of Reform*, 317–18.

47. Fragnoli, *Transformation of Reform*, 320–21; "Ford Indorses Mayor Smith," *Detroit Free Press*, Oct. 31, 1925, clipping, scrapbook 8, DCL, BHC, DPL; "'Silk Stocking' Vote Returned Mayor Smith," *Detroit Free Press*, Nov. 5, 1925, clipping, scrapbook 8, DCL, BHC, DPL; Boyle, *Arc of Justice*, 313, quotation; Jackson, *Ku Klux Klan in the* City, 142.

48. Executive Secretary to George H. Fenkell, Aug. 25, 1920, Correspondence, A–G, 1920 folder, box 6, Detroit Citizens League Papers, BHC, DPL. These observations are

based on studying all of the issues of the *Detroit Labor News* published during the decade. On the specific referenda mentioned in this paragraph, see *Detroit Labor News*, Aug. 6, 1920; Oct. 22, 1926. On how DFL-endorsed candidates fared in the 1925 election, see *Detroit Labor News*, Oct. 2, 1925; Oct. 30, 1925; Nov. 6, 1925.

49. On the DFL's endorsements in school elections, see *Detroit Labor News*, Apr. 3, 1925; Mar. 25, 1927; Mar. 1, 1929; Mar. 29, 1929. For examples of the DFL's candidate endorsements in various council races, see *Detroit Labor News*, Nov. 2, 1923; Oct. 2, 1925; Sept. 30, 1927. For the DFL's rationale in supporting Smith, see *Detroit Labor News*, Sept. 12, 1924; Oct. 24, 1924.

50. *Detroit Labor News*, Aug. 19, 1927.

51. "Nine Are Indorsed by Civic League"; William Lovett to Walter F. Arndt, Nov. 11, 1925, A folder, box 13, Detroit Citizens League Correspondence, BHC, DPL.

52. Thomas Merrill to Members of the Detroit Board of Commerce, Dec. 21, 1925, Board of Commerce-Chicago Regional Planning Assoc., 1925–26 folder, box 2, MS Rapid Transit Commission, BHC, DPL.

53. *Financial Statistics of Cities with Populations over 30,000*; City of Detroit, *Annual Report* for the years 1923–27; William Lovett to Karl S. Betts, Jan. 24, 1927, D folder, Detroit Citizens League Correspondence, BHC, DPL; *Detroit Labor News*, Oct. 21, 1927; City of Detroit, *Annual Report . . . 1929*, 340–41; *Detroiter*, Sept. 19, 1927, 10, quotation. The recreation commission was renamed the Department of Recreation in the early 1920s.

54. "City Tax Rate Is Made $22.56, Gain of $2.18," June 15, 1926, clipping, scrapbook 9, DCL, BHC, DPL; *Detroit Labor News*, Oct. 21, 1927; City of Detroit, *Annual Report*, 1924–27; Abt, *Museum on the Verge*, 121.

55. Davis, *Conspicuous Production*, 170–71, 173 (quotation); "Facts on Rapid Transit," *Civic Searchlight*, Mar. 1929.

56. Davis, *Conspicuous Production*, 170–74.

57. Boyle, *Arc of Justice*, 109–11, 145, 342–43; Levine, *Internal Combustion*, 41–42, 54, 129–31; Wolcott, *Remaking Respectability*, 135, 137–40; Thomas, *Life for Us Is What We Make It*, 89–93, 101; U.S. Census Bureau, *Fifteenth Census of the United States: 1930*. On immigrant restriction, see, for example, Mae M. Ngai, *Impossible Subjects: Illegal Aliens and the Making of Modern America* (Princeton, NJ: Princeton University Press, 2004), ch. 1.

58. Levine, *Internal Combustion*, chs. 3–4; Thomas, *Life for Us Is What We Make It*, 26, ch. 3; Wolcott, *Remaking Respectability*, 49–50, 53–64. On Garvey and the United Negro Improvement Association in Detroit, see, for instance, Beth Tompkins Bates, *The Making of Black Detroit in the Age of Henry Ford* (Chapel Hill: University of North Carolina Press, 2012), 70. On the NAACP in 1920s Detroit and especially its battle in the Sweet case, see Boyle, *Arc of Justice*. The quotation appears in Boyle, *Arc of Justice*, 119.

59. Levine, *Internal Combustion*, 119–20; Thomas, *Life for Us Is What We Make It*, 58.

60. Jayne Morris-Crowther, "Municipal Housekeeping: The Political Activities of

the Detroit Federation of Women's Clubs in the 1920s," *Michigan Historical Review* 30 (Spring 2004), 32, 42–48; *Club Woman*, Oct. 1921, 61. *Club Woman* was the official publication of the Detroit Federation of Women's Clubs and included reports of member groups. On women's politics in 1920s Detroit in general, see also Jayne Morris-Crowther, *The Political Activities of Detroit Clubwomen in the 1920s: A Challenge and a Promise* (Detroit: Wayne State University Press, 2013). Morris-Crowther's book has different concerns than this study and, thus, does not directly compare female political activism at the municipal, state, and federal levels. Nonetheless, the evidence that Morris-Crowther presents accords with my discussion here. On food safety and the living conditions of female prisoners, see Morris-Crowther, *The Political Activities of Clubwomen in the 1920s*, 101, 112.

61. For examples of the DFWC's and its member organizations' charitable efforts, see *Club Woman*, Dec. 1920, 205–11; *Club Woman*, Apr. 1921, 454–56; *Club Woman*, June 1921, 590, 594; *Club Woman*, June 1929, 405–6. On women's clubs educating members about various issues and the positions of political candidates, see, Morris-Crowther, "Municipal Housekeeping," 49–50; Morris-Crowther, *The Political Activities of Detroit Clubwomen in the 1920s*, 49–50, 57–58; *Club Woman*, Sept. 1927, 29; *Club Woman*, Nov. 1927, 132; *Club Woman*, June 1928, 462. The Wayne County League of Women Voters similarly prioritized educational efforts in local politics. See, for instance, *Michigan Women*, Apr. 1925, 10; Summer 1925. *Michigan Women* was the official magazine of the Michigan League of Women Voters and included reports on the activities of the Wayne County branch. On female candidates for office, see Morris-Crowther, "Municipal Housekeeping," 41–42; Morris-Crowther, *The Political Activities of Detroit Clubwomen in the 1920s*, 126–28. On Doremus, see box 3, Lucia I. V. Grimes Papers, Bentley Historical Library [BHL], University of Michigan [UM].

62. *Club Woman*, June 1921, 591–92. For the Legislative Council of Michigan Women, see Lucia I. V. Grimes Papers, boxes 1–3, BHL, UM; the Ella H. Aldinger Papers, BHL, UM; *Michigan Women*, Sept. 1924, 6; *Club Woman*, Sept. 1923, 9. The League of Women Voters followed a similar pattern. While the Wayne County branch primarily fostered educational forums, voter registration drives, and get-out-the-vote activities, at the state and national level the league fought on behalf of specific policies. For instance, see *Michigan Women*, Mar. 1926, 18–20; May 1926.

63. Fragnoli, *Transformation of Reform*, 321–24. For a definition of the "tip-over raid," see Sidney Fine, *Frank Murphy: The Detroit Years* (Ann Arbor: University of Michigan Press, 1975), 393–94.

64. *Detroit Labor News*, Sept. 16, 1927; Aug. 19, 1927; Sept. 30, 1927; Oct. 7, 1927; Fragnoli, *Transformation of Reform*, 325–26; "250,000 Vote is Predicted in Elections," *Detroit Free Press*, Nov. 6, 1927, clipping, scrapbook 9, DCL, BHC, DPL, includes quotation.

65. "Lodge Favors Sewer Bonds," *Detroit News*, Apr. 1, 1928, clipping, scrapbook 10, DCL, BHC, DPL; "Sewer Bonds Win at Polls," *Detroit News*, Apr. 3, 1928, clipping, scrapbook 10, DCL, BHC, DPL; "Mayor Lodge Outlines 10-Year Improvement Program," *Detroit News*, Jan. 15, 1929, clipping, scrapbook 10, DCL, BHC, DPL; "$540,000,000 Civic

Program Outlined," *Detroit News*, Jan. 16, 1929, clipping, scrapbook 10, DCL, BHC, DPL.

Chapter 3. Philadelphia

1. Christopher Morley, *Travels in Philadelphia* (Philadelphia: David McKay, 1920), 64, 66.

2. "Chamber Takes Referendum on Statement of Principles Designed to Bring 100% Home Rule," *Philadelphia Chamber of Commerce News Bulletin* [*News Bulletin*], Mar. 1, 1919.

3. "Need $30,000,000 to Place City Streets in Condition," *News Bulletin*, June 16, 1919; "Chamber Revives Project to Hold Sesqui-Centennial Exposition Here in 1926," *News Bulletin*, Aug. 1, 1919; "Consider Building Big Stadium Here," *News Bulletin*, Mar. 15, 1920.

4. Drayer, "J. Hampton Moore," 38–40, 50–53, quotations on 51 and 52.

5. "Moore and the Mayoralty," *Philadelphia Evening Bulletin*, July 26, 1919, clipping, folder 12, box 344, J. Hampton Moore Papers (Collection 1541), Historical Society of Pennsylvania [HSP]; Drayer, "J. Hampton Moore," 96–97.

6. Drayer, "J. Hampton Moore," 98–99; Philadelphia Charter Committee, *Report of the Sub-Committee on the Charter*.

7. Drayer, "J. Hampton Moore," 103, 135–36.

8. "Mayor's Opportunity to Attack Dual Government," *Philadelphia Evening Public Ledger*, Oct. 13, 1920, clipping, J. Hampton Moore (JHM) Scrapbooks, HSP; Drayer, "J. Hampton Moore," 150–51.

9. "Judge Brown's $1,000,000 Roll Has 606 Names," *Philadelphia Public Ledger*, Oct. 31, 1920, clipping, JHM Scrapbooks, HSP; "My Door Open to All Says Penrose in Move to Unite Party Here," *Philadelphia Evening Public Ledger*, Oct. 15, 1920, clipping, JHM Scrapbooks, HSP, includes quotation; "Women Hammer at Weglein, Burch," *Philadelphia Inquirer*, Dec. 23, 1920, clipping, JHM Scrapbooks, HSP; Drayer, "J. Hampton Moore," 150–51.

10. "Health Director Probes His Office to Support Mayor," *Philadelphia Public Ledger*, Dec. 28, 1920, clipping, JHM Scrapbooks, HSP; "Moore Organization Forming as Ax Falls on Disloyal at Hall," *Philadelphia Public Ledger*, Dec. 28, 1920, clipping, JHM Scrapbooks, HSP; "22 Lose City Jobs; Mayor Opens Drive upon Brown's Ward," *Philadelphia Inquirer*, Dec. 30, 1920, clipping, JHM Scrapbooks, HSP; "Moore Followers Engage Quarters," *Philadelphia Public Ledger*, Dec. 31, 1920, clipping, JHM Scrapbooks, HSP, includes quotation; "A Few Words with Mayor Moore," *Philadelphia Inquirer*, Jan. 3, 1921, clipping, JHM Scrapbooks, HSP; Robert Douglas Bowden, *Boies Penrose: Symbol of an Era* (New York: Greenberg, 1937), 264–65.

11. "People in All Walks Rally to the Mayor's Extravagance Fight," *Philadelphia Public Ledger*, Dec. 23, 1920, clipping, JHM Scrapbooks, HSP; "Civic Club Out for Moore; Wrath Amazes Politicians," *Philadelphia Public Ledger*, Dec. 30, 1920, clipping, JHM

Scrapbooks, HSP; "See Quaker City as Storm Center in Legislature," *Philadelphia Inquirer*, Jan. 2, 1921, clipping, JHM Scrapbooks, HSP; Drayer, "J. Hampton Moore," 151–57.

12. "Chamber Revives Project to Hold Sesqui-Centennial Exposition Here in 1926"; "Exposition Plans Early, Mayor Says," *Philadelphia Inquirer*, Mar. 4, 1921; "Big Fair Site Still Mystery," *Philadelphia Public Ledger*, Jan. 22, 1922, clipping, JHM Scrapbooks, HSP; "Park Site Is Chosen for 1926 Exhibition by Unanimous Vote," *Philadelphia Inquirer*, Mar. 15, 1922; "The Sesqui-Centennial Exhibition: Message of the Mayor to the Council," folder 1, box 223, J. Hampton Moore Papers, HSP.

13. "Named to Plan 1926 Celebration," *Philadelphia Public Ledger*, Jan. 16, 1921, clipping, JHM Scrapbooks, HSP; "Mayor's War over 1926 Fair May End," *Philadelphia Inquirer*, Feb. 23, 1921; "Council Yields to Aid Big 1926 Exposition," *Philadelphia Inquirer*, Apr. 8, 1921; "Sesqui Committee Flayed by Mayor in Caustic Speech," *Philadelphia Inquirer*, Dec. 23, 1921; Steven Conn, *Museums and American Intellectual Life, 1876–1926* (Chicago: University of Chicago Press, 1998), 234.

14. "Sesqui Committee Flayed by Mayor in Caustic Speech"; "Sesqui Outgrowth of Ten Years' Effort," *Philadelphia Evening Bulletin*, May 29, 1926, clipping, JHM Scrapbooks, HSP.

15. "Mayor Vents Anger on Sesqui Critics," *Philadelphia Inquirer*, Feb. 18, 1922. For signs of Moore having taken offense, see "Mayor Raps Plans to Make Outsider Exposition Chief," *Philadelphia Inquirer*, Feb. 19, 1922.

16. "Johnson and Potter Resign from Sesqui Board of Directors," *Philadelphia Inquirer*, June 20, 1922; "Sesqui-Centennial Swept Nigh to Ruin by Tornado of Talk," *Philadelphia Inquirer*, July 9, 1922.

17. "Brush Nominated as Exposition Head," *Philadelphia Inquirer*, June 1, 1921; "Vauclain Proclaims Opposition to Fair As Interest Wanes," July 11, 1922, *Philadelphia Inquirer*.

18. "Vauclain Will Lead Town Pump Party," *Philadelphia Inquirer*, Oct. 27, 1922.

19. "Vauclain Will Lead Town Pump Party"; "Stotesbury Resigns Financial Leadership of $20,000,000 Sesqui," *Philadelphia Inquirer*, Nov. 4, 1922. See also "Stotesbury Repeats Big Fair Opposition," *Philadelphia Inquirer*, Oct. 6, 1922.

20. "Prefers Fair's Delay to Opening It with Display Incomplete," *Philadelphia Inquirer*, June 16, 1922; "Johnson and Potter Resign from Sesqui Board of Directors."

21. "Mayor Quits Sesqui Is City Hall Report," *Philadelphia Record*, Feb. 14, 1923, clipping, JHM Scrapbooks, HSP; "Sesqui Directors Hope to Put Life into Plans," *Philadelphia Record*, Feb. 21, 1923, clipping, JHM Scrapbooks, HSP; "Asks Kendrick to Be Honorary Head of Sesqui," *Philadelphia Public Ledger*, Nov. 23, 1923, clipping, JHM Scrapbooks, HSP.

22. "Sesqui Directors Snub the Mayor," *Philadelphia Public Ledger*, Nov. 29, 1923, clipping, JHM Scrapbooks, HSP.

23. "Town Meeting Votes Down Big Sesqui, 10 to 1," *Philadelphia Public Ledger*, Dec. 1, 1923, clipping, JHM Scrapbooks; "Oppose Sesqui by Vote, 403 to 43," *Philadelphia Record*, Dec. 1, 1923, clipping, JHM Scrapbooks, HSP.

24. Vitiello, "Machine Building and City Building," 416–19, first quotation on 416; Brownlee, *Building the City Beautiful*, 63–65, 75, second quotation on 65;

25. Brownlee, "Building the City Beautiful," 65–67; "Mayor Instigates Probe of Art Museum Contracts," *Philadelphia North American*, Jan. 11, 1923, clipping, JHM Scrapbooks, HSP; "An Amazing Revelation," *Philadelphia Public Ledger*, Feb. 6, 1923, clipping, JHM Scrapbooks, HSP; "Art Museum Work Paid For Twice, Engineer Admits," *Philadelphia Public Ledger*, Mar. 16, 1923, clipping, JHM Scrapbooks, HSP.

26. "Mayor Instigates Probe of the Art Museum"; "An Amazing Revelation"; "Mayor Charges Law Was Broken in Use of Art Museum Money," *Philadelphia Evening Public Ledger*, Feb. 28, 1923, clipping, JHM Scrapbooks, HSP; "Museum Work Done on Cost Plus Basis," *Philadelphia Inquirer*, Mar. 1, 1923, clipping, JHM Scrapbooks, HSP; "No Graft Shown in Art Museum Work," *Philadelphia North American*, Mar. 1, 1923, clipping, JHM Scrapbooks, HSP; "Park Board Yields on Contracts," *Philadelphia Evening Public Ledger*, Mar. 21, 1923, clipping, JHM Scrapbooks, HSP; "City Park Board Halts Laxity in Museum Jobs," *Philadelphia Public Ledger*, June 15, 1923, clipping, JHM Scrapbooks, HSP; "They Promise to Be Good," *Philadelphia Public Ledger*, June 15, 1923, clipping, JHM Scrapbooks, HSP, quotation.

27. Museum administrators eventually satisfied the requirements of Elkins's estate by organizing a temporary exhibition in the basement of the uncompleted building in 1924. Brownlee, *Building the City Beautiful*, 64–65, 67; "Trigg to Members of Sesqui. Exhibition Association," folder 3, box 30, Albert M. Greenfield Papers (MSS 1959), HSP.

28. Drayer, "J. Hampton Moore," 203–6; Brownlee, *Building the City Beautiful*, 72–74; "Library Stone Laying," *Philadelphia Inquirer*, Jan. 24, 1923. For the building's seventy-fifth anniversary, the Free Library of Philadelphia posted an online history that provides the best available account of the building's construction: "Construction, 1920–1926," 2002, http://libwww.freelibrary.org/75th/construction.htm?page=his.

29. Farnham, "A Bridge Game," 330; Arthur P. Dudden, "The City Embraces Normalcy," in Weigley, *Philadelphia: A 300-Year History*, 569.

30. *Handbook of the Board of Public Education . . . City of Philadelphia*, 1922; *Boyd's Philadelphia City Directory*, 1918; *Polk's Philadelphia City Directory*, 1924 and 1929; *Philadelphia Social Register*, 1920, 1925, and 1929.

31. *Annual Report of the Superintendent of Public Schools of the City of Philadelphia for the Year Ending December 31, 1922*, 9.

32. For Broome's recommendations along these lines, see *Annual Report of the Superintendent of Public Schools . . . 1921*. For an example of a statement from Broome about the civic and economic purposes of schooling, see *Annual Report of the Superintendent of Public Schools . . . 1923*, 3.

33. *Annual Report of the Superintendent of Public Schools . . . 1924*.

34. "Chamber Takes Referendum on Statement of Principles Designed to Bring 100% Home Rule."

35. "Mayoralty Booms Are Now Being Inflated," *Philadelphia Record*, Jan. 22, 1923, clipping, JHM Scrapbooks, HSP; "Mayoralty Booms Set for Next Week," *Philadelphia*

Evening Bulletin, Mar. 10, 1923, clipping, JHM Scrapbooks, HSP; "Vare Faces Test of Strength Today," *Philadelphia Public Ledger*, Aug. 24, 1923, clipping, JHM Scrapbooks, HSP.

36. "Plan Fight for Complete Ticket," *Philadelphia Record*, July 6, 1923, clipping, JHM Scrapbooks, HSP; "Business Men to Check Kendrick," *Philadelphia Record*, July 7, 1923, JHM Scrapbooks, HSP; "Anti-Combine Men to Work Together," *Philadelphia Inquirer*, July 18, 1923, clipping, JHM Scrapbooks, HSP; "Form Committee of 100 to Select Next Mayor," *Philadelphia Record*, July 21, 1923, clipping, JHM Scrapbooks, HSP; "Caven Suggested for Mayoralty," *Philadelphia Public Ledger*, July 7, 1923, clipping, JHM Scrapbooks, HSP; "Independents Hit When Patterson Declines to Run," *Philadelphia Evening Public Ledger*, Aug. 3, 1923, clipping, JHM Scrapbooks, HSP; "Ward Chiefs Block Patterson's Plans," *Philadelphia Public Ledger*, Aug. 4, 1923, clipping, JHM Scrapbooks, HSP.

37. Drayer, "J. Hampton Moore," 257–58; *Boyd's Philadelphia City Directory*, 1918; "Powell Evans Willing to Run for Mayoralty," *Philadelphia Public Ledger*, July 2, 1923, clipping, JHM Scrapbooks, HSP; "Evans Indorsed by Independents Against Combine," *Philadelphia Evening Public Ledger*, Aug. 9, 1923, clipping, JHM Scrapbooks, HSP.

38. "Temperamental" quotation is from Drayer, "J. Hampton Moore," 258; "Second Hampy Moore" quotation is from "Why the Mayoralty Campaign Foozled," *Philadelphia Public Ledger*, Sept. 2, 1923, clipping, JHM Scrapbooks, HSP.

39. "Mayoralty Booms Set for Next Week"; "Kendrick Helped as Golder Quits," *Philadelphia Inquirer*, Sept. 5, 1923, clipping, JHM Scrapbooks, HSP; "Vare Yields Two to Get Harmony," *Philadelphia Record*, Sept. 12, 1923, clipping, JHM Scrapbooks, HSP; "Combine Is United as Sellers Quits," *Philadelphia Evening Public Ledger* Sept. 17, 1923, clipping JHM Scrapbooks, HSP; Drayer, "J. Hampton Moore," 257.

40. "Launch Kendrick Mayoralty Boom," *Philadelphia North American*, May 2, 1923, clipping, JHM Scrapbooks, HSP; "Vice Presidents for Kendrick Committee," *Philadelphia North American*, Aug. 27, 1923, clipping, JHM Scrapbooks, HSP; Philadelphia Charter Committee, *Report of the Sub-Committee on the Charter*.

41. "Kendrick Formally Seeks Mayoralty," *Philadelphia Public Ledger*, June 13, 1923, clipping, JHM Scrapbooks, HSP.

42. "Kendrick Opens Campaign with Keynote Speech," *Philadelphia Public Ledger*, Aug. 18, 1923, clipping, JHM Scrapbooks, HSP.

43. Drayer, "J. Hampton Moore," 258; "Combine Dazed by Kendrick's Great Sweep," *Philadelphia Public Ledger*, Sept. 20, 1923, clipping, JHM Scrapbooks, HSP; "Kendrick Beats Evans by 225,117," *Philadelphia Public Ledger*, Oct. 5, 1923, clipping, JHM Scrapbooks, HSP; "Business Men Gave $60,000 to the Kendrick Campaign," *Philadelphia Public Ledger*, Nov. 3, 1923, clipping, JHM Scrapbooks, HSP.

44. "Combine Dazed by Kendrick's Great Sweep"; "Kendrick Picks Biles, Sproule and Grakelow," *Philadelphia Evening Public Ledger*, Dec. 17, 1923, clipping, JHM Scrapbooks, HSP; *News Bulletin*, Jan. 1924, 16.

45. "Kendrick to Lead Reorganizing Fair," *Philadelphia Bulletin*, Dec. 3, 1923, clipping, JHM Scrapbooks, HSP. Kendrick first came out in favor of the fair in October 1923,

a month after winning the primary. "Kendrick Out for Sesqui on Big Lines," *Philadelphia Public Ledger*, Oct. 16, 1923, clipping, JHM Scrapbooks, HSP.

46. *Financial Statistics of Cities*, 1923 and 1929; "$200,000,000 Loans in Kendrick Regime," *Philadelphia Inquirer*, Apr. 18, 1927, clipping, JHM Scrapbooks, HSP.

47. "New Vast Public and Private Improvements Now Are Being Set Under Way for Benefit of Philadelphia," *News Bulletin*, Aug. 1925, 5.

48. "Kendrick Pledges Rule by Business," *Philadelphia North American*, Sept. 8, 1923, clipping, JHM Scrapbooks, HSP.

49. "Sweeping Traffic and Parking Changes in New Ordinances Now Ready for Mayor's Signature," *News Bulletin*, Sept. 1925, 8; "The Gas Commission," *News Bulletin*, July 1925, 28; "Chamber of Commerce Brings Start in New Building Code," *News Bulletin*, Jan. 1927, 10.

50. "Chamber of Commerce Inspects Broad Street Subway," *News Bulletin*, Aug. 1927, 15.

51. Dudden, "The City Embraces Normalcy," 596; Free Library of Philadelphia, "Opening Day, June 2, 1927" (2000), http://libwww.library.phila.gov/75th/openingday.htm?page=his.

52. "Revive Sesqui Under New Plans," *Philadelphia Record*, Apr. 25, 1924, clipping, JHM Scrapbooks, HSP, includes quotation; "Seeks Ideas for Sesqui on His Visit to Europe," *Philadelphia Record*, June 5, 1924, clipping, JHM Scrapbooks, HSP; "Sesqui Outgrowth of Ten Years' Effort"; "Sesqui-Centennial Exposition Takes on Renewed Activity with the Appointment of Director-General," *News Bulletin*, Mar. 1925, 14. See also folders 28 and 29, box 24, Greenfield Papers, HSP.

53. "City's Tax Yield Will Be Increased from $26 to $3500," *Real Estate Magazine*, June 1925, 2.

54. "City's Tax Yield Will Be Increased from $26 to $3500"; "Waste Land in South Philadelphia Rapidly Vanishing," *News Bulletin*, Dec. 1926, 35, includes quotation.

55. "South Philadelphia Improvements Are Beneficial to All," *Real Estate Magazine*, June 1925, 2, quotation. For the Real Estate Board's estimate of forty thousand homes, see Horace Groskin, "Philadelphia the City of Progress—Philadelphia the City of Opportunity," *Real Estate Magazine*, Dec. 1925, 6.

56. *Sesquicentennial News Bulletin*, Aug. 27, 1925, folder 19, box 25, Greenfield Papers, HSP; Dudden, "The City Embraces Normalcy," 572–73.

57. Arthur Dudden similarly notes the fair's long-term legacy. Dudden, "The City Embraces Normalcy," 575. On the failures of the sesquicentennial, see Conn, *Museums and American Intellectual Life*, ch., 7, quotation on 233.

58. Dudden, "The City Embraces Normalcy," 569; "Broad Street Subway Finally Reaches City Hall," *News Bulletin*, Jan. 1926, 18. See also Greenfield Papers, folder 29, box 37, HSP. For the development of northern, northeastern, and western sections of the city see, for example, Harry E. Thomson, "Philadelphia's Northeast Section Rich in Historic Possessions Potent with Possibilities for Greater Philadelphia," *Real Estate Magazine*, May 1927, 5, 34; "West Philadelphia Is Making Real Estate History," *Real Estate*

Magazine, Dec. 1926, 7, 41; Raymond Nelson, "Broad Street Subway Will Increase Values All over North Philadelphia," *Real Estate Magazine*, Sept. 1925.

59. "Philadelphia Must Hold First Place as 'City of Homes,'" *Realtor's News*, Aug. 1923, 2.

60. "The Eve of a Great Building Revival," *Realtor's News*, Feb. 1922, 27.

61. Sam Bass Warner Jr., *The Private City: Philadelphia in Three Periods of Its Growth* (Philadelphia: University of Pennsylvania Press, 1987 [1968]), 172, 172n13; "Address by J. Wilson Smith," *Real Estate Magazine*, Feb. 1929, 33.

62. *Annual Report of the Superintendent of Public Schools . . . 1930*, 49; "Philadelphia to Spend Total of $10,000,000 to Construct Buildings to Meet Growing Need," *News Bulletin*, Nov. 1925, 14–15; "Building Program of Board of Education Makes Progress," *News Bulletin*, Nov. 1926, includes quotation.

63. Dudden, "The City Embraces Normalcy," 583.

64. McCaffery, *When Bosses Ruled Philadelphia*, 139.

65. Drayer, "J. Hampton Moore," 264–72; Dudden, "The City Embraces Normalcy," 574–75.

66. Vincent P. Franklin, *The Education of Black Philadelphia: The Social and Educational History of a Minority Community, 1900–1950* (Philadelphia: University of Pennsylvania Press, 1979), 60–64; Francis Ryan, *AFSCME's Philadelphia Story: Municipal Workers and Urban Power in the Twentieth Century* (Philadelphia: Temple University Press, 2011), 9–10, 27; Charles Ashley Hardy III, "Race and Opportunity: Black Philadelphia During the Era of the Great Migration, 1916–1930" (Ph.D. diss., Temple University, 1989), 481–82, 558. Scholars have debated the degree to which political machines in the nineteenth and early twentieth centuries benefited their working-class constituents. Peter McCaffery provides an excellent overview of these debates and finds few reasons to laud the practices of machine politicians in Philadelphia. McCaffery, *When Bosses Ruled Philadelphia*.

67. Hardy, " Race and Opportunity," 487–88.

68. Drayer, "J. Hampton Moore," 103–5.

69. Hardy, "Race and Opportunity," 491–94, 503–4, 511, 512–13; "Hell's Half Acre Is Passing Away," *Philadelphia Inquirer*, Jan. 4, 1921, clipping, JHM Scrapbooks, HSP.

70. "City Contract for Negro," *Philadelphia Evening Public Ledger*, Dec. 31, 1920, clipping, JHM Scrapbooks, HSP.

71. "City Contract for Negro"; "$100,000 Gift for Hall Ward," *Philadelphia Bulletin* Jan. 21, 1922, clipping, JHM Scrapbooks, HSP; Hardy, "Race and Opportunity," 513; "Recreation Costs Called Extravagant," *Philadelphia Inquirer*, Jan. 21, 1922," clipping, JHM Scrapbooks, HSP; "Streak of Economy Suddenly Hits Council," *Philadelphia Record*, Jan. 21, 1922, clipping, JHM Scrapbooks, HSP; *Report of the Controller, City of Philadelphia*, 1923.

72. Hardy, "Race and Opportunity," 527, 530–32, 534, 558.

73. Franklin, *The Education of Black Philadelphia*, 41, 66–67.

74. Franklin, *The Education of Black Philadelphia*, 40, 71, 74–86.

75. For an overview of immigration to Philadelphia in the early twentieth century,

see especially Caroline Golab, *Immigrant Destinations* (Philadelphia: Temple University Press, 1977). On the political experience of Jewish immigrants, see Sandra Featherman, "Jewish Politics in Philadelphia, 1920–1940," in *Jewish Life in Philadelphia, 1830–1940*, ed. Murray Friedman (Philadelphia: Institute for the Study of Human Issues, 1983), 276–82. On Greenfield, see Dan Rottenberg, "The Rise of Albert M. Greenfield," in Friedman, *Jewish Life*, 216–21; "Newspaper Reprint and Editorial Comments," June 24, 1929, folder 6, box 29, Greenfield Papers, HSP; Senate Report 1197, 69th Congress, 2nd Session, Part 2, Dec. 22, 1926, p. 15; Dan Rottenberg, *The Outsider: Albert M. Greenfield and the Fall of the Protestant Establishment* (Philadelphia: Temple University Press, 2014). On immigrant settlement in areas of machine strength, see also John L. Shover, "The Emergence of a Two-Party System in Republican Philadelphia, 1924–1936," *Journal of American History* 60 (Mar. 1974), esp. 989.

76. Ryan, *AFSCME's Philadelphia Story*, 26; Stefano Luconi, *From Paesani to White Ethnics: The Italian Experience in Philadelphia* (Albany: State University of New York Press, 2001), 60–61, 64–65; *Handbook of the Board of Public Education . . . City of Philadelphia*, 1925.

77. Luconi, *From Paesani to White Ethnics*, 65; Shover, "The Emergence of a Two-Party System in Republican Philadelphia," 990–99.

78. Francis Ryan, *AFSCME's Philadelphia Story*, 30–31; Dudden, "The City Embraces Normalcy," 591–92.

79. "Moore Welcomes Aid from Women," *Philadelphia Inquirer*, Aug. 26, 1919, clipping, JHM Scrapbooks, HSP; "Women Spur Voters by Telephone Drive," *Philadelphia Inquirer*, Aug. 27, 1919, clipping, JHM Scrapbooks, HSP; "Women Committee Will Help Moore," *Philadelphia Inquirer*, Sept. 7, 1919, clipping, JHM Scrapbooks, HSP.

80. "Women in Doubt Regarding Mayor," *Philadelphia Public Ledger*, Dec. 31, 1920, clipping, JHM Scrapbooks, HSP.

81. For instance, see "Mayor Appoints Woman," *Philadelphia Evening Public Ledger*, Aug. 15, 1923, clipping, JHM Scrapooks, HSP; "Mrs. Jump Gets City Welfare Post," *Philadelphia Public Ledger*, Oct. 5, 1923, clipping, JHM Scrapbooks, HSP.

82. "Council Slate Is Upset by Women," *Philadelphia Public Ledger*, Sept. 1, 1923, clipping, JHM Scrapbooks, HSP.

83. "Council Slate Is Upset by Women"; Drayer, "J. Hampton Moore," 269.

84. Walter Licht, *Getting Work: Philadelphia, 1840–1950* (Philadelphia: University of Pennsylvania Press, 1992), 181, first quotation; Abernethy, "Progressivism," 548, second quotation.

85. Licht, *Getting Work*, 178–81, quotation on 179. See also Howell John Harris, *Bloodless Victories: The Rise and Fall of the Open Shop in the Philadelphia Metal Trades, 1890–1940* (New York: Cambridge University Press, 2000).

86. Licht, *Getting Work*, 115–16, 117–18; Philip Scranton and Walter Licht, *Work Sights: Industrial Philadelphia, 1890–1950* (Philadelphia: Temple University Press, 1986), 119–20; Philip Scranton, *Figured Tapestry: Production, Markets, and Power in Philadelphia Textiles, 1885–1941* (New York: Cambridge University Press, 1989), ch. 6.

87. Scranton, "Large Firms and Industrial Restructuring," 428, 438; Vitiello, "Machine Building and City Building," 421–23, 426–27.

Chapter 4. Atlanta

1. "Pertinent Paragraphs from the President's Desk," *City Builder*, Apr. 1919, quotation. On Samuel Candler Dobbs, see, for instance, Garrett, *Atlanta and Environs*, 767–68; Bartow J. Elmore, *Citizen Coke: The Making of Coca-Cola Capitalism* (New York: W. W. Norton, 2015), 41–44.

2. "Senate Declined to Accept Report," *Atlanta Constitution*, Aug. 15, 1918; "$1,000,000 Bond Issue Called," *Atlanta Constitution*, Jan. 24, 1919.

3. "Bonds and Higher Tax Are Indorsed," *Atlanta Constitution*, Feb. 21, 1919; "Slogan Adopted by Bond Workers," *Atlanta Constitution*, Feb. 26, 1919; Sudheendran, "Community Structure in Atlanta," 209; "Plans for Success of Bond Election," *Atlanta Constitution*, Feb. 19, 1919, quotation.

4. "Higher Tax Rate for Atlanta Beaten; Voters Favor $1,000,000 Issue of Bonds," *Atlanta Constitution*, Mar. 6, 1919; "People May Vote Again on Higher Taxes and Bonds," *Atlanta Constitution*, Mar. 11, 1919; "Atlanta Will Vote Again on $1,000,000 Bond Issue by Order of City Council," *Atlanta Constitution*, Mar. 18, 1919.

5. Bayor, *Race and the Shaping of Twentieth-Century Atlanta*, 17. For a discussion of the politics that drove disfranchisement campaigns in Georgia and in the South more generally, see Michael Perman, *Struggle for Mastery: Disfranchisement in the South: 1888–1908* (Chapel Hill: University of North Carolina Press, 2001).

6. "Higher Tax Rate for Atlanta Beaten"; "A Good Beginning," *Atlanta Constitution*, Mar. 7, 1919.

7. Clifford Kuhn, Harlon E. Joye, and E. Bernard West, *Living Atlanta: An Oral History of the City, 1914–1948* (Athens: University of Georgia Press, 1990), 9–10. See also Bayor, *Race and the Shaping of Twentieth-Century Atlanta*, part 3. The editorial from the *Atlanta Independent* is described in Sudheendran, "Community Structure in Atlanta," 213–14.

8. Bayor, *Race and the Shaping of Twentieth-Century Atlanta*, 202–4; Godschalk, *Veiled Visions*, 248–50; Sudheendran, "Community Structure in Atlanta," 209–13. For a discussion of shifts in African American political activism in Atlanta in the years preceding the 1919 bond elections discussed here, see Jay Winston Driskell Jr., *Schooling Jim Crow: The Fight for Atlanta's Booker T. Washington High School and the Roots of Black Protest Politics* (Charlottesville: University of Virginia Press, 2014). On the 1919 bond elections themselves, see also Driskell, *Schooling Jim Crow*, ch. 5.

9. Jacqueline Anne Rouse, *Lugenia Burns Hope: Black Southern Reformer* (Athens: University of Georgia Press, 1989), 26, 64–68; Hunter, *To 'Joy My Freedom*, 136–42; Godschalk, *Veiled Visions*, 229–46.

10. Quoted in Sarah Mercer Judson, "Building the New South City: African American and White Clubwomen in Atlanta, 1895–1930" (Ph.D. diss., New York University, 1997), 204, and Godschalk, *Veiled Visions*, 249.

11. Bayor, *Race and the Making of Twentieth-Century Atlanta*, 18; Sudheendran, "Community Structure in Atlanta," 214; "Registration Urged by Colored Women," *Atlanta Constitution*, Apr. 14, 1919, quotation.

12. "Plan for Success of Bond Election," *Atlanta Constitution*, Mar. 28, 1919; "Negroes of Atlanta Hear Talks on Bonds," *Atlanta Constitution*, Apr. 7, 1919; Sudheendran, "Community Structure in Atlanta," 213, quotation.

13. "Bonds and Higher Tax Lose at Polls," *Atlanta Constitution*, Apr. 24, 1919; Sudheendran, "Community Structure in Atlanta," 214–15.

14. "The Chamber: A More Representative Body," *City Builder*, Nov. 1919; "New By-Laws Adopted by Membership," *City Builder*, Nov. 1919; "The Chamber Opens Its Doors to Women," *City Builder*, Jan. 1920, includes quotation; "City Planning Commission Will Work to Stimulate Development of Atlanta," *Atlanta Constitution*, Dec. 30, 1919; "Chamber Drive to Begin Today," *Atlanta Constitution*, Mar. 1, 1920.

15. "500,000 Population for Atlanta Planned," *Atlanta Constitution*, Dec. 2, 1919.

16. "Atlanta Urged to Prepare for Population of 500,000 in Mayor Key's Message," *Atlanta Constitution*, Jan. 6, 1920.

17. "Chamber Drive to Begin Today."

18. "'500,000 City' Drive to Start," *Atlanta Constitution*, June 23, 1920; "Launch Campaign for 500,000 City," *Atlanta Constitution*, July 2, 1920, quotation; "Atlanta Enjoys Glorious Fourth," *Atlanta Constitution*, July 6, 1920.

19. "Launch Campaign for 500,000 City"; "Eugene Black Dies of Heart Attack," *New York Times*, Dec. 20, 1934. On Ivan Allen Sr., see Gary M. Pomerantz, *Where Peachtree Meets Sweet Auburn: The Saga of Two Families and the Making of Atlanta* (New York: Scribner, 1996), ch. 5.

20. Newspaper clipping, [ca. July 4, 1920], scrapbook 3 (1920–1921), Atlanta Woman's Club Collection (MSS 353), Kenan Research Center [KRC], Atlanta History Center [AHC].

21. "City Planning Commission Will Work to Stimulate Development of Atlanta."

22. "Hot Fight Coming on Plan to Levy Emergency Taxes," *Atlanta Constitution*, Jan. 1, 1921; "Bond or Special Tax," *Atlanta Constitution*, Jan. 5, 1921, includes quotation.

23. "The Public Schools and the Bond Issue," *Journal of Labor*, Oct. 3, 1919; "Three Million Bond Issue for Schools Urged by Atlanta Federation of Trades," *Journal of Labor*, Oct. 10, 1919; "Atlanta Woman's Club First to Endorse Plans of Federation of Trades," *Journal of Labor*, Oct. 31, 1919; "Superintendent Dykes Pleads for Schools Before Rotary," *Journal of Labor*, Nov. 21, 1919.

24. "Hot Fight Coming on Plan to Levy Emergency Taxes"; "Dealers in Food Favor Bond Issue and Oppose Taxes," *Atlanta Constitution*, Jan. 12, 1921; "Business and Bonds," *Atlanta Constitution*, Jan. 13, 1921; "Voters of Atlanta Will Pass at Polls March 8 on $8,850,000 Bonds for Civic Improvements," *Atlanta Constitution*, Jan. 21, 1921; "Mayor Re-elected by 2,742 Majority," *Atlanta Constitution*, July 29, 1920; Sudheendran, "Community Structure in Atlanta," 103–4. For Goodhart's biography, his backers, and the

quotation, see "Harry Goodhart Will Make Race for Mayor; Platform Is Outlined," *Atlanta Constitution*, July 14, 1920.

25. "Voters Will Pass at Polls March 8 on $8,850,000 Bonds for Civic Improvements."

26. Judson, "Building the New South City," 220–21; "Organizing for Bonds," *Atlanta Constitution*, Jan. 27, 1921; "Directors of Chamber Indorse $8,850,000 Bonds," *Atlanta Constitution*, Feb. 1, 1921; "Chamber Is Backing the $8,850,000 Bond Issue," *City Builder*, Feb. 1921, 9; "Bond Issue Committee Appointed by Mayor Key," *Atlanta Constitution*, Feb. 13, 1921.

27. "Bond Issue Committee Appointed by Mayor Key"; "With Ashcraft as President Great Progress Is Predicted for Chamber of Commerce," *Atlanta Constitution*, Dec. 16, 1920.

28. Sudheendran, "Community Structure in Atlanta," 216–17; Racine, "Atlanta's Schools," 184; Judson, "Building the New South City," 219–20; "Sentiment of Negroes Is for Issue of Bonds," *Atlanta Georgian*, Feb. 16, 1921, clipping, folder 9, box 2, Kate Lumpkin Papers (MSS 627), KRC, AHC, quotation. On African American activism and the 1921 bond election, see also Driskell, *Schooling Jim Crow*, 232–33.

29. "Waterworks Chief Shows Bond Needs; Expert Is Coming," *Atlanta Constitution*, Feb. 18, 1921, quotation; "Minutes of the Colored Women's Council," folder 12, box 2, Lumpkin Papers, KRC, AHC.

30. "Minutes of the Colored Women's Council."

31. Judson, "Building the New South City," 227–29; "Municipal Bonds Fast Gain Impetus," *Journal of Labor*, Feb. 18, 1921; "Bond Issue Committee Appointed by Mayor Key"; Letter of Mrs. Albert E. Thornton, Feb. 9, 1921, folder 8, box 2, Lumpkin Papers, KRC, AHC; Lumpkin to Spalding, Feb. 25, 1921, folder 8, box 2, Lumpkin Papers, KRC, AHC.

32. "Be on the Safe Side," folder 7, box 2, Lumpkin Papers, KRC, AHC.

33. "Bonds, Only, Can Save Atlanta's Commercial and Civic Life," folder 14, box 2, Lumpkin Papers, KRC, AHC.

34. "Bonds, Only, Can Save Atlanta's Commercial and Civic Life." See also "Some Reasons Why Atlanta Should Vote for the Present Bond Issue," folder 12, box 2, Lumpkin Papers, KRC, AHC.

35. "Be on the Safe Side."

36. Judson, "Building the New South City," 231–32; "Bonds, Only, Can Save Atlanta's Commercial and Civic Life"; "Federation of Trades Puts Stamp of Approval on $8,850,000 Bonds," *Atlanta Constitution*, Jan. 27, 1921; "Atlanta Realty Board Indorses Big Bond Issue," *Atlanta Constitution*, Feb. 3, 1921; "Chamber Is Backing $8,850,000 Bond Issue;" "Gaines Is Gratified over Tax Election," *Atlanta Constitution*, Sept. 2, 1921.

37. Bayor, *Race and the Shaping of Twentieth-Century Atlanta*, 205; Racine, "Atlanta's Schools," 203; Howard L. Preston, *Automobile Age Atlanta: The Making of a Southern Metropolis, 1900–1935* (Athens: University of Georgia Press, 1979), 107; Driskell, *Schooling Jim Crow*, 233.

38. "City Planning Commission Will Work to Stimulate Development of Atlanta."

39. Preston, *Automobile Age Atlanta*, 149; "City Planning Commission Will Work to Stimulate Development of Atlanta"; "Greater Atlanta Given a Boost by 1920 Council," *Atlanta Constitution*, Jan. 6, 1920.

40. Preston, *Automobile Age Atlanta*, 149; Perman, *Struggle for Mastery*, 281–98; "Joel Hurt, Pioneer and City Builder, Claimed by Death," *Atlanta Constitution*, Jan. 10, 1926.

41. "Planning Board Ready," *Atlanta Constitution*, Feb. 18, 1920.

42. "Give First Place to Urgent Needs," *Atlanta Constitution*, Mar. 11, 1920.

43. "Planners Accept Whitten's Offer to Visit Atlanta," *Atlanta Constitution*, Mar. 4, 1920.

44. "City Planning Expert Urges Zoning System," *Atlanta Constitution*, Nov. 15, 1921, quotation; "Big Losses Charged to Lack of Planning," *Atlanta Constitution*, July 22, 1921. On Robert Whitten's vision for Atlanta and the 1922 zone plan, see also LeeAnn Lands, *The Culture of Property: Race, Class, and Housing Landscapes in Atlanta, 1880–1950* (Athens: University of Georgia Press, 2009), 143–50, 152–54.

45. "City Planning Expert Urges Zoning System."

46. "Needs of Zoning System Shown," *Atlanta Constitution*, Feb. 16, 1922.

47. "Needs of Zoning System Shown."

48. "Civic Engineers and Realty Men Favor Zone Plan," *Atlanta Constitution*, Feb. 17, 1922.

49. Preston, *Automobile Age Atlanta*, 96–97, 102–103; "Council to Consider Zoning Plan Action," *Atlanta Constitution*, Jan. 3, 1922; "Real Estate Men Denounce Zoning Plan for Atlanta," *Atlanta Constitution*, Mar. 10, 1922; "City Zoning Plan Praised and Hit by Civic Leaders," *Atlanta Constitution*, Mar. 11, 1922; "Civic Engineers and Realty Men Favor Zone Plan"; "Legislative Committee Report," *Journal of Labor*, Mar. 3, 1922; "Zoning Plan Needed, Says Chamber Head," *Atlanta Constitution*, Apr. 2, 1922; Clipping, Mar. 13, 1922, scrapbook 3 (1920–1921), Atlanta Woman's Club Collection, KRC, AHC.

50. "Zone Plan for Atlanta Ready for Meeting of Commission Monday," *Atlanta Constitution*, Jan. 1, 1922; Bayor, *Race and the Shaping of Twentieth-Century Atlanta*, 54–55; Preston, *Automobile Age Atlanta*, 101; Lands, *Culture of Property*, 154. In 1926, Georgia's supreme court ruled other facets of Atlanta's zoning ordinance unconstitutional as well, proclaiming that the provisions of Atlanta's city charter did not, by themselves, empower the city to implement a zoning ordinance. The state constitution was amended soon thereafter to allow Georgia municipalities to zone. Atlanta passed a new zoning law accordingly in 1928. Barbara J. Flint, "Zoning and Residential Segregation: A Social and Physical History, 1900–1940" (Ph.D. diss., University of Chicago, 1977), 275–77; Blaine A. Brownell, *The Urban Ethos in the South, 1920–1930* (Baton Rouge: Louisiana State University Press, 1975), 182.

51. Jackson, *The Ku Klux Klan in the City*, 30, 38; Kuhn, Joye, and West, *Living Atlanta*, 313, quotation.

52. Jackson, *The Ku Klux Klan in the City*, 37.

53. Jackson, *The Ku Klux Klan in the City*, 37. On populism and antielitism in the 1920s Klan in the South, see especially Nancy McClean, *Behind the Mask of Chivalry: The Making of the Second Ku Klux Klan* (New York: Oxford University Press, 1994).

54. "Two Ward Rallies Hear Platforms of Candidates," *Atlanta Constitution*, Aug. 2, 1922.

55. "Walter Sims Announces Platform in Mayor's Race," *Atlanta Constitution*, Aug. 20, 1922, first quotation; "Councilman Sims Is Out for Mayor," *Atlanta Constitution*, July 16, 1922, second quotation.

56. "Councilman Sims Is Out for Mayor"; "Sims Raps School Board; Green and Karston Defend," *Journal of Labor*, Dec. 14, 1923; Jackson, *The Ku Klux Klan and the City*, 38–39; "Mayor Ragsdale," *City Builder*, Dec. 1926, 28, quotation.

57. "Move Launched for Atlanta Central Park," *Atlanta Constitution*, Feb. 25, 1923.

58. "Move Launched for Atlanta Central Park"; The Central Park Committee, "The Lungs of a City," *City Builder*, Aug. 1923.

59. "Move Launched for Atlanta Central Park," first quotation; "Central Park's Appeal," *Atlanta Constitution*, May 15, 1923, second quotation.

60. "Civic Leaders Indorse Move for New Park," *Atlanta Constitution*, Feb. 25, 1923; Central Park Committee, "The Lungs of a City"; "Effort Will Be Made to Cut Size of Central Park," *Atlanta Constitution*, May 19, 1923, quotation.

61. "Joint Committee Would Leave Park Area to Council," *Atlanta Constitution*, May 30, 1923; "Park Boundaries Fixed by Board," *Atlanta Constitution*, June 16, 1923; "Council to Pass on Bond Issue for City," *Atlanta Constitution*, July 23, 1923.

62. "Council to Pass on Bond Issue for City," includes quotation; "County Board to Appropriate Sum for Central Park," *Atlanta Constitution*, Apr. 22, 1923.

63. Central Park Committee, "The Lungs of a City."

64. Benjamin J. Davis, "The Colored Man Bottled In," *Atlanta Independent*, Aug. 20, 1923.

65. "Why Bonds Failed," *Atlanta Constitution*, Sept. 7, 1923; "Labor Chief Sees Waste in Schools," *Atlanta Constitution*, Aug. 23, 1923; "Gross Mismanagement of Bond Money Charged to the Bond Commission," *Journal of Labor*, Aug. 24, 1923; Sudheendran, "Community Structure in Atlanta," 218.

66. "$2,000,000 City Hall Bond Issue Proposal Approved by Council," *Atlanta Constitution*, July 7, 1925; "Voters Urged to Support New City Hall Bond Issue by Sims and W. R. C. Smith," *Atlanta Constitution*, Sept. 13, 1925; "Adams Advocates Big City Hall Bond Issue," *Atlanta Constitution*, Sept. 20, 1925.

67. "Two Million Dollar Bond Issue," *Atlanta Independent*, Sept. 10, 1925.

68. Sudheendran, "Community Structure in Atlanta," 219–20, 232.

69. Dudley Glass, "Let's Tell the Nation About Atlanta," *City Builder*, Oct. 1925, 3–4; "Campaign to Advertise Atlanta Gets Under Way," *Journal of Labor*, Oct. 2, 1925.

70. "Campaign to Advertise Atlanta Gets Under Way."

71. "We Have Faith in Atlanta," *Journal of Labor*, Oct. 9, 1925.

72. Jackson, *The Ku Klux Klan in the City*, 39–42, quotation on 42.

73. "Let's Put the Bonds Over," *Atlanta Independent*, Mar. 18, 1926.

74. "Let's Put the Bonds Over," quotation; "Local Branch N.A.A.C.P. Holds Mass Meeting," *Atlanta Independent*, Feb. 25, 1926; "Negroes Indorse Bond Proposal at Mass Meeting," *Atlanta Constitution*, Mar. 23, 1926; "A.M.E. Ministers Favor City Bonds for Improvements," *Atlanta Constitution*, Mar. 24, 1926. The *Atlanta Independent* ran many advertisements and other pieces urging its readers to register in the lead up to the campaign. See, for instance, "Qualify for the Big Bond Issue, Both City and State," *Atlanta Independent*, Mar. 4, 1926; G. H. Andrews, "Registration and the City Bond Issue," *Atlanta Independent*, Mar. 11, 1926.

75. "Bonds over the Top," *Atlanta Independent*, Mar. 25, 1926, first quotation. "Gulch" is from "Planning Board Adopts Initial Organization."

76. "Bond Election Date Fixed for March 24 by Vote of Council," *Atlanta Constitution*, Feb. 16, 1926; "Approval Is Given City Bond Issues," *Atlanta Constitution*, Feb. 26, 1926; "Atlanta's Realtors Giving Support to Bond Issue," *Atlanta Constitution*, Mar. 14, 1926; "Clubwomen Favor Bond Issue Plans," *Atlanta Constitution*, Feb. 25, 1926; "Federation of Trades Maintain Bond Views," *Atlanta Constitution*, Mar. 11, 1926; Sudheendran, "Community Structure in Atlanta," 221, 232. On the Atlanta Improvement Association, see "Leaders Join Forces to Back City Hall Move," Sept. 2, 1925; "Improvement Body Aids Many Projects," *Atlanta Constitution*, Dec. 12, 1926.

77. "Vigorous Drive for Bonds Launched by Ward Leaders," *Atlanta Constitution*, Mar. 2, 1926; "City Bond Leaders Launch Intensive City-Wide Drive," *Atlanta Constitution*, Mar. 15, 1926; "Mammoth Demonstration Urges Support of Bonds," *Atlanta Constitution*, Mar. 24, 1926; "William Candler Will Head Body to Direct Expenditure of City's $8,000,000 Bonds," *Atlanta Constitution*, Mar. 12, 1926; "Hartsfield Urges All to Register for Bond Election," *Atlanta Constitution*, Feb. 28, 1926. Frank Neely, head of Rich's Department Store and a leader of the Atlanta Improvement Association, replaced Candler as the chair of the bond commission soon after the election. "A Very Fortunate Selection," *Journal of Labor*, Aug. 27, 1926.

78. "$8,000,000 Bond Victory Foreseen in Voting Today; Seven Candidates Seek Two County Vacancies," *Atlanta Constitution*, Mar. 24, 1926, quotation; "$8,000,000 Municipal Bond Program Is Ratified," *Atlanta Constitution*, Mar. 25, 1926.

79. "$8,000,000 Municipal Bond Program Is Ratified."

80. "Candler Favors City Hall Bonds," *Atlanta Constitution*, Sept. 11, 1925, quotation; Sudheendran, "Community Power Structure in Atlanta," 17–19, 222–23.

81. "Art Commission in First Meeting," *Atlanta Constitution*, Nov. 30, 1918; Carolyn Gaye Crannell, "In Pursuit of Culture: A History of Art Activity in Atlanta 1847–1926" (Ph.D. diss., Emory University, 1981), ch. 10. See also folders 7 and 8, box 1, Helen Knox Spain Papers (MSS 196), KRC, AHC.

82. Crannell, "In Pursuit of Culture," 326.

83. Crannell, "In Pursuit of Culture," 318.

84. "An Art Museum for Atlanta," *City Builder*, Aug. 1923.

85. "A Museum of Fine Arts," *Journal of Labor*, Oct. 23, 1925; "High Residence Given

for Atlanta Museum of Art," *Atlanta Constitution*, May 9, 1926; Crannell, "In Pursuit of Culture," 327–30.

86. Racine, "Atlanta's Schools," 204; Sudheendran, "Community Power Structure in Atlanta," 142–43; Bolden, "The Political Structure of Charter Revision Movements in Atlanta During the Progressive Era," 236–41.

87. Sudheendran, "Community Power Structure in Atlanta," 145–48.

88. Racine, "Atlanta's Schools," 215–19, quotation on 219; Sudheendran, "Community Power Structure in Atlanta," 154–59.

89. These figures exclude money spent to finance municipal debt.

Chapter 5. Businessmen's Social Politics Beyond the Civic Welfare State

1. For examples of works that portray corporate social politics in the 1920s primarily through the lens of welfare capitalism, see Cohen, *Making a New Deal*; Colin Gordon, *New Deals: Business, Labor, and Politics in America, 1920–1935* (New York: Cambridge University Press, 1994); Dumenil, *The Modern Temper*; Hawley, *The Great War and the Search for a Modern Order*; Leuchtenburg, *The Perils of Prosperity*. On businessmen and community chests, see Katz, *In the Shadow of the Poorhouse*, 161–62; Roy Lubove, *The Professional Altruist: The Emergence of Social Work as a Career, 1880–1930* (Cambridge, MA: Harvard University Press, 1965), 180–219; Morrel Heald, *The Social Responsibilities of Business: Company and Community, 1900–1960* (Cleveland: Press of Case Western Reserve University, 1970), ch. 5. As mentioned in the notes to the introduction, a leading exception to these broader patterns is the work of George B. Tindall, who began to move toward a more expansive account of corporate social politics in the 1920s through a discussion of business-friendly governors in the South. Tindall, "Business Progressivism," 92–106.

2. David Burner, "1919: Prelude to Normalcy," in *Change and Continuity in Twentieth Century America: The 1920's*, ed. John Braeman, Robert H. Bremner, and David Brody (Columbus: Ohio State University Press, 1968), 10–11; Noggle, *Into the Twenties*, 76; "Unemployment Survey, 1920–21 with Standard Recommendations," *American Labor Legislation Review* 11 (Sept. 1921), 194–95; "Our Immediate Duty to Find Jobs for the Jobless," *Literary Digest*, Sept. 10, 1921, Unemployment, Publicity, 1921, Sept.–Oct. folder, box 662, Commerce Papers (CP), Herbert Hoover Presidential Library [HHL].

3. Udo Sautter, *Three Cheers for the Unemployed: Government and Unemployment Before the New Deal* (New York: Cambridge University Press, 1991), 95–96; Leah Hannah Feder, *Unemployment Relief in Periods of Depression: A Study of Measures Adopted in Certain American Cities, 1857 Through 1922* (New York: Russell Sage Foundation, 1936), 20–23, 31–33.

4. Katz, *In the Shadow of the Poorhouse*, 39, 48; Feder, *Unemployment Relief in Periods of Depression*, 46–70.

5. Feder, *Unemployment Relief in Periods of Depression*, 98–125, 174–77, 185–88; Katz, *In the Shadow of the Poorhouse*, 151–53; Alexander Keyssar, *Out of Work: The First*

Century of Unemployment in Massachusetts (New York: Cambridge University Press, 1986), 254–55.

6. Feder, *Unemployment Relief in Periods of Depression*, 189–244; "Unemployment Survey, 1914–1915," *American Labor Legislation Review* 5 (Nov. 1915), 495–589, esp. 497–500, 498n2, 516–17, 522–29, 564, 543–44, 547–48.

7. David Burner, "1919: Prelude to Normalcy," 6, 8–9; Noggle, *Into the Twenties*, 69–72; Neil A. Wynn, *From Progressivism to Prosperity: World War I and American Society* (New York: Holmes and Meier, 1986), 201–2. Bruce Seely is one of the few historians who mentions the 1919 roads bill, but he does not describe its origins nor its relationship to unemployment relief. Bruce E. Seely, *Building the American Highway System: Engineers as Policy Makers* (Philadelphia: Temple University Press, 1987). John Oscar Davis notes in passing the relationship of the 1919 legislation to concerns over unemployment. John Oscar Davis, "Anti-Depression Public Works: Federal-Aid Roadbuilding, 1920–1922" (Ph.D. diss., Iowa State University, 2002), 1–2.

8. "$200,000,000 for Roads," *New York Times*, Jan. 26, 1919; U.S. Congress, Senate, Committee on Post Offices and Post Roads, *Post Office Appropriation Bill*, 65 Cong., 3 sess., Jan. 27, 1919, 10, quotation.

9. Committee on Post Offices and Post Roads, *Post Office Appropriation Bill*, 3, 4.

10. *Congressional Record*, 65 Cong., 3 sess., Feb. 19, 1919, 3777.

11. *Congressional Record*, Feb. 19, 1919, 3780.

12. *Congressional Record*, Feb. 19, 1919, 3780.

13. *Congressional Record*, Feb. 19, 1919, 3782.

14. "Road Funds Stays in Bill," *New York Times*, Feb. 20, 1919.

15. Thomas MacDonald to Otto Mallery, Oct. 6, 1921, Unemployment, Public Works—Roads and Highways, Correspondence, 1921, Sept.–Oct. folder, box 661, CP, HHL; Davis, "Anti-Depression Public Works."

16. *Report of the President's Conference on Unemployment* (Washington, D.C., 1921), 19–22, quotation on 20. For a discussion of Hoover, the president's conference, and the longer history of unemployment relief in the United States, see Daniel Amsterdam, "Before the Roar: U.S. Unemployment Relief after World War I and the Long History of a Paternalist Welfare Policy," *Journal of American History* 101 (March 2015), 1123–43. See also Carolyn Grin, "The Unemployment Conference of 1921: An Experiment in National Co-operative Planning," *Mid-America* 55 (April 1973); Vincent Gaddis, *Herbert Hoover, Unemployment, and the Public Sphere: A Conceptual History, 1919–1933* (Lanham, MD: University Press of America, 2005). On the 1921 roads bill, see Grin, "The Unemployment Conference of 1921," 98–99.

17. Amsterdam, "Before the Roar," 1131–32.

18. "Unemployment Survey, 1920–21 with Standard Recommendations," 191–93.

19. Press release, Jan. 6, 1922, Unemployment, Press Releases, 1921 and undated folder, box 659, CP, HHL; press release, Feb. 8, 1922, Unemployment, Press Releases, 1921 and undated folder, box 659, CP, HHL. Grin states that 225 mayor's committees were formed, but this seems a misreading of the press releases. Grin, "Unemployment

Conference of 1921," 93. Citing Grin, David Burner states the same. David Burner, *Herbert Hoover: A Public Life* (New York: Knopf, 1978), 165. The number of mayor's committees was likely closer to half this many. The highest count I could find was 109. See Unemployment, Committee on Community, Civic & Emergency Measures, 1921–1923 folder, box 637, CP, HHL; Otto T. Mallery, "The Long Range Planning of Public Works," in Committee of the President's Conference on Unemployment, *Business Cycles and Unemployment* (New York: McGraw-Hill, 1923), 241–42.

20. Letter from Arthur Woods to American Mayors, Nov. 4, 1921, Unemployment, Committee on Community, Civic & Emergency Measures, 1921–1923 folder, box 637, CP, HHL; Harry L. Lurie to H.J. Case, Oct. 21, 1921, Unemployment, Cities: Michigan—Detroit, 1921, Aug.-Nov. folder, box 627, CP, HHL; James Couzens to Arthur Woods, Oct. 10, 1921, Unemployment, Cities: Michigan—Detroit, 1921 folder, box 627, CP, HHL. On Detroit's unemployment campaign, see also Gaddis, *Herbert Hoover, Unemployment and the Public Sphere*, ch. 6.

21. Lurie to Case, Oct. 21, 1921; Couzens to Woods, Oct. 10, 1921; Woods to American Mayors, Nov. 4, 1921; Gaddis, *Herbert Hoover, Unemployment, and the Public Sphere*, 97.

22. *Report of the President's Conference on Unemployment*, 9; Woods to American Mayors, Nov. 4, 1921; Couzens to Hoover, Oct. 12, 1921, Unemployment, Cities, Michigan—Detroit, 1921, Aug.-Nov. folder, Box 627, CP, HHL; "Plans of One City for Unemployed," *New York World*, Oct. 30, 1921, clipping; Report of Agent J. S. Apelman, "Unemployment Situation in Detroit District," Nov. 5, 1921, Unemployment, Cities, Michigan—Detroit, 1921, Aug.–Nov. folder, box 627, CP, HHL; Gaddis, *Herbert Hoover, Unemployment, and the Public Sphere*, 97–98.

23. "Detroit Now in a Fair Way to Take Care of Her Jobless," *New York World*, Nov. 6, 1921, clipping, Unemployment, Cities: Michigan—Detroit, 1921, Aug.–Nov. folder, box 627, CP, HHL; Apelman, "Unemployment Situation in Detroit"; "Married Women's Jobs for Unemployed Men," *New York Herald*, Nov. 7, 1921, clipping, Unemployment, Cities: Michigan—Detroit, 1921, Aug.–Nov. folder, box 627, CP, HHL; Gaddis, *Herbert Hoover, Unemployment, and the Public Sphere*, 97–98.

24. Gaddis, *Herbert Hoover, Unemployment, and the Public Sphere*, 97–98.

25. Gaddis, *Herbert Hoover, Unemployment and the Public Sphere*, 101; "How Mayor Couzens of Detroit Is Solving the Problems of Government," *New York World*, Mar. 26, 1922, clipping, Unemployment, Cities, Extra Public Works Expenditures, 1921–1922 folder, box 636, CP, HHL, quotation.

26. Levine, *Internal Combustion*, 84; Juan R. Garcia, *Mexicans in the Midwest, 1900–1932* (Tucson: University of Arizona Press, 1996), 45; Zaragosa Vargas, *Proletarians of the North: A History of Mexican Industrial Workers in Detroit and the Midwest, 1917–1933* (Berkeley: University of California Press, 1993), 80–84; Cybelle Fox, *Three Worlds of Relief: Race, Immigration, and the American Welfare State from the Progressive Era to the New Deal* (Princeton, NJ: Princeton University Press, 2012), 86–87.

27. Gaddis, *Herbert Hoover, Unemployment and the Public Sphere*, 98; J. S. Apelman,

"Unemployment Situation in Detroit District"; "Employers Taboo All the Vanities," *New York World*, Nov. 6, 1921, clipping, Unemployment, Cities, Michigan—Detroit, 1921, Aug.–Nov. folder, box 627, CP, HHL; Couzens to Woods, Dec. 15, 1921.

28. Pennsylvania State Unemployment Office, Semi-monthly Report, October 1, 1921, Cities, Pennsylvania—Philadelphia, 1921–1922 folder, box 632, CP, HHL; *Report of the President's Conference on Unemployment*, 13.

29. "Mayor Moore Moves to Get Jobs for Idle," *Philadelphia North American*, Oct. 3, 1921, clipping, Unemployment, Publicity, 1921, Sept.–Oct. folder, box 662, CP, HHL; "Philadelphia to Carry Out U.S. Plan to Aid Unemployment," *Philadelphia North American*, Oct. 3, 1921, clipping, Unemployment, Publicity, 1921, Sept.–Oct. folder, box 662, CP, HHL; "Act on Hoover's Advice," *Philadelphia Record*, Oct. 4, 1921, clipping, Unemployment, Publicity, 1921, Sept.–Oct. folder, box 662, CP, HHL; "Make First Move Here to End Unemployment," *Philadelphia Record*, Oct. 6, 1921, clipping, Unemployment, Publicity, 1921, Sept.–Oct. folder, box 662, CP, HHL.

30. "Make First Move Here to End Unemployment."

31. "Make First Move Here to End Unemployment."

32. "Job Finding Task to Begin Tonight," *Philadelphia Public Ledger*, Oct. 21, 1921, clipping, Unemployment, Cities, Pennsylvania—Philadelphia, 1921–1922 folder, box 632, CP, HHL; "City Police Stations to Aid Jobless Group," *Philadelphia Inquirer*, Oct. 21, 1921, clipping, Unemployment, Cities, Pennsylvania—Philadelphia, 1921–1922 folder, box 632, CP, HHL; John Buchanan to Herbert Hoover, Oct. 7, 1921, Unemployment, Cities, Pennsylvania—Philadelphia, 1921–1922 folder, box 632, CP, HHL; "Seek House Repair Jobs for Idle Men," *Philadelphia North American*, Oct. 30, 1921, clipping, Unemployment, Cities, Pennsylvania—Philadelphia, 1921–1922 folder, box 632, CP, HHL; J. F. McDevitt, "Unemployment Situation in Philadelphia and Vicinity," *Philadelphia North American*, Nov. 3, 1921, clipping, Unemployment, Cities, Pennsylvania—Philadelphia, 1921–1922 folder, box 632, CP, HHL; "4,000 Jobs Offered to Unemployed as Night Watchmen," *Philadelphia Public Ledger*, Dec. 27, 1921, clipping, Unemployment, Cities, Pennsylvania—Philadelphia, 1921–1922 folder, box 632, CP, HHL; Ernest Trigg to Woods, Dec. 1, 1921, Unemployment, Cities, Pennsylvania—Misc. 1921 folder, box 627, CP, HHL, quotation.

33. McDevitt, "Unemployment Situation in Philadelphia and Vicinity"; "Report to the Public Relations Committee of the Engineer's Club," Cities, Pennsylvania—Philadelphia, 1921–1922 folder, box 632, CP, HHL; "Mayor Moves to Get Jobs for Idle," *Philadelphia North American*, Oct. 3, 1921, clipping, Publicity, 1921, Sept.–Oct. folder, box 662, CP, HHL; press release dated Jan. 21, 1921, Press Releases, 1921 & Undated folder, box 659, CP, HHL; Grin,"Unemployment Conference of 1921," 93; Philip Klein, *The Burden of Unemployment* (New York: Russell Sage, 1923), 78–81, 100.

34. H. E. Hixon to James Key, Nov. 7, 1921, Cities, Georgia—Atlanta, 1921–1922 folder, box 623, CP, HHL; Woods to Mayors, Jan. 7, 1922, Committee on Community, Civic & Emergency Measures, 1921–1923 folder, box 637, CP, HHL; report of Agent Chastain, Dec. 19, 1921, Cities, Georgia—Atlanta, 1921–1922 folder, box 623, CP, HHL;

report of Agent Chastain, Nov. 3, 1921, Cities, Georgia—Atlanta, 1921–1922 folder, box 623, CP, HHL; "Draft of Statements, Used in Bulletin," Dec. 19, 1921, Cities, Georgia—Atlanta, 1921–1922 folder, box 623, CP, HHL; letter to Woods [author's name difficult to discern], Mar. 19, 1922, Cities, Georgia—Atlanta, 1921–1922 folder, box 623, CP, HHL.

35. Mary Van Kleeck to Woods, Dec. 6, 1921, Van Kleeck, Mary, 1921–1922 folder, box 672, CP, HHL. Van Kleeck's complaints were given further expression when her colleagues at Russell Sage produced a study of local relief programs in the winter of 1921–1922. The resulting report by Philip Klein gave the President's Conference and the relief efforts that followed an overwhelmingly negative review. Klein, *The Burden of Unemployment*. One of Hoover's aides, E. E. Hunt, later contended that Klein's criticism was rooted "in the subordinate position given the social workers in the recommendations of the conference." E. E. Hunt to Hoover, May 22, 1923, Unemployment, Civic and Emergency Relief Commissions, 1921–1923 folder, box 636, CP, HHL.

36. Woods to Van Kleeck, Nov. 19, 1921, Van Kleeck, Mary, 1921–1922 folder, box 672, CP, HHL.

37. Stuart D. Brandes, *American Welfare Capitalism, 1880–1940* (Chicago: University of Chicago Press, 1970), 5–6.

38. Sanford M. Jacoby, *Modern Manors: Welfare Capitalism Since the New Deal* (Princeton, NJ: Princeton University Press, 1997), 11.

39. Brandes, *American Welfare Capitalism*, 31–33. Quotation is from Jacoby, *Modern Manors*, 13.

40. Brandes, *American Welfare Capitalism*, 25–26.

41. Brandes, *American Welfare Capitalism*, 27–28; Katz, *In the Shadow of the Poorhouse*, 195–96; Jacoby, *Modern Manors*, 20, 24, 26–31; Cohen, *Making a New Deal*, 160–61; David Brody, "The Rise and Decline of Welfare Capitalism," in *Workers in Industrial America: Essays on the Twentieth Century Struggle* (New York: Oxford University Press, 1980), 59–60; National Industrial Conference Board, *Industrial Relations Programs in Small Plants* (New York: National Industrial Conference Board, 1929), 13, 16.

42. Jacoby, *Modern Manors*, 20.

43. Brandes, *American Welfare Capitalism*, 30–31.

44. Brody, "The Rise and Decline of Welfare Capitalism," 48.

45. Brody, "The Rise and Decline of Welfare Capitalism," 51–52.

46. Cohen, *Making a New Deal*, 162–76, 186; Jacoby, *Modern Manors*, 20–24; Brody, "The Rise and Decline of Welfare Capitalism," 54–59. Stuart Brandes offers a useful overview of many of these programs. Brandes, *American Welfare Capitalism*.

47. Cohen, *Making a New Deal*, 176–79; Brandes, *American Welfare Capitalism*, ch. 8.

48. I am indebted to Steven W. Usselman for this characterization.

49. Cohen, *Making a New Deal*, 163, 165; Brandes, *American Welfare Capitalism*, 59–60, 68 (quotations).

50. Jacoby, *Modern Manors*, 23–24, 25; Brody, "The Rise and Decline of Welfare Capitalism,"60; Cohen, *Making a New Deal*, 190–91, 194–95.

51. Cohen, *Making a New Deal*, 193.

52. Cohen, *Making a New Deal*, 184–86, 195 (quotation).

53. The National Industrial Conference Board, *Industrial Relations in Small Plants*, 16.

54. Lubove, *The Professional Altruist*, 180–84, 189–92; Katz, *In the Shadow of the Poorhouse*, 161–62; Heald, *The Social Responsibilities of Business*, 118, 120, 121.

55. "Board Moves to Amalgamate Charitable and Social Agencies," *Philadelphia Chamber of Commerce News Bulletin*, Nov. 1, 1920, quotation; Lubove, *The Professional Altruist*, 183, 200, 209; Katz, *In the Shadow of the Poorhouse*, 162; Heald, *The Social Responsibilities of Business*, 121.

56. Heald, *The Social Responsibilities of Business*, 125–30; Lubove, *The Professional Altruist*, 212–14.

57. Sydnor H. Walker, "Privately Supported Social Work," *Recent Social Trends in the United States*, vol. 2 (New York: McGraw-Hill, 1933), 1195.

58. Joyce Shaw Peterson, *American Automobile Workers, 1900–1933* (Albany: State University of New York Press, 1987), 54.

59. Detroit Department of Public Welfare, *Annual Report for 1925*, 121, 114 (quotation).

60. Detroit Department of Public Welfare, *Annual Report for 1925*, 120, 122.

61. Detroit Department of Public Welfare, *Annual Report for 1927*, 140 (quotation), 144; Peterson, *American Automobile Workers*, 130.

62. Detroit Department of Public Welfare, *Annual Report for 1927*, 146.

63. Detroit Department of Public Welfare, *Annual Report for 1929*, 280.

64. Detroit Department of Public Welfare, *Annual Report for 1929*, 281–82.

65. Sunie Davis, "The Underdevelopment of Public Welfare in Philadelphia, 1913–1931," Working Paper 8, folder 8, box 1, Social History Project Papers (MS 80), University Archives, State University of New York at Buffalo.

66. United States Bureau of the Census, *Special Report: Relief Expenditures by Governmental and Private Organizations, 1929 and 1931* (Washington, D.C.: Government Printing Office, 1932). For a discussion of disparities in relief spending in different regions of the United States during the period, including the South, see Fox, *Three Worlds of Relief*.

Epilogue

1. U.S. Census Bureau, *Financial Statistics of Cities*, 1919 and 1929. These debt figures are for gross indebtedness and have not been adjusted for inflation.

2. Eric H. Monkkonen, *The Local State: Public Money and American Cities* (Stanford, CA: Stanford University Press, 1995), 96–97; Mark I. Gelfand, *A Nation of Cities: The Federal Government and Urban America, 1933–1965* (New York: Oxford University Press, 1975), 31; Fine, *Frank Murphy*, 246–47, 298–99.

3. Gelfand, *A Nation of Cities*, 31, 32 (quotation).

4. Gelfand, *A Nation of Cities*, 33; Fine, *Frank Murphy*, 305 (quotations), 313–15.

5. Fine, *Frank Murphy*, 313, 325–27, quotation on 327.

6. Fine, *Frank Murphy*, 262.

7. Fine, *Frank Murphy*, 261–96, 320, 379; Monkkonen, *The Local State*, 97.

8. Drayer, "J. Hampton Moore," 318–20, 322, 325.

9. Drayer, "J. Hampton Moore," 314 (quotation), 315.

10. Bonnie R. Fox, "Unemployment Relief in Philadelphia, 1900–1932: A Study in the Depression's Impact on Voluntarism," *Pennsylvania Magazine of History and Biography*, 93 (Jan. 1969), 87, 91–106.

11. Kuhn, Joye, and West, *Living Atlanta*, 201, quotation. Douglas Lee Fleming, "Atlanta, the Depression and the New Deal" (Ph.D. diss., Emory University, 1984), 118.

12. Fleming, "Atlanta, the Depression and the New Deal," 106–8, 111–12; Roger Biles, *The South and the New Deal* (Lexington: University Press of Kentucky, 1994), 29.

13. Fleming, "Atlanta, the Depression and the New Deal," 100–101, 106, 108; Kuhn, Joye, and West, *Living Atlanta*, 206.

14. David M. Kennedy, *Freedom from Fear: The American People in Depression and War* (New York: Oxford University Press, 1999), 57–58; Glen Jeansonne, *The Life of Herbert Hoover: Fighting Quaker, 1921–1933* (New York: Palgrave Macmillan, 2012), 206–13, 267.

15. Albert U. Romasco, *The Poverty of Abundance: Hoover, the Nation, the Depression* (New York: Oxford University Press, 1965), 144–45. On PECE, see also citations in note 16 immediately below.

16. James Stuart Olson, *Herbert Hoover and the Reconstruction Finance Corporation, 1931–1933* (Ames: Iowa State University Press, 1977), chs. 6 and 7; Glen Jeansonne, *The Life of Herbert Hoover*, chs. 9, 11; Jason Scott Smith, *Building New Deal Liberalism: The Political Economy of Public Works* (New York: Cambridge University Press, 2006), 26–28; Anthony J. Badger, *The New Deal: The Depression Years, 1933–40* (Chicago: Ivan R. Dee, 2002), 44–46, 49; Kennedy, *Freedom from Fear*, ch. 3; Ellis W. Hawley, "Herbert Hoover, Associationalism, and the Great Depression Relief Crisis of 1930–33," in *With Us Always: A History of Private Charity and Public Welfare*, ed. Donald T. Critchlow and Charles H. Parker (Lanham, MD: Rowman and Littlefield, 1998).

17. Jacoby, *Modern Manors*, 33; Cohen, *Making a New Deal*, 238–46.

18. See note 4 in the introduction on the definition of the social welfare state used in this book.

19. For an overview and useful evaluation of the extensive literature on this matter, see Hacker and Pierson, "Business Power and Social Policy," quotation on 299.

20. On the influence of southern congressmen on New Deal social legislation, see especially Ira Katznelson, *Fear Itself: The New Deal and the Origins of Our Time* (New York: W. W. Norton, 2013).

21. On construction through New Deal public works programs, see Smith, *Building New Deal Liberalism*.

22. Leading works on the War on Poverty and Great Society that emphasize these themes include Michael B. Katz, *The Undeserving Poor: America's Enduring Confrontation with Poverty* (New York: Oxford University Press, 2014); Annelise Orleck,

"Introduction: The War on Poverty from the Grass Roots Up," in *The War on Poverty: A New Grassroots History, 1964–1980*, ed. Annelise Orleck and Lisa Gayle Hazirjian (Athens: University of Georgia Press, 2011); Alice O'Conner, *Poverty Knowledge: Social Science, Social Policy and the Poor in Twentieth-Century U.S. History* (Princeton, NJ: Princeton University Press, 2002).

23. On welfare reform, see especially Michael B. Katz, *The Price of Citizenship: Redefining the American Welfare State, Updated Edition* (Philadelphia: University of Pennsylvania Press, 2008).

24. On shifts in the federal government's role in education, see especially Patrick J. McGuinn, *No Child Left Behind and the Transformation of Federal Education Policy, 1965–2005* (Lawrence: University Press of Kansas, 2006). On the "new paternalism," see David Whitman, *Sweating the Small Stuff: Inner-City Schools and the New Paternalism* (Washington, D.C.: Thomas B. Fordham Institute, 2008). For a recent presidential speech that lauds education as "the best anti-poverty program around," see President Barack Obama's 2010 State of the Union Address. https://www.whitehouse.gov/the-press-office/remarks-president-state-union-address. For an example of a high-profile documentary film along these lines, see *Waiting for "Superman,"* directed by Davis Guggenheim (2010).

25. Daniel Stedman Jones, *Masters of the Universe: Hayek, Friedman, and the Birth of Neoliberal Politics* (Princeton, NJ: Princeton University Press, 2002), 321–27. See also *A Decade of Hope VI: Research Findings and Policy Challenges* (Washington, D.C.: Urban Institute, 2003); Henry G. Cisnernos and Lora Engdahl, eds., *From Despair to Hope: Hope VI and the New Promise of Public Housing in America's Cities* (Washington, D.C.: Brookings Institution Press, 2009).

INDEX

Page numbers in italics represent illustrations.

ACKNOWLEDGMENTS

The research for this book was funded by grants and fellowships from the University of Pennsylvania, the Council on Library and Information Resources, the Mellon Foundation, the American Academy of Arts and Sciences, the Historical Society of Pennsylvania, and the Institute for Political History. I am deeply grateful for their support.

Michael B. Katz was the best mentor a young scholar could hope for—brilliant, engaged, forthright, almost impossibly reliable, and endlessly supportive. Not being able to share this volume with him due to his passing is a source of tremendous sadness.

One of the greatest gifts Michael gave me was bringing me into his circle at the University of Pennsylvania. Sarah Igo profoundly influenced how I think about history. She remains incredibly generous with her time. I can trace many of the questions that sit at the center of this book to work that I did under the guidance of Tom Sugrue, who has since provided advice, encouragement, and support at many crucial moments. Walter Licht helped sharpen my initial thoughts about the project. My conversations with Steve Hahn about political economy were formative. I am also grateful to the members of Penn's urban studies program, most of all Elaine Simon and Mark Stern. I also thank Rogers Smith, who provided extremely helpful comments on a paper related to this book at a forum at Penn. Phoebe Young offered excellent advice and generously humored my bumbling first moments of parenthood while I was working with her.

A number of other people from those days in Philadelphia have been particularly supportive. Greg Downs has been a singular source of encouragement, wisdom, and ideas for over a decade now. Intellectually and in so many other ways, Adam Goodman is family. Tim Weaver and Daniel Stedman Jones have been the perfect comrades. My conversations with Ethan Schrum kept my priorities straight and my mind open. Sarah Manekin offered cheerleading and insight countless times. I also thank Dan Brook, Merlin Chowkwanyun, Michael Clapper, Jo Cohen, Erin Park Cohn, Ed Collet, Julie Davidow, Leah Gordon, Julia Gunn, Clemmie Harris, Andrew Heath, Eric Hintz, Chris Jones, Will Kuby, Jess Lautin, Erik Mathisen, Peter Pihos, Joy Rohde, Sarah Rottenberg, Brett Schaeffer, Perrin Selcer, Karen Tani, Eric Taylor, and Domenic Vitiello.

At Ohio State, Vicki and Harvey Graff welcomed my family and me like we were kin. Harvey has been an especially crucial source of support since then. Dave Steigerwald made relatively small-town Ohio feel almost immediately like home to a family of city slickers and gave me the great gift of batting around ideas with him. Steve Conn showed faith in this project from an early stage and provided guidance, excellent conversation, and much-needed tastes of Philly. Kevin Boyle offered kindness and encouragement, including at an especially pivotal moment, and valuable input on a paper based on portions of this book. I am also grateful to Paula Baker, Jim Bartholomew, Mansel Blackford, John Brooke, Bill Childs, Lilia Fernandez, Peter Hahn, Hasan Jeffries, Dave Staley, David Stebenne, and Judy Wu. Heather Tanner and Molly Cavender tried their best to help me find time to write and did so against steep odds. Rachel Bowen was a generous sounding board.

My thanks to the entire Lincoln Avenue crew: Robb, Julie, Emma, Via, Stuart, Alexis, Hayden, Mason, Mr. Joe, and that whole extended gang. We miss all of you every day. Matt Bruns and Amy Downing: I especially thank you for being such generous and fun friends and for letting us spend time with the magical Ava and Madeline.

Georgia Tech already feels like home, and I am truly thankful to my wonderful new colleagues in the School of History and Sociology for that. Steve Usselman is an ideal chair. My deepest thanks, Steve. I am also grateful to Jackie Royster, dean of Georgia Tech's Ivan Allen College of Liberal Arts, for her encouragement and for her enthusiastic support of research and education in the humanities and social sciences.

A number of people (including some whom I have already mentioned) offered comments on all or parts of drafts of this book. I am especially thankful to Mark Rose and Bob Lockhart. Mark read two versions of the manuscript, each time with incredible speed and attention to detail. Bob offered indispensable feedback along the way. Anyone who has a chance to work with Mark or Bob should jump on it. Julian Zelizer read an early version and offered uniquely helpful commentary that transformed the final product. Miriam Cohen read that early iteration, too. Her suggestions and her interest in the project have been absolute gifts. I am deeply grateful to John Krige for many reasons, including because he generously read a draft in its entirety and offered invaluable input. Angus Burgin, Tracy Neumann, and Tracy Steffes read drafts as well. Their suggestions helped in countless ways. Jamie Pietruska read multiple chapters and has been an important source of wisdom and support. I am also thankful for the commentary offered at various points by Pam Laird, Richard John, Ellie Shermer, Bruce Schulman, Michael Zakim, Jason Scott-Smith, Julia Ott, Ben Waterhouse, Jeff Fear, Elisabeth Clemens, Elizabeth Sanders, Andy Jewett, Jason Petrulis, Pat Spacks, David Levitus, Debbie Becher, and Dawn Coleman. Many thanks as well to the anonymous readers for Penn Press and to the Penn Press production team.

I am profoundly indebted to staff members at various libraries and archives for their assistance, especially at the Herbert Hoover Presidential Library, the Burton Historical Library at the Detroit Public Library, the University of Michigan's Bentley Historical Library, the Historical Society of Pennsylvania, the City Archives of Philadelphia, and the Atlanta History Center. I also thank Andrea Jackson at the Atlanta University Center and Nick Okrent at the University of Pennsylvania. Leanna Simon provided fantastic research assistance that saved me time away from family. I also thank Patrick Potyondy for help with research. I am extremely grateful to Fran and Howard Rottenberg, who very generously allowed me to stay with them during my first research trips to Atlanta, and to the Schrum family for their hospitality in Iowa City.

It is exciting to be able to thank my parents and my sisters as well as the Christmans in this venue. There are many people in my family whom I wish I could thank in person and hand a copy of this book but who have passed away. My grandfather, Morton Amsterdam, who loved history and cherished academic life, would have particularly taken pleasure in seeing this volume published.

To my kids, let the record show that I determined whose name would go first on the dedication page by flipping a coin. Far more important, nothing makes me happier, prouder, or inspires me more than being your dad. Thank you for the imaginary worlds, the probing questions, reading books with me, and for being so loving and full of life.

I have known Kate Christman since I was so young that I remember having age-appropriate flights of fancy in which I thanked her on national television upon winning a Grammy Award. An acknowledgment here is admittedly a shoddy substitute. Kate has let this project be one of the main tasks that we have juggled as we have built our life together. Moreover, she has done so with a humbling degree of generosity, patience, flexibility, grace, and good cheer—far more than this book or I deserved. She also read every page and offered precisely the feedback that I needed when she did. Kate, for all this and for infinitely more, thank you.